A People's Voice

A People's Voice

Black South African Writing
in the Twentieth Century

Piniel Viriri Shava

Zed Books Ltd.
London

Ohio University Press
Athens

A People's Voice was first published by Zed Books Ltd,
57 Caledonian Road, London N1 9BU, UK, and by
Ohio University Press, Scott Quadrangle,
University of Ohio, Athens, Ohio 45701, USA, in 1989.

Copyright © Piniel Viriri Shava, 1989.

Cover designed by Andrew Corbett.
Typeset by EMS Photosetters, Rochford, Essex.
Printed and bound in the United Kingdom
at Bookcraft (Bath) Ltd, Midsomer Norton.

British Library Cataloguing in Publication Data

Shava, Piniel Viriri
  A people's voice: black South African
  writing in the twentieth century.
  1. English literature. South African black
  writers, to 1987– Critical studies.
  I. Title.
  820.9'968

  ISBN 0-86232-684-2
  ISBN 0-86232-687-7 pbk

Library of Congress Cataloging-in-Publication Data

Shava, Piniel
  A people's voice: Black South African writing in
  the 20th century/Piniel Shava.
      p.   cm.
  Bibliography: p.
  ISBN 0-8214-0931-X. – ISBN 0-8214-0932-8 (pbk.)
  1. South African literature (English) – Black
  authors – History and criticism. 2. Protest literature,
  South African (English) – History and criticism. 3.
  Literature and politics – South Africa – History –
  20th century. 4. Blacks – South Africa – Intellectual
  life. 5. Politics in literature. 6. Blacks in literature.
  I. Title.
  PR9358.2.B57S54   1989   89-30980
  820'.9'896068–dc19   CIP

Contents

Acknowledgements

I should like to thank Dr Rowland Smith for sharing with me his inside knowledge of the field of study and for his invaluable corrections and comments. My thanks also to Drs Malcolm Ross and Clayton Myers for furnishing me with information germane to the study and the frank and thought-provoking discussions we had on South African politics and other vital issues of our time. To Dr Ronald Huebert, who discovered my eligibility for the Isaac Walton Killam Memorial Scholarship, I express my heartfelt gratitude. Fungai Mavugara, my parents, and my late uncle Cassius Magomatema Hwata are greatly thanked for their interest in and support for my academic pursuits. Last but not least, thanks to Zed Books for its willingness to publish the book.

Piniel Shava

Introduction

> In the plainest sense, of course, literature is itself one part of the structure, the institutions, the actions of society – like bread or banking. In action, literature is both a reflection and a force. It may simply record the kind of society that the writer knows – its values, problems, structure, events. Or, with bludgeon or rapier, it may attack this very society and its present evils. More often, literature embodies the writer's evaluation of his world, or illuminates its possibilities.[1]

This statement encapsulates the role of literature in any society. The most instructive aspect of the statement is its emphasis on the view that literature neither emerges from nor operates in a vacuum but that, whatever method it employs, the outcome is a close relationship between literature and the society of which it is a product.

This book deals with the relationship between literature and politics in South Africa. Black South African literature is a literature of protest. It protests against social, political, economic and military arrangements which deprive black people of civil rights and the free expression of their aspirations. As a result, this literature has tended to be overwhelmingly political and proletarian in outlook, and concerned with the problems of colour and class. This preoccupation with politics makes it incumbent upon black South African writers to address themselves to the subject in a manner that reveals commitment. By commitment I mean "a matter of orientation, a matter of perceiving social realities and of making those perceptions available in works of art in order to help promote understanding and preservation of, or change in, the society's values and norms."[2] In the South African context, commitment is calculated to inculcate political understanding and to promote change.

Political commitment itself is, nonetheless, not new. In the 19th century Karl Marx and Frederick Engels advocated what they described as, "a faithful portrayal"[3] of social reality through the "reproduction" of "typical characters under typical circumstances".[4] For V. I. Lenin, literature serves a utilitarian function, being "part of the common cause of the proletariat, 'a cog and a screw' of one single great Social-Democratic mechanism . . .".[5] Emphasizing the primacy of freedom over other human pursuits, Jean-Paul Sartre – in the mid-20th century – has maintained that, if literature is to be meaningful, it should "reverberate at every level of man and society".[6] Of course, there is considerable comment on the issue of commitment in literature, but these central attitudes expressed by some of the major thinkers on the topic serve to give some sense of context to my study of a specific manifestation of the theme.

Because of Africa's colonial experience, political commitment has tended to be more pragmatic than theoretical. Twentieth-century writers espouse commitment in various ways. Arguing that colonialism created cultural disorientation, alienation and economic domination[7] for Africans, Chinua Achebe maintains that it is the task of the African writer to help his society regain its lost dignity, identity, values and customs:

> What we need to do is to look back and try and find out where we went wrong, where the rain began to beat us . . . The writer cannot expect to be excused from the task of re-education and regeneration that must be done. In fact he should march right in front. For he is after all . . . the sensitive point of his community.[8]

In another instance, Achebe warns that any African writer who shies away from social and political concerns in his writings runs the risk of becoming irrelevant:

> It is clear to me that an African creative writer who tries to avoid the big social and political issues of contemporary Africa will end up being completely irrelevant – like that absurd man in the proverb who leaves his burning house to pursue a rat fleeing from the flames.[9]

Ngugi wa Thiong'o, the novelist and playwright, advocates a more involved form of political commitment. Like Lenin, Ngugi expresses a belief that:

> . . . literature cannot escape from the class power structures that shape our everyday life. Here a writer has no choice. Whether or not he is aware of it, his works reflect one or more aspects of the intense economic, political, cultural and ideological struggles in a society. What he can choose is one or the other side in the battle field: the side of the people, or the side of those social forces and classes that try to keep the people down. What he or she cannot do is to remain neutral. Every writer is a writer in politics. The only question is what and whose politics?[10]

As his own writings demonstrate, Ngugi is not satisfied with merely criticizing the Kenyan neo-colonial system but wishes to overhaul it and replace it with a socialist one.

Because the political situation in South Africa dominates all aspects of life in that country, commitment among black writers has been seen as a necessity.

> *Apartheid* affects every aspect of a person's life like a virulent form of cancer. Hence many South African writers [and, I would say, nearly all black and 'coloured' South African writers] are concerned with 'fighting' *apartheid*, with demonstrating how monstrous *apartheid* is, with showing how it dehumanizes everybody.[11]

Commitment itself is revealed in many ways. There are writings which merely record the various aspects of apartheid as described in the opening quotation. Other works not only record the injustices of the system but also attack them. The third kind of writing records, attacks and "illuminates" or prescribes a solution to the problem. As in the case of the views of Lenin and Ngugi wa Thiong'o on commitment, this third kind of writing invariably advocates revolution and the subsequent establishment of a socialist political system.

The central objective of this book is to trace and discuss these various forms of commitment as they are expressed in a large body of literature: poetry, drama and prose. While most of these writings are by blacks, some of them have been by whites. I use white writers not as subjects in themselves but as a way of explaining my method.

The approach to this book is basically historical and thematic; works discussed date from as early as 1916 to the present. Chapter One deals with early black writings which expose the deprivation and oppression that follow colonial conquest and occupation. Solomon T. Plaatje's two books, *Native Life in South Africa* and *Mhudi*, focus on the loss of black lands and the nascent racial policies of the white imperialists. The second part of the chapter examines the problems of urbanization and proletarianization which accompany the growth of industrialization. The short stories of R. R. R. Dhlomo and Ezekiel Mphahlele graphically reflect the poverty, violence, exploitation of labour and crowded living conditions of the period.

Chapter Two discusses the strangeness and agony of growing up and working in a police state in the 1950s and early 1960s. The manner of the autobiographical writings and short stories that deal with this period ranges from Mphahlele's dispassionate portrayal in *Down Second Avenue*, through Can Themba's corrosive cynicism in *The Will to Die*, to Bloke Modisane's vexed depiction of the variegated but bitter township life in *Blame Me on History*.

After the Sharpeville Emergency of 1960, black writings reflect different forms of protest. Chapter Three examines the emergence and development of militant politics after the Emergency. Writings range from Peter Abrahams's portrayal of the sabotage campaign in *A Night of Their Own*, to the representation of revolutionary activity by Alex La Guma and Nadine Gordimer in *In the Fog of the Season's End* and *Something Out There*, respectively.

Chapter Four deals with another form of protest (inside South Africa) after Sharpeville. Fear of censorship compels writers like Oswald Mtshali to resort to indirect protest through the medium of poetry. A whole generation of poets, including Mongane Serote, Njabulo Ndebele, Mandlenkosi Langa and Mafika Gwala develops. Because of his persistently direct and angry style, James Matthews is an odd man out among these poets.

Chapter Five addresses itself to the influence of the Black Consciousness Movement, and the role of poetry as an instrument of politicization in the 1970s. The implicit protest of Mtshali and his contemporaries gives way to a militant technique that asserts black identity, pride, dignity and solidarity. Among the angry poets who deal with these concerns are James Matthews and Don Mattera.

Like poetry, drama was used as a vehicle of politicization in the 1970s. Chapter Six discusses a wide range of plays that deal with issues of the black experience analysed in the preceding chapter, while Chapter Seven, as the concluding chapter, examines writings published in the period after the Soweto uprising of 1976 to the present.

The book, therefore, is a comprehensive attempt to analyse and synthesize a wide range of South African literature in the 20th century. The discussion takes into account the problems of earnestness, didacticism, exhortation and, in some cases, partisanship that accompany committed writing. Hence, the book grapples with the conflict between literary values and political goals by consistently discussing the relationship between form and content. In this respect, it is probably one of the few extended critical works that employ this method. Above all, the book approaches literary analysis in a way that subsumes various other subjects such as history, political science, sociology, psychology and philosophy. Each of these supporting disciplines, I hope, will enrich the literary discussions that follow.

Notes

1. Bernice Slote (ed.) foreword to *Literature and Politics* (Lincoln: University of Nebraska Press, 1964) p. v.

2. Chinweizu *et al. Toward the Decolonization of African Literature* (Washington: Howard University Press, 1983) p. 253.

3. Frederick Engels, letter to Minna Kautsky, 26 November 1885, in David Craig (ed.) *Marxists on Literature* (Harmondsworth: Penguin Books, 1975) p. 268.

4. Engels, letter to Margaret Harkness, April 1888, in Craig (ed.) *Marxists on Literature*, p. 23.

5. V. I. Lenin, *On Literature and Art* (Moscow: Progress Publishers, 1970) p. 23.

6. Jean-Paul Sartre, "The Purposes of Writing", quoted in Raymond Williams, *Marxism and Literature* (London: Oxford University Press, 1977) p. 201.

7. For an extended analytical treatment of the impact of colonialism on both the colonized and colonizers, see Frantz Fanon, *The Wretched of the Earth* (New York: Grove Press, Inc., 1968).

8. Chinua Achebe, *Morning Yet on Creation Day* (London: Heinemann, 1975) pp. 44–45.

9. Achebe, p. 78.

10. Ngugi wa Thiong'o, preface to *Writers in Politics* (London: Heinemann, 1981) no pagination given.

11. Peter Nazareth, introduction to *Literature and Society in Modern Africa* (Nairobi: East African Literature Bureau, 1972) p. 2.

1.   Commitment or Reaction?

The Writings of the Mission-educated Elite and other Early Black Writers

Early black South African literature comprises writing in both the vernacular and English languages. This study is concerned with the latter. Written literature arose mainly in response to missionary initiative. Mission stations such as Lovedale School in the Cape Province became centres for the nascent black literature. For the first time, unrecorded oral material was printed either in book form, or in newspapers which were also mostly run by missionaries.

Early literature, like contemporary writing, reflected different varieties of commitment. On the one hand, the commitment was strongly coloured by what had given rise to its emergence: missionary influence. Among other productions, the Lovedale Press published translations of the Bible and collections of hymns. Some of the outstanding novels published in the mid-19th and early 20th centuries contain obvious moralistic themes.

On the other hand, early literature was also committed to political issues of the time. Most of the writers whose works I shall discuss argued that something was desperately wrong with the life they depicted. Whether they named the problem colonial occupation, moral decadence, alienation or economic deprivation, all the early writers (like their contemporary counterparts) believed that the South African situation could be remedied only by changing the political system.

Colonial Penetration and Its Aftermath

By the time early literature was produced, historical events such as the Great Trek,[1] with its far-reaching repercussions, had started. In the interior, after the Mfecane (the scattering of the Ngoni, Shangani and Ndebele ethnic groups to the north, west and south of Southern Africa after their defeat by Shaka), many ethnic groups had settled between the Limpopo River and the Cape, tilling the soil and keeping cattle, goats and sheep. With the coming of the Boers, who were also interested in agriculture and keeping livestock, frontier wars broke out over ownership of resources. As early as the 1940s, C. W. De Kiewiet enlarges on the origin of the conflict:

In the writing of South African history it was long customary to believe that the chronic conflict of the Kafir frontier was the result of the spontaneous hostility of a savage and treacherous people to the presence of a superior race. Actually the conflict of black and white was fed more by their similarities than by their differences. The opposing lines of settlement struggled for the control of the same natural resources of water, grass and soil. It was not a romantic frontier like the American West or heroic like the North-West Frontier of India.[2]

This Black–Boer conflict and its aftermath are at the centre of the writings of some committed early writers. Solomon T. Plaatje, for instance, convincingly portrays the misunderstandings. Plaatje, though the most representative, is not, however, the first to deal with these concerns. They are introduced by early vernacular writers, such as I. W. W. Citashe who, quite early in the history of black literature, reminds his countrymen of the encroachment and dispossession they have suffered at the hands of Boers:

> Your cattle are gone,
> My countrymen!
> Go rescue them! Go rescue them!
> Leave the breechloader alone
> And turn to the pen.
> Take paper and ink,
> For that is your shield.
>
> Your rights are going!
> So pick up your pen,
> Load it, load it with ink.
> Sit in your chair –
> Repair not to Hoho,
> But fire with your pen.[3]

Citashe's plea to resort to the use of the "pen", "ink" and "chair" at once reminds one of the much debated relationship between the writer and his society. To Citashe, literature serves the social and political function of raising people's consciousness, a belief more conspicuous in later writers. Citashe is not, however, a Marxist. His cry derives from sheer political radicalism that seeks to regain what has been lost, and not from the need to overhaul the system and replace it with a new one. Given the return of his land, goats, sheep and rights, Citashe would probably be satisfied with the political system that prevailed before the arrival of the Boers. Nonetheless, his technique is didactic, programmatic and tendentious.

The political concerns that Citashe grapples with find their most extended expression in the works of Solomon T. Plaatje. Though published in the early 20th century, when the gold and diamond mining industries were well established, Plaatje's *Mhudi* and *Native Life in South Africa* do not deal with problems of industrialization and urbanization. Among other themes, the books explore issues related to the Great Trek, such as the frontier wars, racial

prejudice, Boer brutality, inter-racial friendship, Barolong-Griqua collaboration with Boers, the 1913 Land Act and its attendant problems of land and
labour. It is probably the remoteness of his concerns, coupled with what some
critics believe to be missionary influence, which have led critics to assess his
work less than favourably. Janheinz Jahn categorizes *Mhudi* as a work of
"tutelage", "hedging or half-in-half" between "apprentice literature" and
"protest literature".[4] By "apprentice literature" he seems to mean early
experiments at black writing in which the concerns are religious rather than
social, political and economic. According to Jahn, "protest literature" is,
perhaps, mostly associated with what he terms the "skokiaan" culture in his
Muntu.[5]

   Though *Mhudi* is not as openly committed as the "skokiaan" literature, its
portrayal of the arrival of the Boers and their subsequent clashes with blacks
may be sufficient testimony of its political nature. The "skokiaan" culture that
Jahn deems the only committed writing is, after all, the outcome of the events
which Plaatje so thoroughly examines. Whereas in most "skokiaan" writing
protest is direct and stark, in *Mhudi* it is disguised, only implied through
dialogue and situation. Martin Tucker, one of Plaatje's critics, acknowledges
the latter's detached style: ". . . Plaatje's comments on the Boer attitude are not
obtrusive even when they are bitter, and they reflect a wit that bites deeper than
surface humanitarianism."[6] Plaatje's corrosive but restrained bitterness
manifests itself clearly when he writes about the Boer's religious hypocrisy:

> The Boers were God's chosen people, so they argued . . . they remonstrated
> . . . and held it unnatural to reward a kafir for anything he did as liberally as
> if he were a baptized Christian . . . The Boers, a race of proverbial Bible
> readers . . . profess Christianity to the point of bigotry.[7]

His sarcasm is biting. Protest is implied rather than explicitly stated. There is no
neutrality about it all as Jahn claims. Perhaps he could have done Plaatje
justice if he had said something about *Native Life in South Africa*, which
complements *Mhudi* in its thematic treatment. As Tim Couzens argues:

> I believe that *Mhudi* and *Native Life in South Africa* should be read in
> conjunction for they were not only written within a short time of each other,
> but they also show Plaatje's consistent and persistent preoccupations. The
> Native Land Act was devastating in its effect, rendering homeless large
> numbers of Africans throughout the Union and causing untold hardship.
> *Native Life in South Africa* is an explicit and *Mhudi* an implicit attack on the
> Act and the hardship it caused.[8]

   The assessment of Plaatje's *Mhudi* as a work of "tutelage" has been heavily
influenced by the Christian milieu in which he operated. As Stephen Gray has
pointed out, "Plaatje himself was a Lutheran and a laypreacher."[9]
Nonetheless, his church affiliation neither obscures nor seriously blunts his
political consciousness. Unlike some of his contemporaries (such as Thomas
Mofolo and R. R. R. Dhlomo, whose writings praise Christian life unstintingly
and indiscriminately), Plaatje is capable of seeing through the hypocrisy of

some denominations and criticizing them bitterly. He shows how Boers use the Church to legitimize and consolidate their position at the expense of blacks. In *Native Life in South Africa*, for instance, Plaatje is convinced that Boer racism is caused by the Dutch Reformed Church:

> One of the most astounding things in connection with the unjust treatment of the Natives by the whites of South Africa is the profound silence of the Dutch Reformed Church, which practically is now the State Church of South Africa . . . If the predikants of the Dutch Reformed Church would but tell their congregations that it was gross libel on the Christian faith, which they profess, to treat human beings as they treat those with loathsome disease except when it is desired to exploit the benefits, such as their taxes and their labour which these outraged human beings confer upon the Dutch . . . The Dutch almost worship their religious teachers; and they will continue these cruelties upon the Natives as long as they believe that they have the approval of the Church.[10]

In *Mhudi*, his attack on the Dutch Reformed Church is subtle but still acidulated. One example occurs in the conversation that takes place when the first group of Boers arrives at Thaba Nchu, the headquarters of the Barolong tribe. Ostensibly the Boers have left the Cape Colony in search of some "unoccupied territory to colonize and to worship God in peace."[11] Asked by Chief Moroka whether they could not worship God in the Cape Colony, Cilliers, the leader of the group, answers: "We could . . . but oppression is not conducive to piety. We are after freedom. The English laws of the Cape are not fair to us".[12] Though Cilliers uses the Church to conceal his group's ulterior motives, it is apparent from the dialogue that the Boers are in search of land to secure political independence. Thus, by juxtaposing the Boers' claim for freedom of worship with their search for land, Plaatje is demonstrating that, being a racially exclusive denomination, the Dutch Reformed Church can thrive only where the Boers have the upper hand. The Church thus becomes a handmaiden of Boer expansionism and, hence, the State Church. As Nadine Gordimer has rightly commented on this relationship between the Church and politics, ". . . there it was, unashamedly, the ugliest creation of man, and they baptized the thing in the Dutch Reformed Church, called it apartheid."[13]

The driving force behind Boer exclusiveness is racism. Like other aspects of Boer life, it too is buttressed by Church sanction. Plaatje demonstrates this in a very intriguing manner. As soon as the Boers arrive in the interior, a relationship of mutual understanding and friendship develops between a Boer and a black, De Villiers and RaThaga respectively. The former is unwittingly what one may hazard to call an archetypal Christian liberal. The acts of cruelty perpetrated against Hottentot servants by his people invoke pity and compassion in him. Besides relishing RaThaga's company and friendship, De Villiers takes the former's advice seriously. For instance, after their adventurous search expedition in the Matabele region, De Villiers, on RaThaga's advice, develops a promising love relationship with Hannetjie, who is a woman similar to De Villiers in terms of their benign treatment of blacks.

Most important, De Villiers is generous. Towards the end of the novel, he presents Mhudi, RaThaga's wife, with an old wagon for her bravery. It is this gesture that triggers Boer racism:

> The Van Zyls, especially, and the other Boers at Khing, feeling outraged at De Villiers' treatment of the Kaffir and his wife, regarded these acts of generosity as being grossly extravagant. Indeed they began to doubt the sanity of the young man. The Boers were God's chosen people, so they argued, and had never seen a heathen treated with so much consideration, they remonstrated with De Villiers and held that it was unnatural to reward a Kaffir for anything he did as liberally as if he were a baptized Christian.[14]

Plaatje's criticism of the Boer's possessive attitude towards Christianity is unmistakable. Though he is a man of the Church, Plaatje does not endorse a denomination which puts people into watertight compartments of predestined Christians and heathens. Apparently, his community of Christians is the one cited by De Villiers in response to his people's reprehension: "What did Paulus mean, . . . when he said to the Galatians, there is neither Greek nor Jew, bond nor free, male nor female, White nor Black, but are all one in Christ Jesus."[15] Hannetjie, of course, backs up De Villiers' "scriptural rejoinder" to the hilt. Though Hannetjie's brittle faith and belief in Church doctrine may easily lead her into problems of dogmatism, she impresses upon the dumbfounded Boers that the Lord's commandments rise above the prejudices of man.

The most telling example of Boer feelings of racial "purity" and "superiority" manifests itself when RaThaga attempts to drink water from a Boer vessel. The act arouses so much anger among the Boers that they come close to attacking him physically. His familiarity with some of them helps him out of what could have been an uglier scene. A number of observations arise from this episode. First, it shows the limits of liberal intervention. Plaatje supplies the reader with ample information to the effect that De Villiers, the Christian liberal, is aware that Boers never allow blacks to drink anything from their vessels. He is also aware that when blacks visit the Boers, the former are always served from vessels set aside for Hottentot servants. But with all De Villiers's apparent beliefs in non-racism, non-racial discrimination and benignity, nowhere does Plaatje make him raise a finger against these racist restrictions. If it is not the author's failure to create a fully realized liberal character, then Plaatje wants to make the reader conscious that, in a society so polarized by social conflict, a budding liberal may not be completely free and independent in beliefs and values. Sometimes he may have to compromise his principles in the interest of majority opinion and behaviour.

Second, the incident unmasks RaThaga's ambivalent radical consciousness. Brave as he is in maintaining a precarious existence in the forest and fomenting revenge against the Matabele, his critical capacity with regard to Boer attitudes is kept in check by the friendship between himself and De Villiers. Though the incident discourages him from visiting the Boers often, he keeps vacillating between considering the Boers as friends and treating them as enemies. Indeed, in order not to betray their friendship, "RaThaga and De Villiers both agreed not to let Mhudi hear anything of the latest escapade of her husband's friends."[16] Unlike RaThaga, Mhudi is cautious in her dealings with the Boers. Her disenchantment with some of them reaches its climax when she sees Hottentot servants either flogged mercilessly or their ears screwed between the jaws of a vice. Mhudi, however, is careful enough not to condemn the Boers collectively. She believes that, in spite of their unbridled cruelty, there are redeeming personalities among them:

> A pretty Boer girl in the waggon in which I came remonstrated with her mother for keeping quiet while Jan was being beaten for no cause whatever. The Boers are cruel but they sometimes breed angels, . . . and Hannetjie is one of them.[17]

Boer racism and religious exclusiveness are invariably linked with land ownership. The disruptive effects of the 1913 Land Act loom large in Plaatje's works. As Tim Couzens observes, "Throughout Plaatje's writings, a single theme constantly recurs, the loss of the land the African loves and needs."[18] One of his characters demonstrates the importance of land to blacks when Potgieter plans to keep all the land for the Boers and hand over captured cattle to the Barolong after the defeat of the Matabele:

> What an absurd bargain! exlaimed Chief Tauana of the RaTshidi, What could one do with a number of cattle if he possessed no land on which to feed them? Will his cattle run on the clouds! and their grass grow in the air? No, my lords; I would rather leave the Matabele where they are and remain a sojourner with my people in the land of the Selekas under my cousin, Moroka.[19]

To blacks, therefore, "To lose land was to lose the most important foundation upon which tribal life was built."[20] But the South African land problem does not just begin with the 1913 Land Act. It manifests itself as early as the middle of the 19th century. Natal is the breeding ground of what today are termed "Bantustans", areas specially "reserved" for blacks:

> In the late 1840's the British administrator Theophilus Shepstone established his famous system of Native Reserves that became the first large scale scheme for the physical segregation of the races in South Africa, and the blueprint for subsequent 'Native Administration' in the rural areas. Shepstone set aside dispersed land tracts for the exclusive occupation of Africans. This scattering served the dual purpose of making farm labour more easily accessible to White farmers, and of averting the threat of large concentrations of Africans. Subsequent legislation, such as the Native Land Act of 1913 and the Native Trust and Land Act of 1936, expanded and refined the Shepstone system.[21]

The difficulties posed by "Bantustans" will be elaborated upon in later chapters, but it is important to note that the problems of segregation and land deprivation usually associated with the Boers alone, were, in fact, created by the British administration. Despite his apparent respect for Cape liberalism, Plaatje is painfully conscious that "Native Reserves" serve as labour pools for white farms. He denigrates them as "human incubators" that produce black men and women and their children "for a life of serfdom".[22] In both *Mhudi* and *Native Life in South Africa*, Plaatje examines the gradual development of the land problem and the dislocation of traditional life.

In his portrayal he places events in an historical perspective. Though the technique is used in both books, it is more conspicuous in *Mhudi*. As the story opens, Plaatje presents the reader with a portrait of a sedate, well-ordered society. Though the region he deals with is vast and inhabited by different ethnic groups, he portrays a peaceful, unified and idyllic society, totally in control of its resources and the preservation of its traditional culture.

> Two centuries ago the Bechuana tribes inhabited the extensive areas between Central Transvaal and the Kalahari Desert . . . In this domain they led their patriarchal life under their several chiefs who owed no allegiance to any king or emperor. They raised their native corn which satisfied their simple wants and, when not engaged in hunting or in pastoral duties, the peasants whiled away their days in tanning skins or sewing magnificent fur rugs. They also smelted iron and manufactured useful implements which today would be pronounced very crude by their semiwesternized descendants . . . their cattle which carried enormous horns ran almost wild and multiplied as prolifically as the wild animals of the day.[23]

Plaatje does, however, show that traditional life was not all peace and tranquillity. He uses a dispute that arises between RaThaga and some Qoranna hunters, and which involves the attempted murder of RaThaga and the abortive seduction of his wife, Mhudi. Plaatje also demonstrates that the idyllic character of traditional life was later threatened by the Mfecane[24] and the Boer incursion. In terms of style, however, Plaatje's portrayal of a peaceful society is designed to highlight the total erosion and disruption of traditional life that succeeded the idyllic phase. The contrast revolves around the activities of the Matabele and the Boers who are the agents of disruption in the novel.

The Matabele style of life is described as predatory and based on a ruthless subjugation of other ethnic groups. Besides trekking from Zululand and creating a large kingdom at the expense of other ethnic groups, the Matabele impose exorbitant taxes on their subjects. Above all, they are portrayed as warmongers who, in battle, kill all their enemies, men, women and children, without distinction. Worse still, some ethnic groups, such as the Barolong of Kunana, are virtually wiped out by the Matabele. Certainly Plaatje has a purpose in depicting the Matabele in this way. Though they are one of the black ethnic groups, the Matabele share certain characteristics with the Boers. Plaatje's description of the movement of the Matabele from Zululand into the interior is reminiscent of the plundering raid of the Boers from the Cape into the interior:

> Sweeping through the northern areas of Port Natal, they [the Matabele]

advanced along both banks of the Vaal River, driving terror into man and beast with whom they came in contact. They continued their march very much like a swarm of locusts; scattering the Swazis, terrifying the Basụto and the Bapedi on their outposts, they drove them back to the mountains at the point of the Assegai; and, trekking through the heart of the Transvaal, they eventually invaded Bechuanaland where they reduced the Natives to submission.[25]

By employing forceful metaphors and a vocabulary of devastation and plunder, Plaatje succeeds in painting the attributes the Matabele share with Boers. The biblical image of "a swarm of locusts" is a concrete and very effective one, symbolizing invasion and destruction. The description so vividly portrays the terror of the marauders' advance that it is as though it is a depiction of the Boers and not of a black ethnic group. Yet, the terror of statements such as "where they reduced the Natives to submission" is characteristic of colonials' exaggerated descriptions of black inter-ethnic raids and fights. The description is, however, in keeping with Plaatje's dislike for any form of disruption, dispossession and oppression, whether internal or external.

Like the Boers, the Matabele are seen as expansionists and oppressors. Plaatje goes on to reveal more parallels. Whereas the leader of the Qoranna and Moroka, chief of the Barolong, are associated with justice, hospitality and, in the case of the latter, abhorrence of the shedding of blood, both the Matabele and the Boers are associated with brutality, lack of justice, exorbitant taxation, ruthless bloodshed and land-grabbing. To that extent, it may be claimed that Plaatje makes the Matabele harbingers of Boer hegemony. Besides showing the similar contribution that both groups make to the collapse of black society, this parallelism signifies what seems to be Plaatje's conception of history.

This he sees as dialectical and cyclical, reflecting the birth, development and death of epochs. To herald the birth and death of the opposing cycles, Plaatje uses the image of a "star with a long tail (what Tim Couzens terms Halley's comet)". According to Couzens, Plaatje's star symbol appears in 1835 and is seen as foreshadowing the Matabele defeat. It next occurs in 1910 (shortly before the Native Land Act) and is widely viewed as foreshadowing the end of the white man in South Africa.[26] Indeed, as Plaatje himself puts it, the star, portends "the downfall of kings and destruction of nations by war or sickness".[27]

The most obvious manifestation of the prophetic and cyclical nature of Plaatje's conception of history may be found in Mzilikazi's speech. Having been thoroughly defeated by the combined forces of the Boers and the Barolong, Mzilikazi warns:

Those bearded Boers who killed my herdboys and stole my cattle are today helping them to destroy me.

The Bechuana know not the story of Zungu of old. Remember him, my people; he caught a lion's whelp and thought that, if he fed it with the milk of his cows, he would in due course possess a useful mastiff to help him in hunting valuable specimens of wild beasts. The cub grew up, apparently tame and meek, just like an ordinary domestic puppy; but one day Zungu came home and found, what? It had eaten his children, chewed up two of his wives, and in destroying it, he himself narrowly escaped being mauled. So, if Tauana and his gang of brigands imagine that they shall have rain and plenty under the protection of these marauding wizards from the sea, they will gather some sense before long.

Chaka served us just as treacherously. Where is Chaka's dynasty now? Extinguished, by the very Boers who poisoned my wives and are pursuing us today. The Bechuana are fools to think that these unnatural Kiwas (white men) will return their so-called friendship with honest friendship. Together they are laughing at my misery. Let them rejoice; they need all the laughter they can have today for when their deliverers begin to close them with the same bitter medicine they prepared for me; when the Kiwas rob them of their cattle, their children and their lands, they will weep their eyes out of their sockets and get left with only their empty throats to squeal in vain for mercy.

They will despoil them of the very lands they have rendered unsafe for us; they will entice the Bechuana youths to war and the chase, only to use them as pack-oxen; yea, they will refuse to share with them the spoils of victory.[28]

Here Plaatje makes use of an effective allegory couched in local diction like "Kiwas", and an all too familiar fable. Addressed to a highly traditional audience that strongly believes in the meaningfulness of fables, the story of Zungu concretizes the seriousness and prophetic character of Mzilikazi's speech. Exhortatory, declamatory, highly political and emotionally nationalistic in tone, the speech sounds very persuasive. The fable itself becomes a premise on which Mzilikazi develops his trend of political thought. On the face of it, the speech predicts the betrayal of the Barolong by their Boer "friends". On a wider level, it is a universal prophecy concerning the incidence of cycles of power and defeat, a theme which the Matabele hegemony is meant to highlight. It is as though Plaatje is arguing that no matter how oppressive and exploitative they may be, governments come and go. The victorious Boers would, therefore, be vanquished one day. But the only people who would seek to vanquish them are blacks who have been dispossessed of their land. In that case, the speech is an indirect prediction of a revolution[29] against the Boers by blacks.

More important, the speech anticipates the 1913 Land Act and its attendant problems. Later, in *Native Life in South Africa*, the Boers annex the whole territory previously occupied by blacks, confiscate all the land not yet surveyed and pass a law to the effect that all the Barolongs who have access to land may sell their farms only to white people. Plaatje argues that the Act is not the creation of the Boers alone, but is passed with the full consent of both the Boers and the British.

The objectives of the Act as described by Plaatje were segregation and exploitation. First, those blacks who intended to carry out agriculture and pastoralism "freely" would inevitably be encouraged to move to poor, unproductive and crowded "reserves". Second, with no prospect of settling down in the areas set aside for blacks, most dispossessed people would ultimately have to sell their labour to their very dispossessors in order to subsist. Two dominant activities – farming and mining – would be increasingly in need of labour. The arrangement that emerged on white farms was akin to the feudal system whereby serfs were totally dependent on their lords. The black South African labourer was forced to offer his labour in the field and household. In return, "the master" would protect him and accord him the right to practise a limited amount of "independent" agriculture and pastoralism. The black worker was reduced to what Frederick Johnstone later rightly terms an "ultra-exploitable" squatter.[30]

Plaatje sharpens his picture of the underprivileged existence of the black farm workers by cynically comparing their conditions to those of the American slaves:

> A contemplation of the circumstances attending these selfish recommenda-tions leads one to wonder whether the Commissioners suffered from the lack of a sense of humour or an undue excess of it. In North and South America, for instance, we read that the slave-pens were erected and maintained by the farmers at their own cost. That 'the interest of the master demanded that he should direct the general social and moral life of the slave, and should provide especially for his physical well-being'; but the pens proposed by the South African Land Commission, on the other hand, are to be maintained entirely by the slaves, at their own cost, the farmer's only trouble being to come to the gate and whistle for labourers.[31]

Though he implicitly condemns slavery as a system, the parallel Plaatje employs here serves to illustrate the selfish and pitiless exploitation of labour. He makes it clear that the white South African farmer does not care about the social and economic well-being of his worker, his sole concern being the unfailing provision of labour. That is very much in keeping with the Boers' belief that blacks are born to be hewers of wood and drawers of water for whites.

Plaatje is, therefore, a committed writer whose political beliefs are mainly communicated through a convincing foreshadowing technique. Though he does not deal directly with problems of industrialization and urbanization, his discussion of the effects of the 1913 Land Act foreshadows the concerns of what Jahn terms "skokiaan" culture. In *Native Life in South Africa*, Plaatje graphically presents the landlessness, poverty and hopelessness of blacks so that their future condition as farm labourers and workers in the developing gold and diamond mining industry is foreshadowed. Indeed, the directness and anguish with which the book is written leave one in no doubt of its element of protest. In *Native Life In South Africa*, Plaatje, nonetheless, does not advocate revolution. He stirs his countrymen's consciousness by continually harping on the negative effects of the Land Act. His belief in revolution is implicitly and subtly portrayed in *Mhudi*, written a year after the publication of *Native Land in South Africa*. Though devoid of a confrontational tone, *Mhudi* foreshadows a revolutionary future. Using Mzilikazi as a mouthpiece, Plaatje implies that no political enemy is invincible indefinitely. Hence, according to him, a black revolution would dislodge whites from what they believe to be their impregnable fortress of power. To that extent, Plaatje's writings deserve a place in the growing body of protest literature written by blacks in South Africa.

Industrialization and Problems of Urbanization

The rapid development of the mining industry and the ever-increasing urbanization of Johannesburg present Plaatje's successors with newer and more immediate concerns. Invariably, they deal with such issues as blacks' economic need, the conflict between rural and urban values, which could be divided into sub-themes such as blacks' working conditions, their relationship with superiors both black and white, living conditions in urban slums, and "shebeen" life. Early writings on these issues range from R. R. R. Dhlomo's mine stories of the 1920s through the 1930s, to Peter Abrahams's proletarian novels of the late 1940s. Although published in 1973, Modikwe Dikobe's *The Marabi Dance* partly belongs to the same period. A common feature exhibited by all the writers mentioned above is an awareness of the predicament of the black man. Nonetheless, there is a significant difference in what the authors consider to be the underlying cause of that predicament. While Dhlomo attributes the black man's problem to evil, in a Christian sense, Dikobe and Abrahams attribute it to the flaws of capitalism. Abrahams's attribution derives from an unmistakable Marxist perspective.

A dominant theme in all these authors' works is the loss of innocence. In each novel an innocent young man or woman, because of economic need, goes to town to seek employment. The young man generally works in the mines whereas the woman works as a maid or a self-employed shebeen-queen. As time progresses, the once innocent, morally upright country person becomes hardened and corrupted by the temptations and pressures of city life. But not everyone ends up corrupted and deracinated. For some blacks, the experience prompts political awareness.

In *An African Tragedy*, Dhlomo gives a brief and didactic account of the degeneration of a traditional young man. Before leaving home, Robert Zulu is a pious village teacher at a mission school. Once in Johannesburg, his disorientation is first occasioned by his failure to choose friends carefully. Robert's friend, John Bolotwa, is a bad influence. According to Dhlomo, the places to which Robert is introduced by John are embodiments of evil – places in which unbridled drinking, rampant sexuality, murder and senseless assaults are common.

Similarly, Abrahams's protagonist, Xuma (in *Mine Boy*[32]) arrives in Johannesburg raw and disturbingly innocent. Like Dhlomo's Robert, Xuma soon finds himself in the company of people hardened by urban life. Nonetheless, while Robert does not live under the same roof as his "evil" friend John, during his first days in the city Xuma is literally looked after by Leah, a well-known shebeen-queen. The other people in Xuma's orbit are Eliza, an alienated school teacher with bourgeois aspirations, Maisy, an earthy and trustworthy girl who later promises to marry Xuma, Ma Plank, Leah's devoted colleague in the shebeen enterprise, and Daddy, an alcoholic who flirts with Ma Plank. While Dhlomo tells the reader nothing about Robert's working conditions, Abrahams dwells on Xuma's work as a miner. The reader is furnished with descriptions of Xuma's work shifts, his boss-boy duties and execution of them, and the workers' strike that, towards the end of the novel, he initiates and leads.

As in Abrahams's *Mine Boy*, Dikobe's *The Marabi Dance* has a number of characters who are affected by Johannesburg life. In this case, the innocent character is a woman (Ma Ndlovu) whose husband goes to work in the mines but never returns home and ends up a bigamist. With good intentions, Ma Ndlovu follows her husband to the city. Having failed to win back his heart, she decides to subsist by throwing Marabi parties,[33] and this marks the beginning of her downfall. Later, she finds herself in the company of other corrupted residents of Johannesburg, including Mr Tshirongo, a bogus minister who goes by the pseudonym of Reverend Ndlovu, George, a playboy who impregnates girls in every corner of the black township, and Martha, who later marries George.

As mentioned above, these writers view the causes and results of the black man's degeneration and corruption differently. Though the subject matter of their works belongs to the same period, they themselves have different backgrounds. The most senior of them all, Dhlomo, is a contemporary of Solomon T. Plaatje. Like other members of the mission-educated élite (Plaatje himself, Tiyo Soga, D. T. Jabavu, John Dube and Thomas Mofolo), Dhlomo works in a milieu heavily influenced by the Church. His works are edited, approved and published by missionaries. Unlike Plaatje, who refuses to blunt his political vision in the interests of the Church, Dhlomo feels it necessary to examine the blacks' predicament within an overtly Christian framework. Commenting on the obvious Christian influence in Dhlomo's *An African Tragedy*, Stephen Gray rightly says:

> The publishing policy of the Lovedale Press as it affected an earlier novella in English, R. R. R. Dhlomo's *An African Tragedy*, was clear cut . . . the truth about *An African Tragedy* might be that it was so calculated to be "a contribution towards staying the decline of Native life in large cities and towns" in the face of liquor, gambling, whoring and thievery, and so in line with the proselytizing intentions of a press using its printing works for the general propaganda of the Christian message, . . . the very fact that this rudimentary attempt at transforming pamphleteering into fiction has such a publisher's note demonstrates that a missionary press could not contemplate printing a manuscript unless it conformed in some way to its general policy.[34]

Except for parts which describe Robert Zulu's episodic encounters with various people in Johannesburg, a great deal of *An African Tragedy* sounds like a homily, packed with didactic sermons and religious warnings conveyed with righteous anger. Remarking on what he calls "a revolting immoral" life that obtains in the shebeens, Dhlomo pontificates:

> For after all is said and done what is the use of trying to unite our peoples when their offsprings wallow in the mud so to speak? Do Christians who profess to love God, and seek to do His will ever visit such (places) not as they do on Sunday afternoons when the people in the yards are already half mad with drinks and evil (passions) but in the quiet during the week when these people are more amenable to reason?
>
> Does it occur to their minds that these slaves of vice may be the sheep of whose welfare Christ spoke so eloquently, and so feelingly in the 10th Chapter of St. John's Gospel: Verse 16?[35]

Indeed, Dhlomo himself feels the weight of his pessimistic and defeatist preachiness, and soon after the above passage he feels it imperative to make an authorial apology: "Pardon my digression, my poor effort being to write the story of Robert Zulu as he handed it to me for publication, not to presume to teach or preach."[36]

But teaching or preaching is what Dhlomo predominantly does. Towards the end of the novel he employs a genuine religious character, a minister who literally preaches about what Dhlomo piously calls "God's mysterious movement", as Robert languishes with venereal disease on his death-bed. While Abrahams gives the reader ample information about the socio-economic conditions that motivate blacks to behave the way they do, Dhlomo seems to assume that blacks are inherently promiscuous and corrupt. It is rather surprising that he should paint such a superficial and stereotyped picture because his mine stories reflect a thorough and first-hand knowledge of the work experience and living conditions of blacks, and how these affect their lives. On the contrary, *An African Tragedy* is a rushed, unsubstantiated critique of the drinking and licentious habits of blacks. For instance, Dhlomo condemns shebeens in general, but he never indicates why they are there in the first place. Having grown up in a system which imposes oppressive laws on blacks, he must be aware that until 1962 it was a criminal offence in South Africa to sell to "nonwhites" alcoholic beverages of almost any kind, except for traditionally prepared beers, and those only under rigorously specified monopolistic circumstances. As a result, the practice of illicit liquor-drinking flourished, especially in the towns, where it became institutionalized in various forms.[37]

Regarding the drinking itself, no one condones excessive drinking as do Robert and his circle of friends and Daddy in Abrahams's *Mine Boy*, but one's condemnation ought to be thoroughly informed by the various forces at work. Daddy's alcoholism, for example, is the outcome of an oppressive system that denies his talents and aspirations. As Ma Plank sorrowfully puts it to Xuma, Daddy is a man who has been hauled from heights of social importance to the lowest ebb of frustrated drunkenness:

You scorn him, heh? Yet when he first came to the city he was a man. Such a man! He was strong and he was feared and he was respected. And now you scorn him . . . Even the white ones respected him.

He had money then, and many friends. Men thought it an honour to be his friend and women longed for him. And when there was trouble about the passes he stood at the head of the people and he spoke to hundreds of them and the police feared him.

He understood and he fought for his people, but he understood too much and it made him unhappy and he became like Eliza. Only he fought. And listen, Xuma, that one lying there in his own piss is wiser than Eliza. He can read and write even better than she can.[38]

In *An African Tragedy*, other hateful aspects of South African life such as passes and the oppressive police system are simply mentioned in passing. This is very different from the trenchant way Dhlomo exposes police brutality in one of his mine stories, "Special Pass", in which a man is senselessly and uselessly kicked to death because he is not carrying a pass. The satire and humour with which Dhlomo depicts this incident is quite remarkable. In *An African Tragedy*, he merely narrates how Robert encounters the police without a pass, but manages to escape. Later, Robert becomes involved in gambling and a mêlée subsequently ensues in which a Xosa is stabbed to death by a "Blantyre". Again Dhlomo condemns gambling, superficially, and moralizes about it. First, it is important to note that the involvement of a "Blantyre" (Malawian mine worker) is related to the attitude of black South African workers to foreign miners. Workers do not get involved in fights of this nature because they are inherently prone to violent acts. On the contrary, local workers tend to dislike foreign labour (due to competition for jobs) As Tim Couzens argues:

As in *An African Tragedy*, so in 'The Sins of The Fathers', Dhlomo is somewhat disparaging of 'Blantyres', 'boys' from the then Nyasaland. He seems to be following the prejudice of the time: local blacks were against 'foreign natives' because of their competition in the labour market . . .[39]

As for gambling itself, in the black South African context it is partly a township pastime and partly an activity prompted by economic need. In the case of underpaid workers like Robert, the latter motive is more important. At the beginning of his novel, Dhlomo misguidedly describes Robert's banking habits as though Robert makes a lot of money. In *Mine Boy*, by contrast, Abrahams gives an example of a miner whose lungs have been affected by cancer, but who insists on working until he has accumulated the eight pounds he owes:

Listen, Xuma, I have a wife and two children and I have worked it all out. We have a small farm and I owe a white man eight pounds. If I do not give it back to him he will take the farm. And if he takes it, where will my wife and children go? I have worked it all out, Xuma, really I have. *For four months I have been saving and if I save for another three months I will have the eight pounds and there will be a house for my wife and children* (Emphasis mine).[40]

In Dikobe's *The Marabi Dance*, Martha sees a cluster of "Portuguese" Africans bound for home and reminisces about a mine-worker who left the mines on account of low wages: "Tiny's father left many years ago because he complained that the mines make a man work too hard for very little money. I think these men are also glad that they are going back home."[41]

Judging by the tenor of some of his mine stories, Dhlomo is certainly aware of the socio-economic forces that influence black behaviour, but his Christian background militates against him exposing and condemning them. His performance in *An African Tragedy* clearly demonstrates the alienating influence that he absorbed from missionary institutions. Daniel P. Kunene has argued:

> The African intellectual who came out of the missionary school was not only literate, but also he was a changed being. He looked about himself and saw nothing but evil. He saw his 'heathen' brothers singing and dancing and drinking and loving in pursuit, as they thought, of the Good Life, and he shook his head in pity. For suddenly these things had become ugly and sinful . . . The process of alienation had begun, complex and divisive – Christian and non-Christian drifted; worse than that, they began to hate each other.[42]

An African Tragedy is the product of a thoroughly alienated mind. Dhlomo views the activities of his fellow blacks with anger, disdain and insufferable condescension. In keeping with the misconceptions of an alienated black man, he, like the racist Boers, believes blacks are the cursed children of Ham. "No wonder Black Africa is cursed!"[43] he cynically claims. Dhlomo's commitment, therefore, is aggressively moral. His concerns are alcoholism, promiscuity and venereal diseases. Since the book deliberately neglects to examine the material conditions of blacks, and none of the characters in it ever acquire any form of political awareness, it would not contribute much to the understanding of the black man's struggle in South Africa. Unlike characters in *Mine Boy* and *The Marabi Dance*, who are convincingly delineated interacting with other people at shebeens, work places, church and rural reserves, Robert's development as a character is significantly stunted by the Christian straitjacket that encompasses the novel's plot. Robert is only associated with the moral aspects that Dhlomo wants to highlight and this denies *An African Tragedy* the rich and comprehensive analysis which distinguishes *Mine Boy*. Of course the length of *An African Tragedy* is another limiting factor.

While Dhlomo's *An African Tragedy* is the product of a black South African dominated by Christian influence, Abrahams's *Mine Boy* is the child of the Marxist world of the 1930s and 1940s. Though Dikobe does not adopt a Marxist perspective, he shares common concerns with Abrahams. Both writers show an acute awareness of the material conditions of blacks. Instead of disdaining and mocking the drinking, sexuality, violence and trickery of blacks, they view these activities against the backdrop of political oppression and economic deprivation. Abrahams's work is, however, more profound than Dikobe's rather thin portrayal.

The notions of poverty and economic need that Dhlomo introduces are more extensively treated in *Mine Boy* and *The Marabi Dance*. Both books deal with extremely poor characters who struggle to subsist. In the former, Leah's household is composed of people none of whom are related by blood. They are brought together by what they have in common, that is, poverty and homelessness. First, we learn that, in his heyday, Daddy "found Leah in the street and looked after her".[44] As the book opens, Daddy's wealth and power have disappeared and he is in Leah's custody. Eliza is Leah's foundling whom she has educated. Xuma is, of course, an outsider to whom Leah has given accommodation and food. All these people depend on the money that accrues from Leah's "skokiaan" business. The importance of the business is reflected by the division of labour involved in the production and sale of the beer and the solidarity manifested by the residents in the face of police raids. Although towards the end of the novel Leah is arrested for illicit trade, the economic importance of the business is nevertheless underlined. Before she leaves for prison, Leah instructs Ma Plank to take control of the business and maintain the family in her absence. To them, the business is not a hobby but a necessity. Lewis Nkosi succinctly expresses this relentless determination to subsist when he says:

> . . . the African township represented the strength and the will to survive by ordinary masses of the African people. In its own quiet way the township presented a dogged defiance against official persecution, for in the township the moments of splendour were very splendid indeed, surpassing anything white Johannesburg could offer.[45]

In *The Marabi Dance*, economic need is portrayed in shattering terms. As in *Mine Boy*, a female character sells illicit liquor for a living. In this case, however, poverty in general has taught blacks to make money from anything, no matter how dehumanizing. People like Ma Ndlovu are courageous enough to make money even from dead bodies. As George's mother warns him after Madonda's death:

> George, my child, town people make money from dead bodies. They keep the bodies for longer than a week in order to get more people to collect money from. Women claim husbands from whom they have been parted for years. Not because they loved them but to disgrace the women with whom they had been living.[46]

For all its macabre connotations, this mode of earning a living was a reflection of the desperate economic position blacks find themselves in. Poverty renders them insensitive and heartless. When Ma Ndlovu first appears in Johannesburg, she is depicted as a character which evokes sympathy, a woman who has been deserted and cheated by her husband, Madonda. The need to survive in a harsh environment, however, teaches her a sad and callous lesson.

Though published in the late 1960s, Ezekiel Mphahlele's short story, "In Corner B", touches on a similar theme. Like *The Marabi Dance*, the story concerns a man who has been robbed and murdered by township thugs. As the dead man's relatives and friends await his burial, a notorious swindler mounts a stool and starts to collect unauthorized contributions. In normal circumstances, such money is used for purchasing food for guests from afar. In this case, however, the swindler needs part of the money for his own use; it has become his custom to benefit from funerals:

> It was generally known that the . . . young man appeared at every death house where he could easily be suspected to be related to the deceased, and invariably used his initiative to take collections and dispose of some of the revenue.[47]

But, like Abrahams and Dikobe, Mphahlele argues that, by depriving blacks economically, the South African white regime encourages the breeding of swindlers and people who commit murder for material benefit. During the vigil, one of the characters in "In Corner B" asserts: "Now look here you men, these boys don't mean to kill nobody; their empty stomachs and no work to do turns their heads on evil things".[48]

Dikobe's treatment of economic need assumes satirical proportions when Reverend Ndlovu appears on the scene. After accumulating the money that accrues from Madonda's body and a successful Marabi party, Ma Ndlovu invites Reverend Ndlovu to help her count it. While everyone assumes that the Reverend is a truly pious man and a brother to Ma Ndlovu, the truth of the matter is that he is her lover and an imposter who operates under a pseudonym. His true identity is learned only after he has absconded with all of Ma Ndlovu's money. One is struck by the various methods blacks employ to get money in the novel. Mr Tshirongo masquerades as Reverend Ndlovu to swindle Ma Ndlovu and other people. The pseudo-Reverend himself is later driven to a shebeen by a false taxi-driver who hands the former over to bogus policemen. The whole process becomes an endless struggle for survival based on deceit and criminal acts. In such a society, some people simply end up either irredeemably brutalized or withdrawn from their own society and its culture. To others the experience is a revelation that leads to political consciousness. Abrahams and Dikobe depict both categories.

They are convinced that, besides breeding drunkards, murderers and swindlers, the South African system continues to produce alienated people like some of the mission-educated intellectuals. Abrahams, in particular, examines two forms of alienation, both of which derive from a Marxist interpretation. First, he identifies alienation within the context of divorce from one's society and culture due to the overall effect of oppression, exploitation and racial discrimination, with the emphasis on class antagonism. Second, he identifies it within the context of the productive process in an industrial setting with the thrust of his examination on the relationship between the worker and the product of his labour. The first type of alienation involves a number of characters in *Mine Boy*.

By virtue of her academic qualifications, Eliza believes that all the other people in Leah's household are below her social station; she respects Leah only because she had brought her up. In spite of the fact that Eliza's education was financed by money from shebeen sales, she does not play a significant role in the shebeen business. Abrahams invariably depicts her either coming from school or in her room, where she spends most of the time bemoaning the kind of life surrounding her. Because of the crisis of belonging that Eliza faces, her character is highly unpredictable, veering as it does between introversion and impulsive expansiveness. This is partly illustrated by the tenuous and precarious love relationship that she evolves with Xuma. While the latter loves her sincerely, she is half-hearted about the affair. Abrahams implies that the root cause of Eliza's crisis is deep-seated alienation. Eliza herself tells Xuma:

> I am no good and I cannot help myself. It will be right if you hate me. You should beat me. But inside me there is something wrong. And it is because I want the things of the white people. I want to be like the white people and go where they go and do the things they do and I am black. I cannot help it. Inside I am not black and I do not want to be a black person. I want to be like they are, you understand Xuma. It is no good but I cannot help it. It is just so, and it is that that makes me hurt you . . . Please understand.[49]

This is the confession of a totally deracinated black person; Eliza is a black person with a white mask. Her intense drive for social mobility prompts her to resent, and subsequently reject, people of her own kind. By virtue of her academic qualifications, Eliza is technically a member of the petit-bourgeois class. The realization of this, coupled with the poor conditions that surround her, causes her to crave a life beyond that enjoyed by her own class. Judging by her tastes, Eliza is not looking for the company of "poor whites", she wants to be an authentic bourgeois. It is the failure to achieve this status at home that frustrates her and completes her alienation. Ultimately she disappears and engages herself in a quest for the company and life that she needs.

The depiction of Eliza is, however, hardly credible. Her background does not vindicate the bourgeois aspirations she holds. First, she is Leah's foundling, brought up in poverty. Second, she is never described in the company of very rich people or of white friends who could have influenced her aspirations. She is always seen against the background of workers and the *déclassés*. Besides mingling with other teachers at school, one wonders what other influence has kindled her upwardly mobile zeal.

Dr Mini's alienation is somewhat similar to Eliza's. He, nonetheless, has already succeeded in withdrawing himself from his own society entirely. His detachment is reinforced by the anonymity associated with him when he is first introduced. Abrahams simply refers to him as "the black Doctor" until later the doctor introduces himself as Dr Mini. Most of his own people are meeting him for the first time because of an accident that has happened not very far away from his cosy house. After that, Dr Mini literally disappears except for a brief appearance after Daddy's death. His alienation is sharpened by this total withdrawal from his own people; he views whatever happens to them with the eye of an outsider. Like most whites, Dr Mini maintains an independent, rather closed mode of life based on nuclear family connections. To emphasize this, Abrahams implicitly compares Dr Mini's domestic comfort and middle-class values with the life-style of whites.

Daddy's alienation is the most vivid, yet incredibly exaggerated. As pointed out earlier, he used to be a man of consequence but the system has relegated him to the level of a pauper. Besides his excessive drinking and persistent withdrawal, Daddy is also associated with anonymity. "Daddy" is not his name. His real name is Francis Ndabula, but that has become disregarded and replaced by one that fits his degenerate state. "Daddy" is a general and impersonal name given to any man in Daddy's state. Hence, he is a kind of "everyman" representing all the degraded, degenerate and decrepit men in his society. The important thing to note is how the system's pernicious influence leads to loss of identity. As Michael Wade argues:

> . . . urban life for the African in South Africa is fundamentally a process of depersonalization, of stripping the individual of his identity and reducing him to membership of a menial group.[50]

In order to appreciate the effectiveness with which Abrahams employs the second version of alienation, we have first to refer to Marx's own definition. According to him, a worker becomes alienated in this way:

> First, that the work is external to the worker, that it is not a part of his nature, that consequently he does not fulfil himself in his work but denies himself, has a feeling of misery, not of well-being, does not develop freely a physical and mental energy, but is physically exhausted and mentally debased. The worker therefore feels himself at home only during his leisure, whereas at work he feels homeless. His work is not voluntary but imposed, forced labour. It is not the satisfaction of a need, but only a means for satisfying other needs . . . Finally, the alienated character of work for the worker appears in the fact that it is not his work but work for someone else, that it is work that does not belong to himself but to another person.[51]

By using Xuma and his work-mates, Abrahams brilliantly demonstrates the practical dimension of Marx's theory of alienation:

> . . . men gasped for breath and their eyes turned red and beads of sweat stood on their foreheads and the muscles in their arms hardened with pain as they fought the pile of fine wet sand. But the sand remained the same. A truck would come from the heart of the earth. A truck would go up to build the mine-dump. Another would come. Another would go . . . All day long . . . And for all their sweating and hard breathing and for the redness of their eyes and the emptiness of their stare there would be nothing to show. In the morning the pile had been so big. Now it was the same. And the mine-dump did not seem to grow either.
>
> It was this that frightened Xuma. This seeing of nothing for a man's work. This mocking of a man by the sand that was always wet and warm, by the mine-dump that would not grow; by the hard eyes of the white man who told them to hurry up.[52]

Xuma's anxiety about the drudgery and lack of achievement involved in his work, and the weariness and listlessness that it generates encapsulate Marx's point. Xuma's realization of them marks the beginning of his worker-consciousness. As in the case of Reverend Ndlovu, George and Martha in *The Marabi Dance*, Xuma's general experience in the city is a journey towards the realization of this consciousness.

His white colleague, Paddy, helps fuel Xuma's awareness. Whereas at first the latter views black problems in the context of race, the former convinces him that the situation should be seen from the point of view of class. ". . . it is not good to think only as a black man or only as a white man", Paddy advises Xuma. Constructive as Paddy's political conviction may sound, towards the end of the novel it becomes clear that, of all the whites who work in the mines, he is the only one who subscribes to it. After Xuma has engineered a strike, all the white workers except Paddy refuse to support it. Abrahams is grappling with three cardinal aspects of South African politics. First, that though Xuma and Paddy believe that South African problems are rooted in class antagonism, they may not be entirely correct. The problems pertain to both racial and class struggle. The dichotomy often forced between these two issues has polarized radical political opposition. Alluding to the differences among black political movements, the journal *Africa Confidential* says:

> The ANC [African National Congress] makes clear its outright hostility to this post-1960 breakaway [Pan African Congress], led by the late Robert Sobukwe, many of whose objections to the ANC are shared by BCM [Black Consciousness Movement]. For its part, the ANC condemns what it sees as the "black racism" of the PAC . . . the ANC has always been ambivalent, honouring the late Steve Biko [Leader of the BCM] as a charismatic leader but never quite endorsing his beliefs, many of which run counter to the tenets of ANC multiracialism and class-based as opposed to race-based analysis.[53]

Second, the response of white workers to the strike implies that, in times of political upheaval, only liberals are sympathetic to the black cause. Their commitment is, however, characterized by vacillation. When the strike begins to take shape, Xuma and the other black miners stand on the right, the white manager and the *indunas* (selected "trusty" blacks in supervisory positions – hated and despised by the miners) and all the white men are on the left. Paddy, the liberal, is in the centre, a position traditionally associated with neutrality and half-heartedness. Though he later proclaims his support for Xuma and the other black miners, Paddy does not actually stand with them on the right. Most important, the strike leaves Xuma's emergent consciousness in no doubt. Not only is he able to detect the weakness of the system, he is courageous enough to defy its representatives by opting for imprisonment instead of risking his life in an unsafe mine.

In *The Marabi Dance*, political concerns are similarly underlined. Besides, through Martha, condemning South Africa's "homeland" policy and black disdain of traditional life, Dikobe shows development and transformation in some of his characters from positions of corruption and indifference to worker and political awareness. When George is in Johannesburg, he impresses the reader as a character merely interested in casual love affairs and Marabi parties. Having moved to Durban to escape responsibility for Martha's pregnancy, he undergoes a tremendous change. He begins to feel the need for commitment in the face of problems that confront him and other workers. The Bus Company he works for wants to use him as an informer on other workers, but George declines. In a letter to Martha he talks of the formation of a trade union among black workers:

> Our men have formed a trade union and have made some demands to the Company for more money and shorter working hours. The Company is dead scared to meet the workers' representatives, so they want to use some of us to say who are leaders.[54]

Commendable as it is, George's transformation sounds too abrupt. His road towards change lacks the vitality and political challenges a character like Xuma encounters. In Johannesburg, George is a cavalier person predominantly interested in nugatory pursuits. In Durban, the source of his transformation remains nebulous. Instead of dramatizing the conflict between the Bus Company and its employees, Dikobe simply gives a brief and feeble narration of what transpires. No attempt is made to convey the overall political climate of the city. All the reader learns is the overnight formation of a trade union and George's escape from the employers' untoward request.

The bogus Reverend Ndlovu represents the most revealing example of acquired political awareness. But again, how he acquires it is a question that Dikobe fails to answer for the reader. After robbing Ma Ndlovu of her money, Reverend Ndlovu flees to Salisbury. After some time, he, like George, decides to return to Johannesburg. His reason is overtly political, to establish a Church for Africans in which he would preach sermons related to their living conditions. Reverend Ndlovu's church is a reformist denomination calculated to communicate social and political propaganda. The church's teachings, addressing themselves as they do to the forced movement of blacks from the city to the location, are tailored to reinforce the unpopularity of separate development that Dikobe discusses earlier. It is, however, interesting to note that, by establishing an exclusive church like the Dutch Reformed Church the Boers set a dangerous precedent. Reverend Ndlovu's Church is exclusively black:

> The white Mfundisi I worked for had a church for the English people, why shouldn't I also have a church for Africans? The white Christians say, love thy neighbour as thyself and yet they don't love us.[55]

Compared to *Mine Boy*, *The Marabi Dance* is rather thin. For a short novel of its nature, its treatment of so many concerns sounds ambitious. The book can be used as a reference point because it contains most of the concerns found in contemporary black writing. This comprehensiveness, however, is at the expense of a more profound and convincing portrayal. More showing rather than telling would have made the novel more sophisticated and engaging. Though simple and straightforward, the manner in which language is employed lacks energy and can easily have soporific effects on the reader. Nonetheless, the novel is committed, albeit sometimes too earnestly. Statements such as, "My people are suffering. They own nothing on this earth. This Bible is wrong to tell us we must be meek so that we shall enter the Kingdom of God",[56] are based on correct observations but are too direct and nakedly didactic. The familiarity and comprehensiveness with which *The Marabi Dance* is written, however, make it a significant contribution to black writing. It is invaluable running commentary on black life from the 1930s to the present.

Despite the differences in the manner in which they espouse political change, the writers discussed in this chapter form a coherent group. Besides the fact that they belong to a group of writers who produced the earliest black literature, their writings reflect the transitional stages through which this literature passed. The progression from what Njabulo Ndebele calls the literature of morality through the literature of urban consolidation to the literature of protest[57] is clearly represented. The third of these literary phases heralds the central preoccupation of the literature of the 1950s and early 1960s, which the succeeding chapter discusses in detail.

Notes

1. Exodus of Boers from the Cape Province into the interior of South Africa which took place in the 19th century. It was motivated by social, political, 'religious' and economic causes.

2. C. W. De Kiewiet, *A History of South Africa: Social and Economic*, p. 48.

3. I. W. W. Citashe, "Your Cattle are Gone", in *The Return of The Amasi Bird*, (eds) Tim Couzens and Essop Patel, p. 15.

4. J. Jahn, *A History of Neo-African Literature*, p. 90.

5. J. Jahn, *Muntu*, p. 14. "Skokiaan" is an illicit, home-brewed beer drunk in the black townships of the major cities of South Africa, particularly Johannesburg. It is usually sold in private drinking-places called "shebeens", owned and run by "shebeen-queens".

6. Martin Tucker, *Africa in Modern Literature*, p. 257.

7. Solomon T. Plaatje, *Mhudi*, p. 180. In his demonstration of Plaatje's detached portrayal of the stereotypes of Boers, Martin Tucker cites the same passage.

8. Tim Couzens, "Sol Plaatje's *Mhudi*", *Journal of Commonwealth Literature*, Vol. 8, No. 1 (1973) pp. 11–12.

9. Stephen Gray, *Southern African Literature*, p. 172.

10. Solomon T. Plaatje, *Native Life in South Africa*, pp. 129–30.

11. Plaatje, *Mhudi*, p. 83.

12. Ibid.

13. Nadine Gordimer, "Living in the Interregnum", *New York Times Book Review* Vol. 29, Nos. 21–22, (20 January 1983) p. 21.

14. Plaatje, *Mhudi*, p. 184.
15. Ibid.
16. Ibid., p. 119.
17. Ibid., p. 162.
18. Tim Couzens, "Sol Plaatje's *Mhudi*", p. 12.
19. Plaatje, *Mhudi*, p. 142.
20. De Kiewiet, *A History of South Africa*, p. 80. Tim Couzens quotes the same statement in his article.
21. Pierre van den Berghe, *South Africa: A Study in Conflict*, p. 31.
22. Plaatje, *Native Life in South Africa*, pp. xii and xiii.
23. Plaatje, *Mhudi*, p. 25.
24. See J. D. Omer-Cooper, *The Zulu Aftermath: A Nineteenth Century Revolution in Bantu Africa*. The book deals with the scattering of black ethnic groups by Shaka (King of the Zulu Kingdom) and their subsequent establishment of independent Kingdoms in Central and Southern Africa in the early part of the nineteenth century.
25. Plaatje, *Mhudi*, p. 28. My comparison of the social and political attitudes of the Matabele with those of the Boers has been partly influenced by Couzens' article.
26. Tim Couzens, introduction, *Mhudi*, by Solomon T. Plaatje, p. 18.
27. Plaatje, *Mhudi*, p. 149.
28. Ibid., p. 175.
29. Couzens, "Sol Plaatje's *Mhudi*", p. 15.
30. Frederick Johnstone, *Class, Race and Gold*, p. 22. On the same page, J. F. Herbst is quoted as defining the word "squatter" thus: "Whether a Native lives on an occupied or unoccupied farm, whether he pays rent or gives his own service or that of his family, whether or not wages are paid, whether the service is casual labour at call or seasonal or for specified periods, whether he cultivates from a share or produce – in all these cases he is called a squatter. The term therefore covers undefined leasehold, metayage, labour tenancy, part-time service and, in fine, every condition of settlement except fixed leasehold and full time wage service".
31. Plaatje, *Native Life in South Africa*, p. xiii.
32. Peter Abrahams's other early novel, *Song of a City*, deals with similar concerns. Dick Nduli, like Xuma, goes to Johannesburg and finds himself involved with two opposing generations of political activists.
33. Similar to shebeen parties in content and procedure except that they were practised earlier, in the 1930s and 1940s. They were named after a type of dance (Marabi Dance) that reached its climax in the early 1930s.
34. Gray, *Southern African Literature*, p. 173.
35. R. R. R. Dhlomo, *An African Tragedy*, p. 7.
36. Ibid.
37. Michael Wade, "South Africa's First Proletarian Writer", in *The South African Novel in English*, (ed.) Kenneth Parker, p. 96.
38. Peter Abrahams, *Mine Boy*, pp. 115–16.
39. Tim Couzens, introduction, *English in Africa*, Vol. 2, No. 1 (1975) p. 6.
40. Abrahams, *Mine Boy*, p. 152.
41. Modikwe Dikobe, *The Marabi Dance*, p. 114.
42. Daniel P. Kunene, "The African Writer's Response", *Africa Today*, Vol. 15, No. 4 (1968) p. 20.
43. Dhlomo, *An African Tragedy*, p. 5.
44. Abrahams, *Mine Boy*, p. 116.

45. Lewis Nkosi, obituary, *The Will to Die*, Can Themba, p. viii.
46. Dikobe, *The Marabi Dance*, p. 8.
47. Ezekiel Mphahlele, *In Corner B*, p. 113.
48. Mphahlele, p. 112.
49. Abrahams, *Mine Boy*, p. 89.
50. Michael Wade, "South Africa's First Proletarian Writer", p. 104.
51. Karl Marx, *Economic and Philosophic Manuscripts of 1844*, pp. 73–74.
52. Abrahams, *Mine Boy*, pp. 65–66.
53. *Africa Confidential*, Vol. 24, No. 14 (1983), p. 2.
54. Dikobe, *The Marabi Dance*, pp. 114–15.
55. Ibid., p. 118.
56. Ibid., p. 117.
57. Njabulo Ndebele, address, on New Writing in Africa, *West Africa*, No. 3508, (12 November 1984) p. 2267.

2. From Sophiatown to Robben Island

Protest in the Writings of the 1950s and 1960s

The 1950s and 1960s constitute a great period in black writing. The prolific output of black writers and the intensity of their commitment had much to do with the political climate of the time. The 1948 accession to power of the Afrikaner Nationalist party unleashed a spirit of defiance. Political movements such as the Congress Alliance comprising blacks, Indians, "Coloureds" and whites were in open opposition to the government.[1] Yet until historic incidents such as the Defiance Campaign in 1952 and the Sharpeville crisis in 1960, the strict application of apartheid laws did not involve massive police repression.

It was partly because of this relative "freedom" and the ability to forge a kind of multiracial front against the system that Lewis Nkosi called the 1950s a "fabulous decade".[2] A multiracial opposition filled the black intellectual élite with the false hope that a multiracial society was about to be realized. But the period was also "fabulous" because of the great amount of writing produced and the sudden prominence of black writers on the literary scene. Writers took up the defiant mood of the time and began to write works imbued with protest. Nonetheless, at that time the protest was not an index of overt commitment to a particular ideology. It was partly aimed at awakening white consciousness to black frustration.[3] Even more important was the fact that the protest was calculated to raise the political awareness of blacks.

Legislated Segregation and Discrimination: The Portrayal of the Township

Literary protest in the 1950s and 1960s occurs in three genres: autobiography, fiction and poetry. The protest itself is directed at issues such as racial prejudice, violence and prison conditions. The first of these receives the most extended treatment because it pervades virtually all aspects of South African life. While some of the early writers, like Solomon T. Plaatje, deal with a generalized non-legislated form of racial conflict, most of the writers of this period explore the racial segregation and discrimination established by and enshrined in numerous laws and acts.

The manner in which autobiographies reflect the pain of legislated segregation ranges from cool, studied detachment to anger. A common theme is demonstrated through the history of a once cohesive and vibrant black township that is demolished in order to make way for the establishment of a dormitory area far from the so-called "white" district. The destruction of the black township of Sophiatown has become a motif that runs through most of the books that examine this problem.

Sophiatown began as private land belonging to a man called Tobiansky whose aspiration was to establish a European suburb in the west of Johannesburg. As time passed, the Town Council chose the same area for the site of sewage disposal and an African "location". Finding himself in a predominantly black area, Tobiansky sold his land to African, "Coloured" and Asian town dwellers.[4] Later, a township of unique character emerged. There were brick houses, tin shacks, dusty streets, slovenly shops and unsanitary living conditions. As the city expanded, Sophiatown found itself contiguous with the fast-growing white suburbs and parts of the downtown area. It was then, in 1953, that the decision to remove it was taken and implemented.[5]

The main objective of the removal of the township has been disputed. According to popular white opinion, Sophiatown had to be removed because it was dirty and amorphous. The most devoted exponent of this view is Alexander Steward. In a visceral response to Father Trevor Huddleston's analysis of the township and its life, Steward consistently refers to Sophiatown as an "ugly, sprawling slum".[6] Steward's argument constitutes in effect an apologia for apartheid. Father Huddleston, a monk of The Community of the Resurrection and a prominent sympathizer with blacks, concedes that Sophiatown was a slum, but he advances a number of reasonable objections to its removal. The same objections are echoed by black writers.

Father Huddleston argues that the township was eliminated, not just because it was a slum, but because of the need to remove it from a "white" residential area. This, of course, went together with the deliberate abolition of freehold tenure:

> It would be treason to them (those who have lived in Sophiatown) to deny that Sophiatown was a slum. But slum conditions can be removed without the expropriation of a whole area. Indeed the greatest experts in town-planning would agree that only in the last resort should you uproot people from the place they know as home: for in such uprooting you destroy a living organism – the community itself. Sophiatown, then, could have been replanned and rebuilt on the same site: a model African suburb. It could have been, but for the pressure of three things: First, the pressure of white opinion and the political force it represented; secondly, the existence of freehold tenure, thirdly, that which underlies every event of any significance in South Africa: the assumption that white "civilization" is threatened by the very existence of an African community in any way similar to itself.[7]

In some of the autobiographical writings, the protest against the abolition of Sophiatown is earnest. The anguish, cynicism, regret and despair emanating from its removal are epitomized in Can Themba's resigned but accusatory attitude:

Inside of me, I have long stopped arguing, the vindictiveness, the strong-arm authority of which prostrate Sophiatown is a loud symbol.

Long ago I decided to concede, to surrender to the argument that Sophiatown was a slum, after all. I am itchingly nagged by the thought that slum-clearance should have nothing to do with the theft of freehold rights.[8]

Other black writers gave a more extended condemnation of the injustice. In a style that appears rather artificial, Bloke Modisane opens each of the first chapters of his *Blame Me On History* by bemoaning the fate of Sophiatown. The lament, however, is punctuated by fascinating, nostalgic vignettes of the township's once diversified life. The writer who dramatizes the pain of segregation most incisively is Modikwe Dikobe. His approach is historical, calm but, at the same time, satirical. In his novel, *The Marabi Dance*, Dikobe paints a desperate portrait of Sophiatown reduced to rubble. A few people who have the mistaken view that the government might reverse its decision are busy reconstructing a shelter out of corrugated iron sheets. As soon as the policemen on duty notice them, they are arrested and charged with trespassing: "You have no right to be here. Your place is in the Native Location. The Government and the Municipality have built nice houses for you but you still want to make the white man's place stink."[9] Here Dikobe is bent on demonstrating that the removal of Sophiatown marks a further step in the entrenchment of apartheid. While Themba and Modisane merely describe the removal, Dikobe concretizes the process by a dramatic recreation of the action.

Whereas Alexander Steward argues as though the new houses are very comfortable, Dikobe debunks their sleaziness with biting sarcasm: "The Government and the Municipality have built nice houses for you . . .". The critique is extended through the observations of a character called Martha, who goes to inspect her house before she moves in. She notices that the open pit lavatory is uncomfortably close to the house, a few feet away. The house itself is very small with three rooms and a doorway "too narrow for furniture to go in".[10] The walls rasp like sandpaper. There is no ceiling but an ugly criss-crossing of rafters where spiders have already begun to build their webs. Above all, several rows of identical prefabricated houses of this type are not only monotonous but destructive of the inhabitants' individuality. Blacks live in regimented clusters instead of leading free lives on plots of land of their own choice.

This touches on Father Huddleston's second argument which deals with the inhuman nature of "locations". He contends that Sophiatown was ideal for black occupation because it was not a "location". Nadine Gordimer highlighted the degenerate character of "locations" by describing them as ". . . human conglomerations, neither city nor suburb, now called black townships but once more accurately called 'locations', since they are sites chosen by whites to dump blacks outside the limits, after work, just as they choose sites well out of the way for the city trash heap."[11]

It would not be too much of an exaggeration to assert that "locations" are miniature "homelands". Both are usually established in specially prescribed and disadvantaged areas. "Homelands" are characterized by overcrowding, impoverished soil and a lack of viable industrial life. Similarly, "locations" are associated with unattractive living arrangements, inconveniently situated many miles away from work-places and the city centre. "Location" dwellers have no leasehold. The houses in which they live and the land on which they stand belong to the Town Council and the Municipality. Above all, like "homelands", "locations" are meant to be "pools" of cheap labour. These conditions contrast sharply with those in Sophiatown, where blacks had freehold rights and the choice to establish their home wherever they liked.

Lastly, Father Huddleston contends that the removal of the township led to the obliteration of a cosmopolitan community. Blacks, Indians, Chinese and whites had all contributed to the evolution of the township over some 40 years. For a town council to demolish a place of that nature was tantamount to the destruction of a people's history and culture overnight. As Bloke Modisane has argued: "The dying of a slum is a community tragedy, anywhere".[12] Nonetheless, Modisane goes on to point out that, despite its cosmopolitanism, Sophiatown experienced racial conflicts. Citing detailed instances, he demonstrates how colour gradations and special privileges for white residents had threatened to divide the community.

The tenuousness of the multiracialism of the period is more clearly portrayed in short stories. Ezekiel Mphahlele's stories, for instance, show that the multiracialism was fraught with double standards, but Mphahlele is rarely very explicit about his bitterness with the system. His anger is usually expressed neutrally. In "A Point of Identity", however, Mphahlele comes close to overt protest.

In this story, Mphahlele attacks the hypocritical nature of the multiracial co-existence of the 1950s and 1960s. Karel Almeida, a "coloured" who lives among blacks, is required to prove his racial identity by the city authorities. Realizing that if he is declared black he will be expected to carry a pass and earn meagre wages, Almeida sets out to prove that he is a "coloured" of Portuguese descent. This provokes an immediate critical backlash from his black neighbours: "They like us as people to laugh with, not to suffer with. We are the laughing cheerful blacks, the ones they run to when they're tired of being Coloureds, Europeans and Indians."[13] There is something desperate, melancholic, as well as didactic, in this response. The speaker is virtually lecturing the reader on the falseness of racial unity in the townships of the period. A little later, the whites, Indians and "Coloureds" who join blacks in protesting against oppression are accused of hypocrisy.

The passage unmasks Almeida's opportunism. He has one foot in the "Coloured" community, another in the black. But the willingness of the black neighbours to offer help when the "Coloured" is ill and to give him a decent burial when he dies exposes the futility of apartheid. This willingness expresses the triumph of human dignity over colour prejudice. This is the heart of Mphahlele's own racial credo ". . . a multi-racial society in South Africa in which there would be a firm guarantee of basic rights of the individual as well as respect for the dignity of man".[14]

In "Mrs Plum", Mphahlele regrets the lack of such racial harmony. In a satirical way, he exposes the protagonist's theoretical and superficial liberalism. She participates in political demonstrations, attends meetings and writes radical newspaper articles in the interests of blacks. Yet she fails to practise authentic, actual fellowship with the people she fights for. In her own home, she gives dogs precedence over her black servants, and Mphahlele demonstrates this by grotesquely portraying her bestial behaviour. Given Mrs Plum's "humane" attitude towards blacks, Mphahlele's depiction of her bestial conduct interposes an imbalance in her character and indeed in the whole story. But Mphahlele seems to produce the imbalance deliberately in order to highlight the superficiality of liberal values and to condemn them. Mrs Plum's liberalism is hollow because "it is completely impersonal, directed at ideas rather than at people".[15] As the chapter on Black Consciousness will show, Mphahlele is not alone in criticizing this kind of political vacillation. With the growing complexity of the South African situation and the general reluctance of liberals to espouse militant action against the government, all liberals have come under heavier criticism from blacks.

Other short stories protesting against racial policies deal with such commonplace subjects as interracial love affairs doomed to end because of the restrictions of the Immorality Act; the geographical restriction of blacks to townships, and the localized discrimination in "Coloured" families where some of the members are light- and others dark-skinned.[16]

Urban Violence

Violence itself occupies a significant place in black protest writings of the period. Early writers like Solomon T. Plaatje have condemned the violence endured by blacks during wars of conquest, whether perpetrated by fellow black or by whites. With the entrenchment of the apartheid system in the 1950s and 1960s, the rate of violence between black and white and among blacks themselves increased. In his autobiography, *Tell Freedom*, Peter Abrahams records a scene of racial violence that takes place between himself and a group of young white boys. The confrontation is triggered by the white boys' abuse of Abrahams and his boyhood friend as "Bloody Kaffirs" whose fathers are "dirty black bastards of baboons".[17] In the aftermath of the confrontation, Abrahams shows the powerlessness of black people in white-ruled South Africa. Instead of apologizing for the abusive statements made by the white boys, the white adult who later accompanies them to Abrahams's family wants Abrahams to be punished for fighting one of the boys. The warning uttered by Uncle Sam as he reluctantly thrashes Abrahams reflects the level to which blacks have been subjugated: "You must never lift your hand to a white person. No matter what happens, you must never lift your hand to a white person . . .".[18] Though portrayed in a detached way, the sense of humiliation in the scene is vivid and moving. Uncle Sam's impotence and bitterness over the beating, and the domineering demeanour of his white opponents are manifested by his sobbing and his need to apologize to Abrahams over the incident. The bitterness itself is an intense emotional rejection of subjugation shared by the entire family and, on a wider scale, by all blacks.

Ezekiel Mphahlele deals with a similar case of racial violence in his autobiography, *Down Second Avenue*. His manner of protest is much more subdued than it was in his short story, "A Point of Identity". Like Abrahams, Mphahlele tries his best "to cope with his bile, his dislike of whites, with whom his contact mainly involves fear or humiliation".[19] At the sight of Mphahlele and his friends in the Pretoria zoo, an Afrikaner woman petitions her drunken boyfriend to kick one of them for her amusement: "Kick me a kaffir tonight, my lief, won't you, my love? A nice kick on the arse of a nice black kaffir monkey, eh?"[20] Mphahlele and the other blacks respond to the drunken man's aggression by leaving the zoo. Despite this white man's drunkenness, Mphahlele's mother warns: "Beware of the white man, he's very, very strong . . ."[21] She is, of course, not referring to physical strength alone, but to the political power the white man wields.

Mphahlele and the other writers of this period devote part of their protest to the police abuse of political power. Confrontation between the police and blacks invariably leads to violence. Perhaps one of the first novels to deal with the absurdity of police violence is Peter Abrahams's *Mine Boy*. Its portrayal of blacks' sudden disappearance from the street at the sight of a police van and the subsequent unwarranted fight between the protagonist, Xuma, and a police officer demonstrates the mutual fear existing between black and white. To the black, the sight of a policeman signifies violent beating or possible arrest. To the white, every black person is a potential criminal. Abrahams's dislike of the apparent motivelessness of police violence is here conveyed by the sudden solidarity between Xuma and a "Coloured" who is also running away from the police:

> A Coloured man stepped into the road and held up his hands. Xuma braced himself. His heart was pounding but he ran easily . . . Another Coloured man (a second one) stepped into the road. . . . An unbelievable thing happened. The second Coloured man knocked the first one down and ran down the street waving to Xuma . . . They ran into a house and went through a window and over a wall. And into another house and over another wall. And the Coloured people did not seem to mind. Then they walked down a narrow street and slipped into a house.[22]

The incident marks the beginning of Xuma's political consciousness and his opposition to white oppression.

In all the autobiographies of the period, police violence is associated with shebeens and the general surveillance of township life. Because shebeens are illegal, the violence used against people involved in them is much more severe than the violence Xuma experiences. Ezekiel Mphahlele records a painful childhood encounter with the police:

The Black constable had hardly reached my hand when the big white hand crashed full on my cheek so that I seemed to hear my name called, and staggered and hit against a pole that was supporting a vine. The Black man pulled me away with a jerk that sent a pain shooting through my side . . . I got a back-hand on the mouth, and in an instant I tasted something salty. While I held my mouth the big white man caught behind the neck and pressed my face against his other massive hand, so that I began to suffocate . . . With the last word he thrust me away from him. I went down on hard ground.[23]

There is no moralizing in Mphahlele's vivid depiction, but the reader is made acutely aware of the boy's pain. Mphahlele himself emphasizes his vulnerability by consistently contrasting the bigness of the white man with his own fragile body.

While Mphahlele's manner of protest in his autobiography is one of concealed anger and bitterness, Bloke Modisane's attitude is uncompromisingly harsh and polemical. Besides supplying the reader with the facts of frequent confrontation between police and blacks, Modisane gives an aggressively committed and critical commentary on the situation:

Life in a shebeen exposed me to a rude introduction to the South African police, they made me realize the brutal, dominant presence of the white man in South Africa. I saw my mother insulted, sworn at and bundled into the kwela-kwela, the police wagon, so often it began to seem – and I perhaps accepted it – as a way of life, the life of being black. Listening to the young constables screaming obscenities at Ma-Willie emphasized the fact that we were black, and because my mother was black she was despised and humiliated, called 'kaffir meid' and 'swart-hell'.[24]

Modisane goes on to give harrowing accounts of the cross-examination and humiliation that takes place when blacks are arrested. He uses his writing as a safety valve for pent-up anger. Of all the autobiographers who have written about the political ethos of this period, he is probably the only one to give a detailed, analytical critique.

Protest in the 1950s and 1960s is also directed at violence that takes place among blacks themselves and their white sympathizers. Township violence is as old as the processes of industrialization and urbanization in the major cities of South Africa. R. R. R. Dhlomo's short stories[25] published as early as the 1920s depict black gangs as perpetrators of violence in mine compounds and townships. Innocent people are waylaid in dark corners and robbed and murdered.

Discussion of this criminal violence is directed at two targets. Whereas most non-thinking whites believe that this kind of violence is caused by the laziness of blacks who would rather rob than work, black writers and white sympathizers blame the system for frustrating the hopes and wishes of young blacks, thereby encouraging them to indulge in desperate acts of violence in order to gain a living. One of the outspoken exponents of this attitude is Oliver Tambo, the current leader of the African National Congress, who argues that

"South African apartheid laws turn innumerable innocent people into 'criminals'. Young people who should be in school or learning a trade roam the streets, join gangs and wreak their revenge on the society that confronts them with only the dead-end alley of crime or poverty."[26] With the worsening of the blacks' political and economic position, criminal violence has become endemic. But, and this is the second point, while black writers acknowledge that the violence is born of economic deprivation, they deplore its counter-productive nature. Most blacks believe that the chief enemy in the South African situation is the white man's oppressive and exploitative system. Hence, any politically motivated violence should be directed at this system in order to bring about change. The fault of criminal violence, therefore, is that it is not therapeutic because it is aimed at innocent fellow-blacks and white sympathizers, who happen to be the wrong targets.

Alex La Guma is one of the committed writers whose protest against this kind of misdirected violence and its origin is especially effective. His early book, *A Walk in the Night*, demonstrates the power of implicit protest. La Guma's critical realism lays bare the poverty, degeneration and helplessness of blacks. In this novella, a cross-section of his community comprises desperate people on the periphery of society:

> There was a general atmosphere of shabbiness about the cafe, but not unmixed with a sort of homeliness for the unending flow of derelicts, bums, domestic workers off duty, in-town from the country folk who had no place to eat except there, and working people who stopped by on their way home. There were taxi-drivers too, and the rest of the mould that accumulated on the fringes of the underworld beyond Castle Bridge: loiterers, prostitutes, "fah-fee" numbers runners, petty gangsters, drab and frayed-looking thugs.[27]

La Guma's depressing environment is recorded in minute detail and without editorial comment. No shouts of protest are necessary, for the picture alone indicts the society which permits the existence of such inhumane conditions.[28]

Part of the central thrust of *A Walk in the Night* is to show how blacks are made desperadoes by the regime's repressive laws. The protagonist of the novella, Michael Adonis, loses his job for answering back to his white foreman. Frustration and anger prompt him to join a dangerous gang that thrives on robbery in Cape Town's notorious District Six. The cruel intentions and determination of the gang remind one of Anthony Burgess's dystopian world of "droogs" where robbery, murder and rape are committed with savage brutality.[29] Michael Adonis's anger at a system which has sacked him leads him to murder. He unwittingly strikes and kills a degenerate white alcoholic named Doughty. Adonis's fury derives from the fact that Doughty is white and hence a symbol of the source of his frustration. But, despite his whiteness, Doughty, like Adonis, suffers extremely poor living conditions (both live in the same block of flats, a phenomenon of the 1950s but impossible now). In terms of work, the white man is equally frustrated because he is an unemployed, erstwhile actor. His nostalgia for the heyday of his theatrical career is graphically described. The line Doughty recites from Shakespeare's *Hamlet*, "I am thy father's spirit; doomed for a certain term to walk the night",[30] is meant to highlight his own ghostly existence. Poor and neglected, Doughty's life is a kind of death-in-life. Indeed, as Doughty himself puts it, everyone who leads a lowly life similar to his is a ghost: "That's us, us, Michael, my boy. Just ghosts, doomed to walk the night . . .".[31]

Because of this shared suffering, Adonis's murderous fury at Doughty is directed at the wrong target. Here is an index of the former's ignorance of what constitutes social, political and economic classes. Perhaps the ignorance is not his fault because the society in which he lives recognizes only classification based on colour. La Guma would like to demonstrate that the acquisition of class consciousness is a slow and difficult process. From *A Walk in the Night* through *The Stone Country* to *In the Fog of the Season's End*, he shows how the political consciousness of his heroes develops in stages. Each book marks a phase of development and a change in the strategy of grappling with the system. To that extent, La Guma's writings exhibit a definite progression in both the complexity of the political situation and black people's response to it.

In some of the journalistic writings which appeared in *Drum*, a prominent black magazine of the period, similar acts of sterile violence such as that experienced by Doughty are described in strong language tinged with regret. Can Themba vividly describes Henry Nxumalo's political exploits and his wretched appearance on the morning his body is discovered:

> There he lay, the great, gallant Henry Nxumalo, who had fought bravely to bare cruelty, injustice, and narrow-mindedness; there he lay in the broiling sun, covered by two flimsy rags.
>
> He who had accepted the challenge of life and dedicated himself against the wrongs of mankind, now lay on the road-side, his last battlefield the gutter, his last enemies arrant knaves for whom even Henry had raised his trumpet call. And there was a staggered trail of bloody footsteps that told the graphic story of that night's drama.[32]

Whereas La Guma's representation of Doughty's death is fictional, the above instance, is a description of fact. There was a real Henry Nxumalo, an editor of *Drum* who died at the hands of thugs. Can Themba's regret and condemnation of the murder are couched in flamboyant and archaic terms such as "arrant knaves". Though his audience is contemporary, Themba probably employs this diction to emphasize the barbarity and thoughtlessness of the murder. His protest implies that the political and economic motivations of this kind of violence tend to degenerate into an anarchy that seeks violence for its own sake. Bloke Modisane deals with a number of these anarchical murders. The most representative of them involves his father who is waylaid, knocked down and pounded to death with a brick. The barbarity of the act is movingly encapsulated by Modisane's mother when she moans: "We are castoffs in the wilderness. . . . We are orphans, our shield is gone".[33] She refers to the political wilderness created by whites, aggravated by the erosion of humane values that has left blacks rudderless and hostile to each other.

Non-violent Politics and Prison Literature

The 1950s and 1960s were a time of sporadic and turbulent political activism. The need to counter the system's unjust and oppressive laws began with political acts such as the Defiance Campaign (of 1952) in which blacks were to disobey various oppressive laws, suffer arrest, assault and penalty if need be, without violence. The method was to send in carefully trained "volunteers" from the Congress Alliance to abandon the "separate but unequal" facilities set aside for blacks, and to make challenging use of the alternative white facilities. Segregated places like railway stations, waiting-rooms, post offices, public seats and train accommodation were the main targets of the defiance. In addition to this, the flouting of curfew and pass regulations was encouraged.[34] Police response to the Defiance Campaign was mild. A few people were arrested and later discharged. But as black political activities intensified, police response became unprecedentedly violent and Sharpeville became the battleground for the violence.

While the 1952 Defiance Campaign was aimed at violating a variety of oppressive laws, the 1960 Sharpeville crisis was precipitated by a campaign against pass laws only. Organized by the Pan Africanist Congress, all blacks were to leave their passes at home and declare this fact to the police.[35] At a later stage, all blacks would stay at home and refuse to work. In this way, the PAC believed that the economy of the country would be affected. According to the party leader, Robert Sobukwe, a campaign of this nature would bring the government to its knees and force it to implement a policy of one man, one vote which would result in blacks taking over and creating an African socialist democratic state by 1963.[36] The PAC's underestimation of the police capacity to use force ended in tragedy. At Sharpeville, 67 blacks were shot dead and 186 were wounded. The two radical political parties, the African National Congress and the Pan Africanist Congress, were outlawed and went underground. Many of the leaders were arrested and thousands were detained under emergency regulations.[37] The spate of arrests and detentions prompted the emergence of a new and lively literary genre, recording and protesting against prison conditions.

Of the writers on this theme, Alex La Guma, Dennis Brutus and Dan Zwelonke, having been prisoners themselves, portray prison life most convincingly. Their protests differ, according to whether their individual experience derives from solitary confinement or communal imprisonment. The setting of the writings is, however, similar. It is either a prison on the mainland, or Robben Island in Table Bay, site of a maximum security prison. In the case of the latter, the entire island has become synonymous with prison, hence Athol Fugard could later entitle a play *The Island*, knowing that this could mean only one island.

Nonetheless, South African prisons share similar attributes. Alex La Guma, whose experiences are based on a prison in Cape Town, describes the prison itself and its surroundings in menacing terms:

Outside, the facade had been brightened with lawns and flower-beds: the grim face of an executioner hidden behind a holiday mask. The brasswork on the castellated main door was polished to perfection, and the flagged pathway up to it, kept spotless, as if at any moment it would receive some dignitary or other. It waited like a diseased harlot, disguised in finery, to embrace an unsuspecting customer.[38]

La Guma's singular use of imagery, irony and contrast brings out the oppressive character of prison life. The image of the "diseased harlot" masquerading in attractive "finery" is devastating in its effect. Inside, beneath the veneer of the prison's external tranquillity, there is unbearable heat, torture and oppressive loneliness.

Dan Zwelonke, too, graphically describes the claustrophobic and threatening nature of prison life. Basing his portrayal on his experiences on Robben Island, he compares the prison's frightening grip to a nightmare's numbing hold on the body of a dreamer:

I remember well the nightmares that hold a man pressed to the floor, while the creature steadily advances. You want to cry out, but no voice comes; you want to kick, but your legs will not move.[39]

Zwelonke's problem is twofold: to contain his anger and to forget the torture and humiliation he saw and experienced on the Island. Until he can record these experiences, he fails to come to terms with these two problems because each time he is asked about the place, he "would feel exasperated" and his "voice would be choked".[40]

Perhaps one of the most consistently disturbing ideas for the prisoner is the representation of the prison as a replica of South Africa itself. Being a place specifically intended for incarceration and oppression, the Island is a microcosm of the oppressive macrocosm. Nonetheless, while the mainland is notorious for its extensive maltreatment of blacks, Robben Island is infamous for its intensive and systematized punishment of political "offenders". Solitary confinement is one of the punishments. Though published in 1973, *Robben Island*'s lurid tales of the hero's confinement and torture belong to the 1960s. The brutality of the Island is shown in the way Bekimpi dies. Besides the sporadic torture he endures, he is hanged head down so that he dies slowly and painfully:

All he could see properly was the roof and the thin rope which supported his body in extreme tension. His eyes weary of rolling upward to look at the floor. And his neck had strained to breaking point by bending backwards. The floor was two feet below his head.[41]

The horror of Bekimpi's torture is made more poignant by the perverse pleasure the prison officials derive from the dying man's body:

That evening, Du Plessis and two others came to have fun with the hanging man. They let him swing like a hunk of meat in a butchery.

"No, here's better fun: cut the rope with this knife, and see him come down headlong to crash on the floor," Du Plessis said, and tested the rope with a pocket knife.

One of them played with Bekimpi's testicles. "By God, this bastard has a big penis," he shouted merrily, "Just like a donkey's."

Another one slapped Bekimpi's buttocks. Then he took a ballpoint pen and pushed it slowly down the helpless man's anus. The muscles there shrank inward like a snail into its shell. Bekimpi moaned.[42]

Compared to the vivid prison writings of, for example, Alex La Guma, Zwelonke's dialogue is weak and stodgy.[43] But Zwelonke's primary concern, the brutal torture of Bekimpi, is acutely registered. As Lewis Nkosi has argued, "The very rawness of the language, the book's dry and violent factuality, create conditions for our appreciation which are inseparable from its palpable intention to shock us out of our assumed literary poise and professional equanimity."[44] By referring to the scandalous forms of torture Bekimpi undergoes, Zwelonke succeeds in depicting the grimness of Robben Island. The Island's evilness is intensified by the grotesque black humour with which the torture is administered.

Bekimpi's protracted torture is similar to what Elias Tekwane experiences in Alex La Guma's *In the Fog of the Season's End*, ranging from bodily contact with acidic solutions to blindfolding and electric shock. The callousness of Tekwane's torturers is manifested in the remark made by one of them: "We are at war, and your life really means nothing to us . . . If you die we can always say you committed suicide . . .".[45] Indeed, in *Robben Island* and *In the Fog of the Season's End*, both Bekimpi and Tekwane respectively are tortured to death. The torturers' remark is, however, more enlightening in that it exposes the suspicious manner in which real life political figures such as Steve Biko[46] and several others are believed to have died.

The poetry of Dennis Brutus deals in a vivid but different way with similar acts of torture. His setting is also Robben Island. In his "Letters to Martha", besides protesting against the political injustice of confinement, he complains about the loneliness and lack of freedom a single cell imposes on the prisoner. In Letter 17, Brutus describes how the freedom of birds and clouds outside the cell become meaningful to the restricted prisoner:

the complex aeronautics
and the birds
and their exuberant acrobatics
become matters for intrigued speculation
and wonderment.[47]

Brutus's use of the images of birds and clouds has been criticized. Bahadur Tejani, for instance, argues that "The sense of distance which we need when thinking of the cloud or the bird are not present in the poem."[48] Tejani seems to miss the point of these images. His problem is purely contextual. Brutus is using the images in a political context, not a romantic and aesthetic one. He is emphasizing the oppressive lack of freedom that prevails in solitary confinement. By contrast, when he looks outside through the window, he notices the freedom with which the birds and clouds move. R. N. Egudu is right when he argues that:

> The plight of the poet in prison, who lacks freedom and motion, is the direct opposite of the condition of the birds and clouds which are free and moving . . . Brutus is not simply telling us about his being in 'solitary confinement', though this is part of the fact; he is talking of the bleakness, boredom and death-like coldness of a prison situation, all which result from the stagnant, monotonous life in that situation.[49]

While Dan Zwelonke's attitude towards solitary confinement is one of anger, Brutus's vacillates from resignation to frustration. In a number of his *Letters*, he records the desperate acceptance to which the prisoner succumbs in the face of overwhelming oppression:

> Quite early one reaches a stage
> Where one resolves to embrace
> the status of prisoner
> with all it entails,
> savouring to the full its bitterness
> and seeking to escape nothing:
> . . . But the acceptance
> once made
> deep down
> remains.[50]

The acceptance Brutus talks of is not a yielding to the political oppressor but a positive acceptance of suffering in a cause he deems noble. This is borne out by one of his *Letters*[51] in which he expresses pity for blacks who refrain from participating in politics for fear of being sent to Robben Island. The lines quoted above have the direct, simple quality of ordinary speech. There is not a single "poetic" image but rather straightforward statements. The style is radically different from that used in *Sirens, Knuckles, Boots* where complex poetic conventions are employed. As Brutus himself has put it, the technique in poems like the one above marks his new "naked unornamented way"[52] of writing poetry.

Because of the rigours of solitary confinement, Brutus's acceptance of his political situation sometimes snaps. In Letter 11, he flirts with the possibility of militant action against the system:

> And so one comes to a callousness,
> a savage ruthlessness –
> voices shouting in the heart
> "Destroy! Destroy!"
>   or
> "Let them die in thousands!" –
> really it is impatience.[53]

Whereas Brutus and Zwelonke mainly highlight the torture and loneliness of solitary confinement, La Guma deals with the conditions of communal imprisonment. Though there is very little torture, no nerve-racking stone-breaking duties, and no futile interminable labour of digging and carrying sand such as those recorded in *Robben Island* and Fugard's play, *The Island*, the parallel between prison and the outside world as breeding grounds for apartheid policies is well illustrated in *The Stone Country*.

Even in the Cape Town prison of La Guma's story, prisoners are separated according to colour. There are separate cells for blacks, whites and "coloureds". A more interesting form of apartheid concerns the quantity and quality of food prisoners get. Breyten Breytenbach, a white former prisoner, has observed that

> food in South African prisons is still graded according to the race of the prisoner. Even the condemned man's last meal is subject to apartheid. Before being hanged, the white prisoner gets a whole roast chicken. The black prisoner gets half a chicken . . . It's like a kind of reaffirmation of apartheid in the final moment before the gallows.[54]

Breytenbach's grim humour speaks for itself. In La Guma's *The Stone Country* and Dennis Brutus's poem "Cold" similar acts of racial favouritism are portrayed. In the former work, black prisoners are given inferior food, "plain corn mush", while white prisoners are entitled to "mush with milk and sugar and slices of bread".[55] In the latter, Brutus emphasizes the poor quality of the food and the manner in which it is eaten:

> We sit on the concrete,
> stuff with our fingers
> the sugarless pap
> into our mouths.[56]

Unlike the single cells where Brutus suffers from loneliness, the cells La Guma depicts are crowded with various kinds of prisoners. Some are murderers, like the Kid in *The Stone Country*. Others are bullies like Butcherboy. Dangerous characters like these are placed in the same cell as George Adams, the non-violent but politically aware hero of the novel.

La Guma's attitude towards this arrangement is double-sided. First, he condemns a system that encourages harassment and violence by mixing seasoned criminals with non-violent prisoners. As time passes violence erupts in Adams's cell and results in the mysterious death of Butcherboy. La Guma describes a similar case of harassment and violence in his short story, "Tattoo Marks and Nails". A huge bully, named "The Creature", and his henchmen terrorize fellow prisoners, threatening them with physical force and death. The Creature has even gone to the extent of establishing a private mock court in which other prisoners are convicted of nugatory personal crimes, tried and then subjected to the most severe and brutal "sentences". As La Guma puts it: "Mock courts, much more dangerous than real ones, were held in the cells and 'sentence' meted out".[57]

Second, Adams's interaction with other prisoners seems to be La Guma's way of demonstrating the growth of his hero's political consciousness. The reader is presented with a protagonist whose awareness is much more ambitious and qualitatively superior to that of Michael Adonis in *A Walk in the Night*. Whereas Adonis is depicted as an amateurish and blundering "angry young man", Adams comes across as a well-informed ideologue, arrested and detained for distributing leaflets meant to politicize the public. Within the prison, Adams promotes unity and mutual understanding by sharing his food and cigarettes and setting an example of defiance against authority. Thus, he "introduces fellow-feeling among this forgotten criminal population. Where La Guma's earlier protagonists were still learning, Adams is teaching."[58]

The notion of "fellow-feeling" among prisoners is also dealt with in Athol Fugard's play, *The Island*. Fugard's characters, Winston and John, demonstrate solidarity against the injustices of the system. Instead of fighting between themselves, as do some of La Guma's characters, Winston and John co-operate in identifying and criticizing the enemy and the evil he stands for. The enemy is Hodoshe, an agent of oppression and repression whose duty is to supervise the "back-breaking and grotesquely futile labour"[59] of digging and carrying sand and of stone-breaking at the quarry. Besides their willingness to stage together a political play, *Antigone* (a play within a play), the "fellow-feeling" of Winston and John becomes more obvious when the news is broken that John is to be discharged from prison earlier than expected. Winston becomes visibly anxious about the impending companionless suffering: "Your people will take you home . . . You'll tell them about this place, John, about Hodoshe, about the quarry, and about your good friend Winston who you left behind."[60]

While some of La Guma's prison characters are hostile to each other, Fugard's Winston and John resemble the characters of Samuel Beckett and Harold Pinter. Heavily dependent on each other for the production of *Antigone*, and the criticism of the injustices of the system, Winston and John, like Beckett's Vladimir and Estragon (in *Waiting for Godot*) and Pinter's Mick and Aston (in *The Caretaker*), appear indispensable to each other. As in the case of Vladimir and Estragon and Mick and Aston, minor misunderstandings arise between Winston and John but they are quickly resolved without violence and the original state of interdependence and friendship is restored.

Unlike the prisoners who are placed in solitary confinement, communal prisoners are relatively "free" in the sense that they are sometimes taken out for work, exercises and meals. Once outside, the main agents of their restriction and oppression are the guards. In most of the prison writings discussed, guards are portrayed as cruel and repellent administrators of the system's repressive laws. In *The Island*, the guard's name, Hodoshe, is used interchangeably with the name of a green carrion fly. Owing to its association with rotten things, the green fly is normally shunned. Hodoshe's oppressive role is just as revolting as the dirty green carrion fly. To emphasize the association and similarity, Fugard leaves the distinction between the two deliberately vague.

The oppressive role of guards is more graphically portrayed in *The Stone*

Country. La Guma employs the vivid and symbolic parallel of a confrontation between cat and mouse:

> The cat was watching the mouse crouched between its paws. It lay on its belly again, breathing on the dusty-grey creature with the bright eyes and tiny panting jaws. The mouse had its body drawn taut into a ball of tensed muscle, waiting for another opening, refusing to give up hope. A clubbed paw reached out and nudged it. To the mouse it was like the charge of a rhinoceros. Pain quivered through the bunched muscles and the hide rippled, but it remained balled up. Waiting with tiny, beating heart for another chance to escape the doom that waited for it with horrid patience.
>
> Then the cat made a mistake. It rose up on all fours. Without hesitation the mouse streaked staight forward, under the lone belly and out past the swishing tail. There was a vast roaring sound in its ears. It was the laughter of the onlookers.
>
> The cat spun round; too late. The time taken to turn by the cat gave the mouse a few seconds headway and it was off, hurtling across the square again. Something huge and shiny – it was the boot of a guard – tried to block its passage, but it swerved skilfully, and its tiny muscles worked desperately, and it headed into the shade.
>
> The cat was a few inches behind it, but it swerved again and then the blurred, dark hole of a drain-pipe loomed somewhere to its right, seen out of the corner of one pain wracked eye. The mouse dodged a slashing sabred paw by a hair's breadth, and gained the entrance to the hole.
>
> The paw struck again, just as the mouse dashed in, raking the slender tail, but the mouse was gone, and outside the spectators were chuckling over the disappointment of the cat as it crouched waiting at the hole.
>
> Inside, in the cool, familiar darkness the mouse lay panting to regain its breath.[61]

The entire confrontation, the involvement of a guard blocking the mouse's passage and the mouse entering a dark hole, all point to similar experiences endured by prisoners. On a wider scale, the cat is "synonymous with South Africa's authoritarian rule, while the mouse signifies the oppressed downtrodden black and coloured community in its desperate struggle for survival."[62]

The symbolic cat–mouse confrontation introduces a new way of presenting the response of black people to their political situation. While Brutus's response is one of courage and acceptance, Mphahlele's one of concealed anger, Can Themba's one of corrosive cynicism, La Guma's response is to advocate resistance. In *The Stone Country*, La Guma's hero flouts authority time and again. On one occasion, one of the prisoners is so influenced by Adams's political talk that he whispers, "We got to have a revverlution".[63] This trend of thought marks a more radical shift in La Guma's method. He is beginning to transcend the level of critical realism. There is something implicitly prescriptive about some of Adams's reflections: "Even a mouse turns, someday."[64] This thought foreshadows the overt revolutionary commitment that pervades La Guma's *In the Fog of the Season's End*. Adams is, therefore, laying the groundwork for future protagonists such as Beukes and Elias Tekwane.

Exile and Autobiographical Writings

Because of the arrests and detentions of the early 1960s, the literary upsurge of the period was severely affected. Most young writers went into exile and their writings were subsequently banned. Nonetheless, black writing did not come to a complete halt. As Ursula Barnett has rightly observed:

> At the time when *Drum* ceased to be an outlet, and most of the writers had been banned, several of them felt that they were left with a great deal to say and no means of being heard. They therefore turned to the British and American book publishers who were ready to make use of the vogue of African literature . . . Peter Abrahams, Ezekiel Mphahlele, Bloke Modisane and Todd Matshikiza published autobiographical works.[65]

Autobiographical writings were an attempt to come to terms with the rigours of exile against the background of an oppressive, exploitative and racist regime in their own country. "Both the unique quality and daily life in the apartheid state and the need to digest the escaped humiliations of that state are central topics."[66]

Though a few of the exiled writers managed to write autobiographical works, it was clear that a great deal of the literary energy of the period had been lost. Exile had a negative impact on some of the writers. Frustration led them either to commit suicide or drink themselves to death, the fate of Nat Nakasa and Can Themba respectively. Arthur Nortje died of a drug overdose in Oxford. Recently, Ezekiel Mphahlele returned to South Africa after 20 years in exile. His apologia summarizes the frustration that drove him back:

> I am an African humanist and an empiricist, as well as an idealist. I can function here in South Africa . . . Compromise? Life for an oppressed person is one long protracted, agonizing compromise . . . I (realized) the longer I was away from here, the angrier, the more outraged, I felt against the suffering of people here. Out of sheer impotence. In a sense, my homecoming was another way of dealing with impotent anger. It was also a way of extricating myself from twenty years of compromise, for exile is compromise. Indeed, exile had become for me a ghetto of the mind. My return to Africa was a way of dealing with the concrete reality of blackness in South Africa rather than with the phantoms and echoes that attend exile.[67]

Mphahlele's philosophical and rhetorical argument sounds impressive but his return has raised suspicion. His critics do not see it as mere "compromise" as Mphahlele himself would have his readers believe, but as a reactionary yielding to the oppressor. In a letter to him (written in 1976, a year before Mphahlele's departure for South Africa), Dennis Brutus warned against the adverse political repercussions of Mphahlele's projected return to South Africa:

> I must say that I think on logical grounds there is much reason why you should not go – the graves of the school children dying gallantly in opposition seems to me a strong reason for refusing the favours of the racists: if they give you the favour of a visa it is because they *need you* to make them seem less terrible. Let me speak to you directly and appeal to you *not* to go: I believe it will harm our cause – and *our fight* – if you go now when their hands and the soil of our country are drenched with blood of our people. Even if it is very difficult, I urge you to cancel it at this stage: there will be other opportunities. And while you think you can use Ford, *their* use of you – and of black puppets – whom I unequivocally condemn – (Nkele too) is far more pernicious at this stage, and far more perilous for the future than the brutalities of Vorster's gangsters.
>
> . . . I believe you will be glad if you do not go, and that if you do, your own conscience will reproach you and you will wish that you had resolved to make the sacrifice.[68]

The thought of these criticisms, and his working in a "homeland" as an Inspector of Schools and subsequently teaching in a largely white university have not given Mphahlele any peace of mind since his return. The situation has created a new form of exile for him, that of spiritual alienation:

> My return placed me in an immediate moral and political quandary: to work as an Inspector of Schools under the Lebowa authorities or face unemployment. The optimist had not planned for this kind of staged political humiliation. The trap was set and I walked into it. When I think intensely about it, I find that after various circular movements I can rationalize it and live with it. The conclusion, however, fails to give me the sense of release which I experienced after I had made the decision to return . . . It is a matter of style and degree and even as I work at the University of Witwatersrand and in the black communities around me, even as I write the occasional short story and undertake research into oral poetry in the Northern Transvaal, the existential compromise stares me in the face. In exile, it was the literary compromise that bothered me. After my return it is the existential and political compromise which has come to the fore.[69]

Beside contending with the rigours of exile, the writers of the 1950s and 1960s faced a crisis of audience. They found themselves addressing an alien audience with no direct emotional involvement in the political situation of South Africa.

Nevertheless, the period proved to be crucial in the development of black literature. It gave additional impetus to a literary tradition which forerunners like Solomon T. Plaatje and the Dhlomo brothers had established. The political turbulence forced some of the writers to change their literary outlook. For example, whereas Alex La Guma's early writings concentrate on diagnosing and exposing South Africa's political problems, his recent novel, *In the Fog of the Season's End*, openly advocates armed struggle as a means of bringing about change. La Guma insists that it is not enough for the writer merely to record the events of his times; he should in addition participate actively in the liberation struggles to realize that vision of a new world order which will guarantee mankind "happiness and freedom of spirit".[70] Like Ousmane Sembene (in *God's Bits of Wood*) and Ngugi wa Thiong'o (in *Petals of Blood*), La Guma believes that workers and peasants should constitute the vanguard of a grass-roots movement designed to create a new political order.

The turbulence of the period has also given rise to a new generation of poets whose manner of commitment is rather different from that of the writers of the 1950s and early 1960s. The literary censorship that took place after the emergency forced the "new" poets to adopt a non-militant, but at the same time implicitly critical, style. Their concerns range from the familiar aspects of socio-political protest to the affirmation of the identity and dignity of black people. Among the new poets are Oswald Mbuyiseni Mtshali, Mongane Wally Serote, Njabulo Ndebele, Mandlenkosi Langa and many others. Their indirect approach has saved some of their writings from being banned in South Africa.

Although largely supplanted by revolutionary fiction, protest poems and popular drama, the short story and the autobiography proved to be effective modes of protest. With the "advantages" of the relatively minor police repression and the deceptive multiracialism of the 1950s, the short story was the quickest way of registering protest. As Ezekiel Mphahlele has argued: "It is impossible for a writer who lives in oppression to organize his whole personality into creating a novel. The short story is used as a short cut (to get) some things off one's chest in quick time."[71]

By the time the writers were in exile, they turned to autobiography, which provided a more extended means of fixing the strangeness of the past, the very special schizophrenia of growing up as intellectuals; both in an African village and in an apartheid slum and, at the same time, a way of digesting and coming to terms with exile.

Notes

1. For a thorough understanding of the politics of the period, see Albert Luthuli, *Let My People Go*.

2. Lewis Nkosi, *Home and Exile*, p. 1. See also Stephen Clingman's analysis of the multi-racialism of the 1950s in his "Multi-Racialism", *Salmagundi*, No. 62 (1984), pp. 32–61.

3. Nadine Gordimer, "Literature and Politics in South Africa", *Journal of Southern African Studies*, Vol. 2, No. 2 (1976) p. 14.

4. Until its demolition, Sophiatown was one of the very few places in South Africa where blacks could have freehold rights. For a more detailed examination of this confined living arrangement and its effects on blacks, see Father Trevor Huddleston, *Naught For Your Comfort*, pp. 119–20.

5. Ibid., pp. 118–20.

6. Alexander Steward, *You Are Wrong Father Huddleston*, p. 71.

7. Huddleston, p. 193.

8. Can Themba, *The Will to Die*, p. 103.

9. Modikwe Dikobe, *The Marabi Dance*, p. 112.

10. Ibid., p. 108.

11. Gordimer, "Literature and Politics in South Africa", p. 141.

12. Bloke Modisane, *Blame Me On History*, p. 16. This belief and some of those expressed by Father Trevor Huddleston are similarly articulated in relation to any racially polarized society where the oppressed or underprivileged race finds itself either displaced or removed for one reason or another. A classic case is that of the relocation of black Nova Scotians from Africville to Preston in Halifax, Canada. A great many of the relocatees firmly believe that the removal was "a form of race warfare". See Donald H. Clairmont and Dennis W. Magill, *Africville Relocation Report*.

13. Ezekiel Mphahlele, *In Corner B*, p. 69.

14. Ezekiel Mphahlele, "Accra Conference Diary," quoted by Samuel Omo Asein in "The Humanism of Ezekiel Mphahlele", *Journal of Commonwealth Literature*, Vol. 15, No. 1 (1980) p. 40.

15. Ursula A. Barnett, *A Vison of Order*, p. 177.

16. See Richard Rive, *Quartet*, and Cecil Abrahams, "The Context of Black South African Literature", *World Literature Written in English*, Vol. 18, No. 1. (1979) pp. 8–19.

17. Peter Abrahams, *Tell Freedom*, pp. 36 and 37.

18. Ibid., p. 40.

19. Rowland Smith, "Allan Quatermain to Rosa Burger: Violence in South African Fiction", *World Literature Written in English*, Vol. 22, No. 2 (1983) p. 177.

20. Ezekiel Mphahlele, *Down Second Avenue*, p. 104. "Kaffir" is a derogatory term employed by white South Africans to refer to a black person (just as the term "Boer" is extensively applied to the Afrikaner population). In the denotative sense, however, the term is Islamic in origin and means "non-believer" or "infidel"; it is usually applied to non-Muslims.

21. Ibid., p. 104.

22. Peter Abrahams, *Mine Boy*, pp. 31, 32.

23. Mphahlele, *Down Second Avenue*, p. 42.

24. Modisane, pp. 36–7.

25. See Andre De Villiers, (ed.) *English in Africa*, Vol. 2, No. 1 (1975) pp. 13–69.

26. Oliver Tambo, quoted in Colin and Margaret Legum, *The Bitter Choice: Eight South Africans' Resistance to Tyranny*, p. 83. In his *Naught For Your Comfort*, Father Trevor Huddleston gives a detailed analysis of the economic and political forces that prompt the emergence of urban thugs ("tsotsis") in South Africa. See Chapter Five, pp. 80–99.

27. Alex La Guma, *A Walk in the Night*, p. 3.

28. Bernth Lindfors, "Robin Hood Realism in South African English Fiction", *Africa Today*, Vol. 15, No. 4 (1968) p. 17.

29. See Anthony Burgess, *A Clockwork Orange*. The novel is a satirical commentary on the question of individual choice in a mechanized and dehumanized world.

30. La Guma, p. 28.

31. Ibid.

32. Can Themba's *Drum* article which appears in his *The Will to Die*, p. 97.

33. Modisane, p. 27.

34. Luthuli, p. 117.
35. Ibid., p. 222.
36. Muriel Horrell, *Action, Reaction and Counteraction*, p. 29.
37. Thomas G. Karis, "Revolution in the Making: Black Politics in South Africa", *Foreign Affairs*, Vol. 62, No. 2 (1983/84) p. 382.
38. Alex La Guma, *The Stone Country*, p. 17.
39. Dan M. Zwelonke, *Robben Island*, p. 1.
40. Ibid.
41. Ibid., p. 145
42. Ibid.
43. Smith, p. 180.
44. Lewis Nkosi, *Tasks and Masks*, p. 103.
45. Alex La Guma, *In the Fog of the Season's End*, p. 174.
46. See Donald Woods, *Biko*, pp. 242–59, and Daniel P. Kunene, "Ideas Under Arrest: Censorship in South Africa", *Research in African Literature*, Vol. 12, No. 4 (1981) p. 431.
47. Dennis Brutus, *A Simple Lust*, p. 66.
48. Bahadur Tejani, "Can the Prisoner Make a Poet? A Critical Discussion of *Letters to Martha and Other Poems From a South African Prison*", *African Literature Today*, No. 6, p. 137.
49. R. N. Egudu, "Pictures of Pain: The Poetry of Dennis Brutus", *Aspects of South African Literature*, (ed.) Christopher Heywood, pp. 135–6.
50. Brutus, p. 65.
51. Ibid., p. 75.
52. William E. Thompson, "Dennis Brutus: An Interview", *Ufahamu*, Vol. 12, No. 2 (1983) p. 73.
53. Brutus, p. 61.
54. Breyten Breytenbach, interview, "A South African Poet on His Imprisonment", with Donald Woods, *New York Times Book Review* (1 May 1983) p. 24. See also, Breyten Breytenbach, *The True Confessions of an Albino Terrorist*.
55. La Guma, *The Stone Country*, p. 50.
56. "Cold", quoted in William E. Thompson, "Dennis Brutus: An Interview", p. 74.
57. Alex La Guma, "Tattoo Marks and Nails", *A Walk in the Night*, p. 99.
58. J. M. Coetzee, "Man's Fate in the Novels of Alex La Guma", *Studies in Black Literature*, Vol. 5, No. 1 (1974) p. 21.
59. Athol Fugard, "The Island", *Statements*, p. 47.
60. Ibid., p. 70.
61. La Guma, *The Stone Country*, pp. 126–7.
62. Samuel Omo Asein, "The Revolutionary Vision in Alex La Guma's Novels", *Phylon*, Vol. 39, No. 1 (1978) p. 78.
63. La Guma, *The Stone Country*, p. 25.
64. Ibid., p. 127.
65. Barnett, p. 218.
66. Rowland Smith, "Autobiography in Black and White: South African Views of the Past", *Commonwealth*, Vol. 7, No. 2 (Spring 1985) p. 75.
67. Es'kia Mphahlele, *Chirundu*, pp. ix–x.
68. Dennis Brutus, letter to Ezekiel Mphahlele, 26 June 1976, quoted in N. Chabani Manganyi, *Exiles and Homecomings*, p. 293–4. See also, Daniel P. Kunene, "Ideas Under Arrest: Censorship in South Africa", pp. 431–5.

69. Ezekiel Mphahlele's observations in N. Chabani Manganyi, *Exiles and Homecomings*, p. 296.

70. Alex La Guma, quoted in Samuel Omo Asein, "The Revolutionary Vision in Alex La Guma's Novels", pp. 75-6.

71. Ezekiel Mphahlele, "Black and White", quoted in Ursula A. Barnett, *A Vision of Order*, p. 469.

3.   Conflict or Surrender?

The Theme of Political Revolution in the Literature of the
Post-Sharpeville Era

The Transition from Non-violent Politics to Militant Politics

Before the Sharpeville Emergency, black politics were essentially non-violent.
The African National Congress (ANC) and the Pan Africanist Congress (PAC)
believed in bringing about change peacefully. Political campaigns waged in the
1950s were always structured on this credo of non-violence. With the
Sharpeville massacre, younger and radical members of the two parties felt the
need to adopt a new strategy to counter the system's nascent repressive
measures. The crux of the new strategy was to jettison the policy of non-
violence and face the violent government with violence. Advocating the
necessity of the new strategy, Nelson Mandela said:

> During the last ten years the African people have fought many freedom
> battles . . . In all these campaigns we repeatedly stressed the importance of
> discipline, peaceful and non-violent struggle and we sincerely worked for
> peaceful change . . . But the situation is now radically altered. South Africa
> is now a land ruled by the gun . . . All opportunities for peaceful agitation
> and struggle have been closed . . . Today many of our people are turning
> their faces away from the path of peace and non-violence . . . Certainly the
> days of civil disobedience, of strikes and mass demonstrations are not
> over . . . But a leadership commits a crime against its own people if it
> hesitates to sharpen its political weapons which have become less effective.[1]

In 1961, preparations for violent counter-measures were made. Underground
movements such as the *Umkonto we Sizwe* (linked to the ANC), *Pogo* (linked to
the PAC) and the African Resistance Movement (ARM), founded by members
of the Liberal Party, who were later expelled from the Party, were formed.
Their role was to carry out sabotage against such government property as
power stations, police stations, post offices and administrative offices with, if
possible, no loss of human life. The campaign, however, had long-term
objectives beyond mere sabotage. As Joe Slovo has argued, ". . . sabotage was
to form only the opening phase in the unfolding . . . armed struggle".[2] But the
sabotage campaign hastened the government's intention to fragment black
political force. As demonstrated in the previous chapter, most of the leading
political figures, including Nelson Mandela, Robert Sobukwe and Walter

Sisulu, were arrested, tried and subsequently detained on Robben Island. A great many of the followers of the ANC and PAC were either imprisoned or went into exile. The political parties themselves were banned.

Literature and Revolution

While politics were undergoing these radical changes, literature was experiencing revolutionary shifts of a similar kind. Richard Rive's *Emergency*, Peter Abrahams's *A Night of Their Own*, and Alex La Guma's *In the Fog of the Season's End* (subsequently referred to as *In the Fog*) are committed works which trace the trajectory of the emergent black militant politics. Dealing with, and in some cases advocating, revolutionary militancy as do some of these writings, they mark a complete break with the peaceful protest literature of earlier decades. Because so many of those writing of revolution or revolutionaries are themselves politically committed, their fiction frequently contains revolutionary theory. In commenting on that fiction, a critic must analyse the theory as well as the art.

Richard Rive's *Emergency* attempts to fictionalize the incidents that occurred during and after the crisis at Langa and Nyanga. The novel is set in and around Cape Town early in the 1960s. The shooting of demonstrators on 21 March, the arrest of the PAC leadership, the government's declaration of a state of emergency on 30 March and the blacks' protest march to Caledon Square Police Station during that period are all outlined. As the first novel to be set against a background of the crisis,[3] *Emergency* is of historical and political significance. Rive himself refers to this significance:

> Since to my knowledge there is no recorded history of this important and dramatic period in South African history, I have had to rely on my own compilation gleaned from newspapers of the time. Under the circumstances it is as accurate as possible.[4]

Though more competent literary and historical books have been written on the same subject since Rive uttered these words, his novel is still worth considering.

Rive fails to transmute his historical material into convincing fiction. The main characters of the novel, Andrew Dreyer, Justin Bailey, Abraham Hanslo and the white liberal, Braam de Vries, do not really come across as fully realized political figures. They appear to be middle-class idealists engaged in an intellectual discourse as to whether to espouse the gradual political awakening of the people or immediate action against the system. The action that Andrew, Justin and Braam consistently advocate is later portrayed as impetuous activism when Andrew leads a group of demonstrators into an emotional, unplanned riot. The rioters are demanding the release of political leaders; the specific identities, roles and personalities of these leaders are not clearly delineated in the novel. Obviously Justin and Braam, who are among the people arrested during the emergency, are not significant politicians. Kgosana, who is at the head of the march, does not appear until the march takes place when his name is mentioned only three times. The protagonist of the novel, Andrew, sounds confused and selfish. Though by the end of the novel he decides to confront the police rather than go into exile, he lacks the political toughness and determination that befits his central role. Indeed, as Vladimir Klima, Karel Frantisek Ruzicka and Peter Zima have argued:

> Rive is interested not so much in characters as in actions and situations. He recalls certain modern painters who create a characteristic atmosphere by bizarrely applying different colours on the canvas, without caring for details. There is, of course, one disadvantage in this creative method. Rive's works will have documentary value, even at the end of this century, but at that time they will hardly possess the emotional appeal they unquestionably contain for Rive's contemporaries.[5]

At the narrative level, *Emergency* is equally flawed. With the exception of the dramatization of what happens at the protest on Grand Parade and during the march on Caledon Square Police Station, the novel contains too much of telling rather than showing. The major events such as the shootings themselves, the declaration of the state of emergency and the arrest of political leaders are merely reported. As a result, parts of the narrative sound more like journalism than imaginative writing.[6] A case in point occurs in Chapter Seven where Rive lists his characters' reflections and feelings as if he were writing a diary:

> On Monday, March 28th, Mrs Nhlapo of Steenberg felt terribly depressed because she had no black to wear for the funeral at Langa.
> . . . Braam De Vries was convinced that he could compose an epic on Sharpeville and Langa, preferably in free verse.
> . . . Ruth Talbot hoped that Andrew would stay out of trouble. She was so afraid for him.
> . . . Justin Bailey realized the risk involved in canvassing Coloured workers in Woodstock to support the stay-at-home strike.[7]

This journalistic weakness is coupled with the episodic nature of the book. Of course, one sympathizes with Rive in the sense that the incidents he is dealing with did not happen in an ordered manner. But the tenuousness of connecting threads between some of his chapters could have been avoided. As he himself has confessed, *Emergency* "is basically a series of short stories with a particular character in common".[8]

While it espouses political action, *Emergency* is not as militant as Peter Abrahams's *A Night of Their Own* or Alex La Guma's *In the Fog*. In its portrayal of the transitional period between the end of non-violent politics and the beginning of militancy in the 1960s, *Emergency* serves the purpose of foreshadowing the sabotage campaign. This campaign itself has been thoroughly examined by Abrahams, and partly by La Guma.[9]

The militant preoccupation of Abrahams's *A Night of Their Own* and La Guma's *In the Fog* is shown by the kind of people to whom the books are dedicated. The former is dedicated to "Walter Sisulu and Nelson Mandela, and all the others, the captured and the still free, who are at war against the evils of this night of their own." The latter is dedicated to a deceased combatant, "Basil February and others killed in action, Zimbabwe, 1967". The entire action of *In the Fog*, however, is set in South Africa.

Peter Abrahams employs a variety of characters to demonstrate the activities of the underground movement and police reprisals in the early 1960s, but the central thrust of his portrayal involves one chief protagonist who uses the pseudonym, Richard Nkosi. Nkosi's real name is Richard Dube but he uses "Richard Nkosi" because of the significance of political resistance associated with it: "My name isn't really Richard Nkosi. I have just borrowed the name, because the name has now been turned into the spirit and the will of the resistance. It is a symbol now."[10] As the story unfolds, it becomes clear that Richard Nkosi is a political messenger sent to deliver some money to the underground movement within South Africa. As soon as he enters the country, the police discover his presence and a relentless game of hide-and-seek dominates the story.

Abrahams's portrayal does, however, betray an implicit criticism of Nkosi's political outlook. As a protagonist meant to symbolize the revolutionary spirit of the period, Nkosi does not evince the political stamina implied by the symbolism of his pseudonym or the political action relevant to the gravity of the situation he is facing. Early in the story, the reader learns that Nkosi is an artist who has spent ten years in exile. Despite his affiliation to the movement, nothing specific is said about his political activities abroad. Instead, Abrahams depicts him as a cosmopolite who has lived in such major cities as London and Paris mingling with diplomats at bourgeois parties. Interestingly enough, at one of those parties he finds himself rubbing shoulders with a South African diplomat, Karl Van As, a representative of the regime Nkosi is supposed to be fighting at home.

Within South Africa itself, Richard Nkosi's political role is bedevilled by a number of factors. The most immediate concerns Westhuizen, a reactionary opportunist who receives Nkosi when he leaves the submarine. Westhuizen used to be categorized as a white person, but apartheid laws have proclaimed him non-white. His commitment to the underground movement is probably the most spurious in the novel. His role as an intermediary between the movement and people who enter and leave South Africa on political missions is not portrayed as a result of genuine commitment, but as a way of taking revenge against a system which has deprived him of his identity:

> They're going to pay for it. They're going to pay dearly for their foolishness. I'm only one of a number, you know. And if all those people decide on revenge as I'm now doing, they are going to be in real trouble. Deciding who is and isn't white! It's something you see and know and feel! But they'll learn and then they'll come begging.[11]

Westhuizen never exudes any spirit of brotherhood and solidarity which members of most underground movements usually show. In keeping with the racist attitude of unthinking white South Africans, he keeps referring to Nkosi as "Kaffir" instead of treating him as a comrade-in-arms. Westhuizen himself epitomizes an unrepentant and reactionary loyalty to the values of the system when he confesses: "I look like them. I think like them. I feel like them. Nobody and nothing can change that."[12]

Westhuizen's joining of the movement is by no means Nkosi's responsibility, however. The top officials of the movement are to blame for the infiltration and, as soon as Westhuizen's double standards are discovered, it is Naidoo, one of the hard-core members of the movement, who engineers his death. Westhuizen's death and the subsequent police repression of the movement unmask even further Nkosi's feeble commitment to action.

In Alex La Guma's *In the Fog*, the protagonist is actively involved in the planning and implementation of political activities. The protagonist moves from place to place distributing leaflets. The depiction of Nkosi is the complete opposite. While the explosive situation created by Westhuizen's death and the police resolve to liquidate the movement demands action, Nkosi remains a cowardly pacifist. According to him, the act of bringing money to the movement is sufficient political involvement, hence he keeps nagging his protectors, Dee, Dr Nunkhoo and Dick to arrange his speedy return to Europe. In a strong statement of political analysis, Naidoo compares Nkosi with the pacifist leaders of the 1950s:

> I think you know that the foundation of the underground movement is African. For some time the Congress leaders were in complete control. I'm of course talking about the people who led the Congress before it was banned. You will remember they were the moderates: people who saw things as you do, in terms of values; people who urged restraint and who deplored the matching of a white racialism with a black racialism. Luthuli was, and still is, the great spokesman for this view. But this moderate leadership inevitably suffered reverses when the enemy became more brutal. Resistance was driven underground.[13]

Naidoo's comparison is probably justified. In a novel whose central concern is to portray the beginning of militant politics, Nkosi poses as an anachronistic political figure. Like Luthuli and other leading politicians of the old generation, he strongly believes in liberal politics. As Nkosi himself tells Dee, "The point is to accept being uncertain, to accept being afraid, even to entertain the possibility of disaster and still to carry on. We must cultivate self-doubt and introspection in order to remain human."[14] In the author's view, Nkosi's commitment lacks the positive thrust of an authentic revolutionary attitude and, while informed by revolutionary theory, tends to be ineffectual and merely rhetorical. Because of this, Nkosi is never involved in the militants' action in support of the sabotage campaign. He is consistently portrayed as a well-meaning but passive individualist.

Despite the author's implied criticism of Nkosi's passivity, however, there are other characters who are thoroughly militant and who reflect the actual participation of many blacks in this turbulent period. While there are factional fights between Indians and blacks, some of the most committed followers are Indian. From the time Nkosi leaves Westhuizen to the time he departs for

Europe, he is always in the custody of Indians. Among them is Sammy Naidoo, a hard-core militant whose toughness may be comparable to the courage and determination of one of Alex La Guma's central characters in *In the Fog*. Like La Guma's Elias Tekwane, Naidoo is an experienced politician who has seen black politics evolve through various phases such as the non-violent period of the 1950s and the Sharpeville crisis of 1960. With the advent of the sabotage campaign, Naidoo finds himself in the forefront of the struggle, and this is evidenced by his power to engineer the elimination of traitors like Westhuizen. After Westhuizen's death and Nkosi's disappearance, Naidoo becomes a wanted man. Interestingly enough, after his arrest, Naidoo's interrogation is carried out by Karl Van As, a man with relatively liberal values, the former diplomat Nkosi had met at parties in Europe. Naidoo's response to Van As's claim to maintain law and order by cracking down on members of the movement not only reveals his boldness and unfaltering commitment, but explodes the interrogator's pretentious pseudo-liberalism. The following passage is an angry yet acute denunciation of the false compromiser who, in effect, connives with the oppressors of blacks:

> But you work the system: in fact you are its real brains. Without people like you, without your brains and your talents, the wild fanatics of *apartheid* would not be able to operate for long. You and I know that the genuine believer in *apartheid* is a curiously stupid and gullible creature. But it is you, Mr Van As, people like you, who keep the system alive and strengthen it. You are the really guilty men, and you know it. You try to suppress it and some of you go in for coloured women or good services to the so-called natives, but you know it, and we know it too. You know the difference between right and wrong, between good and evil, and all your rationalization cannot hide what you really know you are.[15]

Claiming to sympathize with the plight of the down-trodden, yet at the same time believing in the hegemony of a white minority, Van As finds his political views radically different from those of militants like Naidoo. In a political discussion, his girlfriend Mildred Scott vehemently dismisses his political position:

> What I do know is that there is no hope of any good any more in white rule . . . No hope of good. And when there is no hope of good, then the evil is complete. Black rule may indeed be the terrible thing you fear. From the little we hear and read, it has not been all that terrible in other parts of Africa. But even if it were, because it would be majority rule, there would be hope for good.[16]

Mildred emerges, not as an aquiescent personality forced by racial imperatives to endorse whatever Van As says, but as a politically aware individual totally in support of black rule. It is Mildred's kind of politics that Naidoo espouses, and with such vigour that it offsets the ineffectual inactivity of the protagonist.

Abrahams does, however, employ other characters who are almost as committed as Naidoo, the most outstanding of which is Dee Nunkhoo, Dr

Nunkhoo's sister. In some contemporary African writings, the role of women in such revolutionary circumstances has become prominent. In *God's Bits of Wood,* Ousmane Sembene portrays the heroic endurance and resourcefulness shown by women while their husbands stage a protracted railway strike. In *Petals of Blood*, Ngugi wa Thiong'o describes how women come to terms with the economic deprivations of neocolonialism and, in some cases, how they join revolutionary forces in order to destroy a decadent, neocolonialist political system. Peter Abrahams, too, portrays Dee Nunkhoo in a similarly revolutionary fashion.

With a political outlook that transcends racial and factional boundaries, she advocates unity among members of the underground movement:

> You're supposed to be fighting against prejudice . . . We're all of us caught up in this rotten sickness. It isn't only the whites. It has spread to us. The black people have it too, and the brown people. You and I, and also our movement.
>
> The only way to stop it . . . is by changing our world . . . and the control of power in society.[17]

It is noteworthy that the women in Abrahams's novel articulate this need to combat prejudice and to change the control of power more directly and forcefully than the men. Like Dee, Mildred Scott fervently advocates majority rule; and she loves across colour lines. Depsite the fact that her brother was killed in African–Indian factional fights of 1948, Dee practises her politics of non-factionalism convincingly. While Nkosi's protection involves the efforts of many people, he is mostly depicted in her company. A love relationship develops between them, but it is not only for the sake of the relationship that they are always seen together. In their conversations, Dee comes across as a committed militant whose political ideas are more firmly rooted than Nkosi's in the realities of the South African situation. Her active participation in politics is further evidenced by the fact that she is invariably aware of the covert goings-on in the movement, such as the mysterious disappearance of Westhuizen and the various plans elaborated to make Nkosi's hiding safer. In addition, Dee's attitude towards the police is characteristically bold and confrontational. Towards the end of the novel, she risks arrest by insisting on seeing the ship that takes Nkosi and her brother off. Dee is therefore, one of the key characters in the novel. Without her co-operation and commitment, the protection of Nkosi would have been difficult. She is a rallying point to which most of the leading characters resort for political discourse, encouragement and help.

From both a literary and historical point of view, *A Night of Their Own* is essential reading. The fictionalized historical detail about the multiracial nature of the underground movement and its acts of sabotage and also police reprisals against political "offenders"[18] is meant to be instructive. The entire mood of the period is described and dramatized. The only flaw of the novel is the passive characterization of its protagonist. Since it is a book that describes the beginning of militant politics, one expects a high degree of action from almost every character, particularly from the main protagonist. But Richard Nkosi is portrayed as a burdensome political paper tiger who spends all his time hiding rather than participating actively in the sabotage. The symbolism of resistance associated with him seems to be hopelessly misplaced. A committed politician like Naidoo dies for shielding a sham militant. Abrahams's depiction of Nkosi may, however, have been influenced by the need to observe historical accuracy. Initially, the decision to resort to acts of sabotage was not supported by the whole political leadership of the ANC and PAC. People such as Albert Luthuli had reservations about the use of force against the government. They still believed in the old, non-violent politics of the 1950s. As a result, when Nelson Mandela and other younger radicals in the ANC formed the *Umkhonto we Sizwe*, they did not inform or consult the conservative leaders of the party.[19] To that extent, Nkosi's passive political outlook may have been intended to shed some light on this contradiction.

If Richard Nkosi's personality illustrates the pacifist elements in black politics in the 1960s, the portrayals of Naidoo, Dr Nunkhoo, Dee Nunkhoo and Mildred Scott demonstrate their militant aspects. While Abrahams does not preach that blacks must go on a political rampage, through these characters he shows that the rule of a small minority should be replaced by a popular democracy with full representation of the majority of the population. To bring this about, an entirely new strategy must be devised. The need to endorse this new strategy is symbolized by Old Man Nanda, who is transformed from a hard-core reactionary to a sympathetic fellow-traveller. It is because of Old Man Nanda's timely co-operation that Nkosi's ultimate escape is made possible.

Though Abrahams implicitly supports the advent of militant politics in the 1960s, he does not advocate the creation of a society with a qualitatively different political ideology. To a writer like Alex La Guma, however, the attaining of independence presupposes the creation of a new political system. While both Abrahams and La Guma deal with violence, for the latter it is not confined to sabotage alone. In a distinctly programmatic and ideological style, La Guma portrays a broad-based militancy that involves guerrilla activity in both the urban and rural areas. In *A Night of Their Own*, the sabotage campaign is associated with an élitist group of activists, whereas in La Guma's *In the Fog*, the revolutionary force is proletarian with sympathizers among the bourgeoisie and intelligentsia.[20]

While its focus is the preparation for armed struggle, *In the Fog* is a comprehensive novel that deals with a variety of political events. Employing a series of flashbacks, La Guma illustrates and dramatizes the stages by which the present structure of white South African supremacy was formally established. In some cases, he goes as far back in history as the Great Trek. One of his character's reading material shows this: "The *voortrekkers* wanted to go on keeping slaves and did not agree with the emancipation, so they decided to trek into the interior of the country."[21] This invocation of white conquest is reminiscent of Plaatje's extensive writings. Nonetheless, whereas Plaatje deals with the dawn of white domination to suggest the possibility of black resistance, La Guma mentions it to vindicate the revolutionary activity that dominates his novel.

From the Great Trek, La Guma provides additional background information dealing with industrialization and urbanization and their impact on black life. His objective here is to supply the reader with as much background history as possible in order to demonstrate how the protagonist has become the uncompromising revolutionary that he is in the novel.[22] The reader learns that Elias's father died in a mining accident near Johannesburg. After that, his family subsisted on a meagre pension of two pounds per month provided by the mine authorities. La Guma goes on to show the practice of favouritism where black and white pensioners are concerned. Elias is then portrayed looking for employment in Johannesburg. The usual problems of urban life, such as the pass system and the rough life in townships, are also briefly dealt with. Invariably, La Guma's covert purpose of demonstrating the development of Elias's political consciousness becomes aggressively clear. Like Xuma in Peter Abrahams's *Mine Boy*, Elias's awareness grows in the face of increasing white oppression and exploitation:

> Anger grew inside him like a ripening seed and the tendrils of its burgeoning writhed along his bones, through his muscles into his mind. Why, he thought, why, we are as they are, except that their lands are bigger and they have more money, and all we do is work for them when we are not trying to make a little corn grow among the stones of our own patches.[23]

What at first appears as background history becomes a sharp and didactic critique of the distribution of wealth in the South African society. The dispassionate, critical approach that characterizes La Guma's early writings has given way to a direct and militant style. This technique runs through all the sections he uses as a backdrop to the contemporary issues that follow.

His recreation of the Sharpeville crisis is another case in point. Whereas Peter Abrahams invokes very little of the crisis, La Guma (like Richard Rive in *Emergency*) provides a comprehensive picture by depicting its organization and the people involved. His choice of those involved betrays his proletarian bias. Distinct among them are workers, schoolchildren and elderly people; emphasis is given to the roles of the Washerwoman, the Bicycle Messenger, the Outlaw and the Child. The purpose of this selective representation is to demonstrate what kind of people constitute the proletarian class. David Rabkin has rightly argued that, in the portrayal of character in *In the Fog*, "the rich variety of what La Guma earlier described as the 'human salad' in a novella like *A Walk in the Night* is replaced by a set of typical figures."[24] While the theme is clearly stated and La Guma's political views are fully presented, characters are often reduced to mere illustrations of the author's point of view.

The organization of the struggle in *In the Fog* revolves around the initiative of two major characters, Elias Tekwane and Beukes. Both are seasoned politicians with a long history of suffering at the hands of the system. While Elias is the mastermind ideologue of the liberation movement, Beukes's immediate business is to ensure the distribution of political leaflets and then provide transport out of the country for three recruits.[25] Beukes's character seems to be a continuation and development of George Adams in *The Stone Country* in which the distribution of political leaflets is thwarted by police intervention. In *In the Fog*, the same character has been released from prison and is continuing with his old job, this time more cautiously.

Many of the other characters are depicted as politically unseasoned. The purpose is, probably, to justify the need for "conscientization" and thereby attempt to make Beukes's central role understandable. La Guma is particularly concerned with the passive – or even reactionary – attitude of women in this critical situation, and one element in the novel is the insistence on the need for a radical change in the outlook and involvement of women.

The first woman Beukes meets at the beginning of his itinerary is a maid-servant. Attempts to generate a meaningful political discussion with her fail because of her incorrigible fear of the system. Though she realizes that all unthinking white South Africans grow up to be bigots, her response to the oppressive situation is depicted as defeatist. When Beukes tries to persuade her that her labour is exploited, she resignedly answers: "That's life isn't it?"[26] A little later, her fear manifests itself more keenly when she discourages Beukes from fighting the system: "It's so hopeless. You only get into trouble".[27]

This timidity is further developed in the graphic depiction of Mrs Harris, a "bony woman with a face like a burned biscuit and neat clothes" who moves ". . . with the quiet manner of a nun".[28] This emaciated and wizened old woman exhibits her paranoia and suspicion as soon as Beukes enters the house. Her negative attitude to political discussions is implied by the blatant lie Flotman tells her about Beukes's name and the purpose of his visit: "No, no, Missus Harris, Mister Hendricks goes round selling encyclopaedias. He's trying to sell me a set, but I don't think I need one."[29]

Though motivated by different concerns, Mrs Bennett's political reaction is also noteworthy. The Bennetts are represented as a well-to-do "coloured" family with middle-class pretensions. Their house is equipped with expensive "brass ornaments and polished furniture".[30] Whereas the political demeanour of Mrs Harris and the maid is based on fear, Mrs Bennett's aggressive reaction is predicated on opportunism. Belonging to what she believes to be a well-to-do class of "coloureds", she does not want her family to lose its "privileged" position by embroiling itself in politics. Hence, she is opposed to strikes and political discussions between her husband and Beukes: "There's no time for politics now, Arty. You got a lot to do, hey",[31] she orders her husband. Despite Mrs Bennett's self-confidence, La Guma makes it clear that her family will be moved because the area has been earmarked for white residency.

Several notable exceptions to this fear-ridden condition of the women are to be found in other novels. Plaatje's Mhudi in *Mhudi* is an extremely courageous woman, who not only braves the forests in search of a lost husband, but fervently believes in Barolong autonomy from the autocratic rule of the Matabele. Dhlomo, too, shows how the oppressive system has coarsened and hardened women. In his short stories, some of his female characters are bold to the extent of perpetrating murder. In Peter Abrahams's *Mine Boy*, characters like Leah run shebeens with an iron hand and defy police intervention with remarkable courage and determination.

La Guma's portrayal of women as apolitical is by no means limited to *In the Fog*; in his earlier works, women play peripheral roles. Political toughness and revolutionary fervour are invariably associated with men. Hence, he claims, "To men who are oppressed freedom means many things."[32] In *In the Fog*, however, the peripheral role sometimes becomes indirect participation. Some of the women, like Henry April's wife, are morale boosters for the men who are directly involved in the armed struggle. The women also contribute to the struggle in that they are associated with children who, in La Guma's writings, symbolize an optimistic future.[33]

But in *In the Fog*, political apathy is not associated with female characters alone. The bourgeois political apathy characterized by Mrs Bennett finds its fullest and most absurd expression in Tommy; La Guma's portrayal of Tommy is probably the most caustic in the novel. Juxtaposed with plans for Beukes's distribution of political leaflets are descriptions of Tommy's misplaced values: affected appreciation of classical music, dancing and half-baked interest in middle-class drinks like sherry. As La Guma describes him, Tommy is a totally apolitical character:

> Not only did he avoid any serious kind of discussion, but was incapable of fathoming the things Beukes often talked about. For Tommy reality, life, could be shut out by the blare of dance-bands and the voices of crooners. From this cocoon he emerged only to find the means of subsistence, food and drink. Politics meant nothing to him. He found it easier to live under the regime than to oppose it.[34]

La Guma's attitude towards Tommy's values is disparaging. To La Guma, no other activity is as important as political involvement in white-ruled South Africa. It is this unfaltering commitment that characterizes his polemical manner in *In the Fog*.

If all characters in the novel were similar to the maid, Mrs Harris, Mrs Bennett and Tommy, then the primary objective of *In the Fog* would have been lost. Like all proletarian-oriented novels, *In the Fog* is an optimistic novel. The majority of its characters strongly believe that political change in South Africa is ineluctable. As Elias Tekwane defiantly puts it to his torturers, "You are reaching the end of the road and going downhill towards a great darkness, so you must take a lot of people with you, because you are selfish and greedy and afraid of the coming darkness . . ."[35] This optimism, it is argued, is based on the immense support the revolution is said to receive from various strata of society. While the women characters are apathetic to the revolution, the men associated with them are amenable to Beukes's political mission. Though Mr Bennett is riddled with fear of the system and the reactionary domination of his wife, he gives money to the radicals. Another sympathizer, more committed than Mr Bennett, is the schoolmaster, Flotman, a clandestine radical who condones the reading of revolutionary material by his students:

... they have taken to surreptitious reading of the theories of guerrilla warfare under the flaps of their desks. Don't worry, they're safe. They weren't caught last time ... Some of the young ones are inclined to be pretty romantic about revolution but their hearts are in the right place ...[36]

Despite the partisan tenor of the dialogue, Beukes is not satisfied with only private reading of surreptitious material. He espouses overt politicization of the students: "But there is also the matter of political education for these young people. I will see that you get more material for them, as soon as I can lay hands on some."[37]

Flotman's comprehension of a successful revolution is quickly registered, however. Whereas he appreciates the importance of reading and discussing revolutionary material, he is painfully aware of the futility of amassing theory without putting it into practice: "We bloody teachers need to help. We have talked about the revolution among ourselves too long. All very intellectual."[38] La Guma uses Flotman to warn theorists against the danger of living in ivory towers. At the same time, La Guma wants to demonstrate that, not only does the revolution receive support from schoolchildren; it is also sanctioned by some members of the intelligentsia.

Later, it becomes clear that the revolution has made an impact even on the bourgeoisie, a class traditionally associated with reaction. La Guma's portrayal of the doctor makes use of one of the most tendentious and rhetorical techniques in the novel. A few days after Beukes has been shot by the police, he seeks the help of a doctor. Beukes has previously been treated by the same doctor for a different ailment but, owing to the suspicious nature of his wound on this occasion, he wonders whether the doctor might not betray him. The doctor's lengthy political response is highly charged:

> If the community is given the opportunity of participating in making the law, then they have a moral obligation to obey it ... But if the law is made for them, without their consent or participation, then it's a different matter ... However, even under the circumstances prevailing in our country, I must ask myself, what does this law or that law defend, even if I did not help to make it. If the law punishes a crime, murder, rape, then I could bring myself to assist it. I would consider reporting a murder, a case of assault. But if the law defends injustice, prosecutes and persecutes those who fight injustice, then I am under no obligation to uphold it. They have actually given us an opportunity to pick and choose. Things happen in our country, Mister Beukes. Injustice prevails, and there are people who have the nerve enough to defy it. Perhaps I have been waiting for the opportunity to put my penny in the hat as well.[39]

What Rowland Smith terms "naive rhetoric"[40] is probably at its highest in this speech. Talking endlessly like a person in a frenzy, the doctor debunks the unfairness of the South African legal system and readily endorses the revolution. His anguished accusations remind one of the lawyer's didactic invective against the economic dominance of the neocolonist system in Ngugi wa Thiong'o's *Petals of Blood*. That lawyer exposes how the law is unfairly applied to benefit the Kenyan comprador bourgeoisie:

> We, the leaders, chose to flirt with the molten god, deaf monster who has plagued us for hundreds of years.
> I am a lawyer . . . what does this mean? I also earn my living by ministering to the monster. I am an expert in those laws meant to protect the sanctity of the monster-god and his angels and the whole hierarchy of the priesthood. Only I have chosen to defend those who have broken the laws and who might be excommunicated. For remember, only a few, the chosen few, can find favourable positions in the hierarchy. And mark you, and this is where it pains, it's their sweat and that feeds the catechists, the wardens, the deacons, the ministers, the bishops, the angels . . . the whole hierarchy. Still they are condemned . . . damned.[41]

The indignation of the doctor, the healer, against an injustice which wounds the flesh as well as the spirit is confirmed and intensified in the language of the lawyer whose outrage finds vent in a more elaborate and symbolic utterance. Ngugi wa Thiong'o's ironic use of religious symbols effectively illustrates the flaws in the socio-economic gradation of the Kenyan society. But, while La Guma's doctor unmasks the injustices of the South African system in order to justify the impending revolution, Ngugi wa Thiong'o's lawyer sarcastically describes the decadence of the Kenyan system to highlight how the Mau Mau revolution of the 1950s was hijacked. In other words, whereas the former deals with the struggle for independence, the latter describes post-independence disillusionment.

It is important to bear in mind, however, that while the doctor and the lawyer represent the impact of the suffering of an oppressed people on the minds of men of conscience from the professional classes, the main stress in most of the novels of the period is on the growing resistance and revolt of the disenfranchised people. As a clear example of this major emphasis, one can turn to the conversation between Beukes and Abdullah in *In the Fog*, where the essential role of workers as a vehicle of revolution is hinted at: "If we can only organize the workers proper nowadays".[42] The workers had once before engaged themselves in radical confrontation against the government and had failed because of police repression. As Abdullah emphasizes, however, their role is still considered indispensable:

> We can't neglect the workers just because some official is scared. The workers have acted before in spite of stupid or cowardly officials. Once the workers have seen that they should make a stand, no silly official is going to get in their way.[43]

Indeed, in *In the Fog*, the workers do take a stand in favour of the revolution and this is symbolized by Isaac. As in the case of most of the radical characters in the novel, Isaac is a political firebrand whose hatred of the system is in keeping with La Guma's revolutionary objectives:

> . . . sitting here in the hot, steamy kitchen, he (Isaac) thought that all this kowtowing to stupid idiots who cherished the idea that they were God's Cherished just because they had white skins, had to come to an end. The silly bastards, he thought, they had been stupefied into supporting a system which had to bust one day and take them all down with it; instead of permanent security and justice, they had chosen to preserve a tyranny that could only feed them temporarily on the crumbs of power and privilege. Now that the writing had started to appear on the wall, they either scrambled to shore it up with blood and bullets and the electric torture apparatus or hid their heads in the sand and pretended that nothing was happening. They would have to pay for stupidity the hard way. Isaac felt almost sorry for these people who believed themselves to be the Master Race, to have the monopoly of brains, yet who were vindictive, selfish and cruel.[44]

There is, of course, a similarity in the views of Isaac and the doctor and the lawyer in Ngugi wa Thiong'o's *Petals of Blood*. But it should be noted that Isaac's anger and capacity to act are much more pronounced. Isaac's confidence seems to replicate Elias Tekwane's optimistic conviction that the system is unavoidably going "downhill". Their optimism is based on a theoretical study of the mechanics of guerrilla warfare. Like Elias Tekwane, Isaac has accumulated revolutionary knowledge by reading history books and smuggled handbooks on guerrilla fighting. He differs from Elias Tekwane, however, in that he lacks praxis. But, though police surveillance is ultimately responsible for his sudden departure to join the guerrillas in the bush, Isaac has been contemplating this for a long time: "Corners of his mind were stored with the accumulated knowledge out of technical books and he longed like a lover for the time when he would be able to turn from theory to practice."[45] The use of the simile, "like a lover" reinforces the chilliness of what Isaac is reflecting upon.

With Isaac's departure along with Peter and Paul, Beukes optimistically anticipates the escalation of the armed struggle and the possible collapse of the oppressive system:

> Beukes stood by the side of the street in the early morning and thought, they have gone to war in the name of a suffering people. What the enemy himself has created, these will become battle-grounds, and what we see now is only the tip of an ice-berg of resentment against an ignoble regime, the tortured victims of hatred and humiliation. And those who persist in hatred and humiliation must prepare. Let them prepare hard and fast – they do not have long to wait.[46]

La Guma's conviction that the South African dilemma can be resolved only through revolutionary means is emphasized in these final sections of the novel. Though the doyen of the liberation organization, Elias Tekwane, is arrested and later brutally tortured to death, the reader is made aware that the struggle will still go on as planned. There is no evidence to prove J. M. Coetzee's observation that when Tekwane dies and Isaac takes up the struggle, Beukes looks "backward to the old politics of rallies and speeches".[47] On the contrary, one gets the impression that Beukes and Henry April would continue to recruit and transport new fighters to the north. This is borne out by the militant warnings and triumphant optimism in Beuke's's thought as Isaac, Peter and Paul depart. Throughout the novel the collective struggle is portrayed as destined to succeed. As Samuel Omo Asein has observed, "the pervasive note . . . in La Guma's novels is not that of despair and flight into a protective world of political negativism, but that of hope in the eventual overthrow of the oppressive regime in South Africa".[48] *In the Fog* closes on this note of hope, symbolized by children basking in the early sunshine of a new day.

La Guma's novel mainly offers a portrait of what could happen in the future, not of what is happening now. While the fact that the struggle is still in its infancy may be appreciated, the reader is never brought close to the major fighters themselves. Their activities are always in the background. Isaac, Peter and Paul are mere recruits on their way to the bush; in other words, they are fighters of the future. Guerrilla activity as it occurs in South Africa today has been vividly recorded by Nadine Gordimer.

Focusing on how the actual struggle is carried out, Gordimer's story, "Something Out There", gives an account of the ripening of the revolutionary situation. Although there is a difference of 12 years between the publication of La Guma's *In the Fog* and Gordimer's "Something Out There", both authors deal with the same period. Peter Abrahams's novel, *A Night of Their Own*, only comes to the edge of revolutionary activity but some comparison is possible between *In the Fog* and "Something Out There".

Nadine Gordimer's approach does not reflect an earnest advocacy of revolutionary change similar to that of La Guma, but both writers are optimistic about the future victory of blacks. In "Something Out There", Gordimer evinces this optimism by satirically depicting a selfish, closed and bigoted white population hopelessly duped by a group of guerrillas. She earlier had portrayed what she deemed to be the unavoidable struggle between black and white. In her collection of stories, *Some Monday For Sure*, Gordimer recorded an attempt by a group of supporters of the struggle to hold up a government truck carrying explosives, but the plan is discovered and the group and other recruits go into exile for military training. It is with the hope of the trained guerrillas' return to South Africa to fight for freedom that Gordimer optimistically proclaims: ". . . some perfectly ordinary day, for sure, black South Africans will free themselves and rule themselves".[49] In "Something Out There", similar guerrillas have returned, ready for political sabotage.

But, unlike La Guma, Gordimer does not show her optimism through the statements of a Marxist ideologue who lays down a theoretical formula guerrillas should apply in order to succeed. Although she writes about the struggle at a time when it is already taking place, she does not inject any revolutionary theory into her work. Unlike La Guma, Gordimer is a non-didactic writer who presents a detailed, detached, critical picture of South African life; little authorial commentary is provided. In describing how she works Gordimer states:

> The novelist writes about what sense he makes of life; his own commitment
> to one group or another enters his novel as part of, sometimes the deepest
> part of, the sense he makes of life. If, on the other hand, the commitment
> enters the novel not as part of the writer's own conception of the grand
> design, but as an attempt to persuade other people – then the book is not a
> novel but propaganda with a story. For the novelist does not say, 'This is
> what you must do' but 'This is what I have seen and heard and
> understood'.[50]

Although not all politically partisan novels constitute propaganda, Gordimer
makes it clear that she writes as a detached observer. La Guma, however, writes
as a committed participant.

Like *In the Fog*, the setting of "Something Out There" ranges from the
suburbs through the city to the veld. The story revolves around two plots linked
by the furtive activities of the characters involved. The first concerns a
rampaging baboon which kills pet animals in a white suburban area. Operating
stealthily, the baboon scares outdoor swimmers and tennis players, until it is
ultimately killed. Nadine Gordimer clearly employs the baboon to parallel, and
hence intensify, the clandestine role of guerrillas, whose activities occupy a
larger part of the story.

The whites' speculation about the baboon's identity parallels the mysterious
nature of the guerrillas.[51] No one in the white suburb is completely certain of the
creature's identity:

> A baboon; unlikely . . . A chimpanzee, some insist. Just a large monkey,
> say others.
>
>   It was seen again in the suburbs of wooded gardens where Stanley
> Dobrow took the only photograph so far obtained. If you could call that
> image of clashed branches a likeness of anything.[52]

Similarly, when the guerrillas, a white couple and two male blacks, settle in the
suburb they operate under borrowed identities. The white couple, Charles and
Joy, tell their neighbours, the Kloppers, that they are Australian. Eddie and
Vusi pose as garden "boys" for the white couple whereas they are guerrillas
trained abroad. Neighbours do not know their names or habits and have only a
hazy idea of their appearance. Each time an intruder approaches, Charles and
Joy hide the two guerrillas. Most of the preparations for blowing-up a power
station that occurs later in the story take place at night when people are asleep.

The suburban residents' plea to pay for the confinement of the baboon to a
zoo or a circus, where they believe it belongs, is reminiscent of the segregatory
and discriminatory tendencies of apartheid. The baboon becomes a symbol of
the entire black population confined to segregated townships and bantustans
by draconian and selfish laws. As Paul Gray argues, ". . . whites in South
Africa have already paid, to keep the majority of blacks in an 'appropriate'
place, a price yet to be reckoned".[53] The price, of course, is one of constant war.

Ironically, the baboon's continued roaming parallels Vusi's and Eddie's stay in the suburb. Not only are the white neighbours unaware that their principles of segregation and discrimination are being constantly violated but that they are indirectly feeding "subversives" who are undermining their system. Mrs Klopper, for instance, offers a biscuit tin full of rusks,[54] which Joy and Vusi relish together. The South African police traditionally search for guerrillas in black townships and rural areas while – the novella shows – the white community itself is unwittingly harbouring guerrillas in its own suburbs.

Gordimer's portrayal of the guerrillas' activities is succinct and witty. She, like Alex La Guma, feels the need to indicate to the reader how the guerrillas' past lives have moulded their present circumstances. Vusi, the most experienced of them all, provides a classic example. His past is recorded in the form of reminiscences:

> Around him in the dark, an horizon darker than the dark held the cold forms in which the old real, terrible needs of his life, his father's life and his father's father's life were not so strangely realized. He had sat at school farting the gases of an empty stomach, he had seen fathers, uncles, brothers, come home without work from days-long queues, he had watched, too young to understand, the tin and board that had been the shack he was born in, carted away by government demolishers. His bare feet had been shod in shoes worn to the shape of a white child's feet. He had sniffed glue to see a rosy future. He had taken a diploma by correspondence, to better himself. He had spoken nobody's name under interrogation. He had left a girl and baby without hope of being able to show himself to them again.[55]

In a passage such as this, the sense that armed struggle is necessary and inevitable is very clear. The content of this passage is similar to La Guma's portrayal of Elias Tekwane's background in *In the Fog*. There are differences in the tone and attitude of the two accounts, however. Gordimer is not only non-polemical and distanced but despite her awareness of evil-doing, always compassionate. La Guma writes with restrained anger. Nevertheless, despite her objectivity and compassion, Gordimer is clearly impatient with and critical of the system.

Another difference between the two writers is clearly seen in their protagonists' relationship with the masses. La Guma, because of his ideological inclination, is always intent on pointing out that the revolution must be broadly based: the solitary revolutionary figure must never lose touch with the urban (or rural) masses.[56] Gordimer shows her revolutionaries as detached, aloof from the masses, close and yet cut off from them. Vusi, Eddie and the white couple stay far from black townships and when Eddie visits the city (Johannesburg), he avoids contact with the masses:

> He roamed again towards the West end, to the queues from which he could catch a bus to get him part of his way back. He bought a carton of curried chicken and ate as he went along. Outside a white men's bar a black girl singled him out with a sidling look, and approached. He smiled and walked

on: no thanks, *sisi*. With the prostitute's eye for the stranger in town, she was the only one in the city to recognize him: someone set apart in the crowd of his own kind from which he appeared indistinguishable.[57]

Having provided background information about her characters Gordimer moves on quickly to tell how they prepare for a major assault. Her inside knowledge of these preparations is surprisingly detailed. She writes familiarly about weapons, and her narration of the establishment of a base and subsequently, the assault itself, is equally detailed:

As their brothers had for generations carried coal and sacks of potatoes, they unloaded and stowed in the pit they had dug the AKM assault rifles and bayonets, the grey limpet mines with detonators and timing devices, the defensive and offensive hand-grenades. The pit was lined and covered with plastic sheeting and covered again with earth, grasses and small shrubs uprooted in the dark. The shelter for the two men was far less elaborately constructed. The stope was there; with Charles they hitched a sheet of plastic overhead to hold the loose earth and put down a couple of blankets off the mattresses in the back bedroom, some tins of food and packs of cigarettes. The entrance to the stope, already concealed on all but one side by the rocks, was covered with branches cut from the single free-standing tree that grew among them.

On a Saturday night towards 2 a.m. there was an extensive power failure over the Witwatersrand area of the Transvaal.[58]

This kind of "inside" knowledge is not found in La Guma's *In the Fog*, in which the reader learns only that a wave of guerrilla activity is impending from the north.

Without doubt, Gordimer is a more accomplished writer than La Guma. Her very objectivity, her great formal skill and her ability to see deep into her characters set her apart from other writers I have discussed. Significantly, her objectivity lends credence to and enhances the impact of her implied rejection of the whole South African regime.

But, in assessing the revolutionary literature of the period, it is also important to stress the less "finished" and less "literary" novels of black writers who, through their own involvement from the 1920s to date, have experienced a crisis which forced them to think in terms of collective, rather than individual, strategies and which often pushes them beyond compassion and anger.

By the end of the decade, despite the repressive mood of the early 1960s, a surging support for revolution was manifested in black South African literature and politics. Organizations such as the South African Students' Organisation (SASO), Black People's Convention (BPC) and others, whose primary objective was to raise the political consciousness of black people, were influential throughout the country.

Notes

1. Nelson Mandela, quoted in Colin and Margaret Legum, *The Bitter Choice: Eight South Africans' Resistance to Tyranny*, p. 93.

2. Joe Slovo, in Basil Davidson, Joe Slovo and Anthony R. Wilkinson, *Southern Africa: The New Politics of Revolution*, p. 187.

3. Ursula A. Barnett, *A Vision of Order*, p. 129.

4. Richard Rive, prologue, *Emergency*, p. 13.

5. Vladimir Klima, Karel Frantisek Ruzicka and Peter Zima, *Black Africa*, pp. 258–9.

6. Vladimir Klima, Karel Frantisek Ruzicka and Peter Zima have expressed a similar view in their book, cited above.

7. Rive, pp. 44 and 45.

8. Rive, quoted in Ursula A. Barnett, *A Vision of Order*, p. 130.

9. Although not a black writer, C. J. Driver deals with the same subject in his *Elegy For a Revolutionary*.

10. Peter Abrahams, *A Night of Their Own*, p. 218.

11. Ibid., p. 12.

12. Ibid.

13. Ibid., p. 42.

14. Ibid., p. 35.

15. Ibid., pp. 165–6.

16. Ibid., pp. 207–208.

17. Ibid., pp. 104 and 105. In his novel, *Emergency* (discussed earlier), Richard Rive portrays the problem of racial prejudice in greater detail.

18. Richard Rive's *Emergency* and C. J. Driver's *Elegy For a Revolutionary* contain similar information, especially on police repression in the face of black resistance.

19. Colin and Margaret Legum, p. 77.

20. J. M. Coetzee, "Man's Fate in the Novels of Alex La Guma", *Studies in Black Literature*, Vol. 5, No. 1 (1984) p. 21.

21. Alex La Guma, *In the Fog of the Season's End*, p. 88.

22. This perspective has also been expressed by David Rabkin who argues that in La Guma's *In the Fog*, "Where characters are provided with personal history, its function is to illustrate how they came to adopt their present stance". See Rabkin's "La Guma and Reality in South Africa", *The Journal of Commonwealth Literature*, Vol. 8, No. 1 (1973) p. 60.

23. La Guma, p. 79.

24. Rabkin, p. 60.

25. Paul A. Scanlon, "Alex La Guma's Novels of Protest: The Growth of a Revolutionary", *Okike*, No. 16 (1979) p. 45.

26. La Guma, p. 11.

27. Ibid.

28. Ibid., p. 22.

29. Ibid., p. 21.

30. Ibid., p. 22.

31. Ibid., p. 21.

32. Ibid., p. 58.

33. Coetzee, p. 22. See also, Samuel Omo Asein, "The Revolutionary Vision in Alex La Guma's Novels", *Phylon*, Vol. 39, No. 1 (1978) p. 86.

34. La Guma, p. 53.

35. Ibid., p. 6.

36. Ibid., pp. 88 and 89.

37. Ibid., p. 88.

38. Ibid., p. 90.

39. Ibid., p. 161.

40. Rowland Smith, "Allan Quatermain to Rosa Burger: Violence in South African Fiction", *World Literature Written in English*, Vol. 22, No. 2 (1983) p. 179.

41. Ngugi wa Thiong'o, *Petals of Blood*, pp. 163–4.

42. La Guma, p. 96.

43. Ibid.

44. Ibid., pp. 114–15.

45. Ibid., p. 119.

46. Ibid., pp. 180–81.

47. Coetzee, p. 21.

48. Asein, p. 86.

49. Nadine Gordimer, introduction, *Some Monday For Sure*.

50. Nadine Gordimer, "The Novel and the Nation in South Africa", *African Writers on African Writing*, (ed.) G. D. Killam, p. 38.

51. In his article, "The Plot Beneath the Skin: The Novels of C. J. Driver", in *Aspects of South African Literature*, (ed.) Christopher Heywood. Rowland Smith describes (p. 152) what he considers to be the unconvincing character of similar underground fighters in C. J. Driver's *Send War In Our Time, O Lord* as "shadowy".

52. Nadine Gordimer, *Something Out There*, pp. 131 and 147.

53. Paul Gray, "Tales of Privacy and Politics", review of *Something Out There*, by Nadine Gordimer, *Time*, No. 23 (July 1984).

54. Gordimer, *Something Out There*, p. 136.

55. Ibid., pp. 145–6.

56. Though there is contact between guerrillas and the people in C. J. Driver's *Send War In Our Time, O Lord*, the role of the collective is partly undermined by the author's undue emphasis on the importance of competent leadership. Driver also does not seem to view the question of individual and collective participation from a strictly Marxist perspective, unlike La Guma. His central concern is merely the necessity of armed struggle rather than the ideological organization and implementation of the revolution.

57. Gordimer, p. 175.

58. Ibid., pp. 191 and 195.

4. Ideas under Arrest

Direct and Indirect Protest in the Poetry of the Late 1960s and Early 1970s

After Sharpeville: A "New" Wave of Poetry

The arrests, exiles and bannings that occurred in the wake of the Sharpeville crisis produced two new techniques for recording the South African political situation. As demonstrated in the previous chapter, for those writing in exile (like Alex La Guma and Peter Abrahams) who were thus immune from South Africa's banning laws, the new style reflected and, in the case of Alex La Guma, promoted a militant attitude towards the system. For those writing inside South Africa, to record militant activities like the sabotage campaign, or to project a revolutionary future would have meant playing into the hands of the regime's censorship and banning board or even courting arrest. Hence, for a period of five years after the crisis, little writing from blacks was published inside the country and some people were anxiously looking forward to another literary renaissance[1] akin to that which had taken place in the 1950s. This five-year silence proved to be a kind of gestation period that finally produced a "new" crop of writers who emerged with a technique compatible with the repressive mood of the period. These writers realized that, for the anticipated literary revival to succeed, they had to adopt a non-militant style that would protect them from banning while at the same time allow them to criticize the injustices of the system. Nadine Gordimer was the first to point out that:

> Black writers have had to look for survival away from the explicit if not to the cryptic then to the implicit, and in their case they have turned instinctively to poetry.[2]

Although some of the poems written by these "new" black poets were very direct statements of political anger and pain, the use of poetry itself reflects a more indirect mode of political expression.

Profundity beneath Apparent Simplicity: Oswald Mtshali and his Contemporaries

This "new" wave of committed poetry was first made prominent by Oswald Mtshali. When his first collection of poetry, *Sounds of a Cowhide Drum*, was published, Mtshali was working as a motor-scooter messenger[3] in Johannes-burg. The poetry, which was generally well received at its publication by both blacks and whites, deals with the familiar concerns of race and politics similar to those examined by older poets such as Dennis Brutus, but it is the manner in which these concerns are expressed that has made *Sounds of a Cowhide Drum* so successful. Mtshali's cynical and sarcastic[4] attitude, his oblique and ironic use of vivid, suggestive similes and images, and the profound meaning that lies beneath the apparent simplicity of his poetry, all contribute towards their total effect. This technique, however, is said to have disgruntled younger, radical writers like Mbulelo Mzamane, who wanted to see "revolutionary fire"[5] in Mtshali's poetry.

Child characters feature frequently in black South African writings. In some short stories, children are associated with parks, swings and other public facilities to which, by virtue of their colour, they have no access. In many autobiographies, experiences of township violence, poverty and disparity in opportunities and privilege are partly seen through the eyes of children. The "new" poetry of the late 1960s and early 1970s also employs children to highlight certain injustices of the system.

In "The Shepherd and His Flock", Mtshali uses the pastoral convention to criticize the economic and educational deprivation of black children. The poem opens with familiar pastoral simplicity reminiscent of William Blake's "Songs of Innocence":

> The rays of the sun
> are like a pair of scissors
> cutting the blanket
> of the dawn from the sky.
>
> . . . The young shepherd
> drives the master's sheep
> from the paddock
> into the veld.
>
> A lamb strays away
> enchanted by the marvels
> of a summer morning;
> the ram
> rebukes the ewe
> "Woman! Woman!
> Watch over the child!"[6]

Mtshali's use of the simile and imagery in the first stanza and his graphic representation of the shepherd's world in the succeeding two stanzas are concrete and effective. The portrayal not only suggests a mood of innocence, but a state of harmony between the shepherd and his environment. But as the poem progresses, it soon becomes clear that the harmony is constantly undermined by a sense of the utter frustration that the shepherd experiences.

Using similes and images in his characteristically effective and ingenious[7] manner, Mtshali satirically implies the shepherd's poverty: "His bare feet/kick the grass/and spill the dew like diamonds/on a cutter's table."[8]

The final stanza ironically offsets the mood of innocence and pastoral harmony by registering an implicit protest. In a manner akin to William Blake's assault on the family, the church and the political system of his time, Mtshali subtly exposes the discrepancy in educational opportunities between black and white children. The shepherd salutes his master's children as they go to school and rhetorically asks: "O! Wise Sun above/will you ever guide/me into school?"[9] The question is put to the Son of God who is represented by the pun "Sun" above.[10] This "religious" allusion is in keeping with the mood of innocence that pervades three-quarters of the poem.

While critics like Mbulelo Mzamane have attacked what they consider to be an over-emphasis on this Blake-like innocence and simplicity,[11] they have overlooked the fact that what at first appears to be a poem celebrating innocence and the rapport between the shepherd and his environment becomes a biting critique of the system's inequality; this is entirely compatible with the indirect approach Mtshali sets out to adopt.

Mtshali's manner of protest is reiterated in another poem that also focuses on a child character, and the technique of rhetorical questioning is again effectively employed. Like the shepherd in "The Shepherd and His Flock", the boy in "Boy on a Swing" is a type-character representing the suffering majority of blacks. Nadine Gordimer has perceptively described this singular representation that characterizes the "new" poetry saying, "'I' is the pronoun that prevails, rather than 'we', but the 'I' is the Whitmanesque unit of multi-millions rather than the exclusive first person singular."[12]

Like "The Shepherd . . .", "Boy on a Swing" opens with innocence and is then followed by an oblique, querulous section that registers Mtshali's protest. The boy is happily playing on a swing but soon asks:

> Mother!
> Where did I come from?
> When will I wear long trousers?
> Why was my father jailed?[13]

The tone is non-declamatory[14] but the avalanche of rhetorical questions coupled with such similes as, "His blue shirt/billows in the breeze/like a tattered kite"[15] captures various ugly aspects of South African life. The political implications of the questions distract attention from the swinging game and focus it on the problems of poverty, unsettled family background and repression indirectly suggested. Hence, the bitterness of the final stanza belies the apparent pleasure depicted in the first three stanzas.

Though published only a year after the appearance of Mtshali's *Sounds of a Cowhide Drum*, James Matthews's poetry goes beyond indirect protest. In its use of children to express criticism, his poetry combines oblique stylistic devices such as rhetorical questions, irony and cynicism with unambiguous statements and a direct cry of anger; at times the bitterness becomes overt. Justifying this style, Matthews himself has proclaimed that:

> To label my utterings poetry
> and myself a poet
> would be as self-deluding
> as the planners of parallel development
> I record the anguish of the persecuted
> whose words are whimpers of woe
> wrung from them by bestial laws
> They stand one chained band
> silently asking one of the other
> will it never be the fire next time?[16]

Nonetheless, some of his poetry reflects certain elements of form and content that approximate to Mtshali's manner of writing. This is exemplified in his poem, "Two Little Black Boys".

In this poem, two black boys argue about the possibility of using a whites-only public lavatory. The poem aims to debunk the discriminatory laws of the white regime. Matthews emphasizes the boys' physical stature in order to highlight the innocence of their age: "One not bigger than a grasshopper/the other a head of hair taller."[17] The bigger boy represents the voice of experience, hence he is aware of the discriminatory nature of the system, "the tall one said, pointing to the board/it's white people only."[18] The shorter boy's rejoinder and attitude towards this warning form the crux of the poem: "puzzled, the grasshopper replied, don't white people shit like me?"[19] Innocent as the response may sound, it unmasks the irrationality and selfishness of privilege by combining the Mtshali-like innocence and rhetorical questioning with an undertone of anger.

Casey Motsisi's poem, "The Efficacy of Prayer", is an ironic critique of the lack of opportunities faced by blacks. The poem revolves around the futile prayer of a little girl called Sally for a career, but it opens with the depiction of a character often met in black prose writings: an incorrigible alcoholic whose personality has been fashioned by the regime's economic policies. By virtue of his mysterious family background and alcoholism, the character is closely reminiscent of Peter Abrahams's Daddy in *Mine Boy* and Alex La Guma's Doughty in *A Walk in the Night*:

> They called him Dan the Drunk.
> The old people refuse to say how old he was,
> Nobody knows where he came from – but they all
> Called him Dan the Drunk.
> He was a drunk, but perhaps his name was not
> really Dan.
> Who knows, he might have been Sam.
> But why bother, he's dead, poor Dan.
> Gave him a pauper's funeral, they did.
> Just dumped him into a hole to rest in

eternal drunkenness.
Somehow the old people are glad that Dan the
Drunk is dead.[20]

Motsisi successfully captures the anonymity and mystery that surround township malcontents like Dan. The indifference with which elders treat Dan during his lifetime and at his death is also effectively portrayed. The motive for this indifference is that parents resent the admiration their children have for him. Prompted by the music Dan plays for her and other children, the child Sally expresses a wish to emulate him when she grows up:

> 'I'm going to be just like Dan the Drunk',
> a little girl said to her parents of a night
> cold while they crowded around a sleep brazier.
> The parents looked at each other and their eyes
> prayed.
> 'God Almighty, save our little Sally.'
> God heard their Prayer
> He saved their Sally.
> Prayer. It can work miracles.
> Sally grew up to become a nanny . . .[21]

Besides showing that no job other than that of a nanny is accessible to a black girl like Sally, Motsisi makes it clear that the social, economic and political deprivation imposed on blacks denies them the opportunity to produce meaningful role models for the younger members of their society.

This lack of models has been passionately articulated by Lewis Nkosi:

> I write so much at length about the hero of Alan Paton's novel not in any effort to give a full critique of the novel as a work of art, but in order to show that when we entered the decade of the fifties we had no literary heroes, like generations in other parts of the world. We had to improvise because there were no models who could serve as moral examples for us in our private and public preoccupations. On the other hand by the time we were through living in the fifties we had given white writers a milieu and characters who were recognisably modelled upon our lives.[22]

Given some of the early, non-religious and committed works by Plaatje, Dhlomo and Abrahams, Lewis Nkosi's argument may be overstated. It could, however, serve to illustrate Motsisi's notion behind "The Efficacy of Prayer", especially if applied to non-intellectual and non-élitist blacks. Their "models" are mainly people without a chance, like the disorderly drunkard in the poem and the urban thugs who harass the townships day and night.

In his poem, "Her Name is 'Dooti'", Wally Serote paints a more desperate picture of the lack of opportunities for black girls. Dooti's future is bleak:

> Dooti is a girl with a great future;
> She has the world's greatest keys
> In those excursions of the heart,

> Or wherever it is we hold these keys;
> Hullo–Goodbye;
> Between that stands her name and needs,
> And her face; silent.
> We of the world have grown tired of listening
> To names and needs;
> We have closed curtains lately
> To the future.[23]

Serote's attitude here is not one of defeatism but bitterness and impatience.

In "Burning Cigarette", he portrays a similar aura of hopelessness among township boys. Depicting the wasted life of a little boy, Serote says:

> This little black boy
> Is drawn like a cigarette from its box,
> Lit
> He looks at his smoke hopes
> That twirl, spiral, curl
> To nothing.
> He grows like cigarette ashes
> As docile, as harmless;
> Is smothered.[24]

The image of a "box" signifies the trapped lives blacks lead. Like Mtshali's shepherd and Serote's Dooti, the little boy in "Burning Cigarette" has no future to look forward to. The best he can do is to find a menial job similar to that of a nanny. Yet, while Serote's portrayal is cool, it is heavy with protest.

One of the most forceful poems to mock a political system that promotes this abject lack of opportunities is by Oswald Mtshali. In his usual, satirical style, he invokes the hollow career of a representative boy:

> He enrolled at Life University
> whose lecture rooms were shebeens;
> hospital wards and prison cells.
>
> He graduated cum laude
> with a thesis in philosophy:
> 'I can't be black and straight
> In this crooked white world!
>
> If, I tell the truth
> I'm detestable
> If I tell lies
> I'm abominable.
> If, I tell nothing
> I'm unpredictable.
> If I smile to please
> I'm nothing but an obsequious sambo'[25]

The "philosophic" section of the poem emphasizes the perennial lack of trust of blacks by whites. Mtshali enlarges on this in his poem, "Always A Suspect", where a young black man is depicted walking beside a white woman and is presumed to be about to rob her.

Njabulo Ndebele examines the absence of opportunities and its corollary, frustration, in a more detailed and fresh manner. He consistently and effectively operates at the metaphorical and imagist level. His protagonist, who is much older than Mtshali's and Serote's characters, is initially presented as a person doing relatively well in town, perhaps working as a miner or garden "boy". Once having lost his source of livelihood, he hopelessly searches for alternatives in the "homelands":

> I hid my love in the sewerage
> Of a city; and when it was decayed,
> I returned:
> I returned to the old lands.[26]

Ndebele has managed to protest against two injustices without necessarily stating them in these lines. The "old lands" to which the protagonist returns symbolize the depth of the black people's suffering and deprivation. James Matthews, Gladys Thomas[27] and Ndebele himself have thoroughly demonstrated that "homelands" have very little to offer except poverty, overcrowding, disease and palpable dullness. Hence, searching for fulfilment in such a wasteland ends in despair and desperate introspection:

> Below the bottom of life,
> My love – lay drowned in the stench,
> Of – course I knew it
> I knew my love was dead;
>
> I knew I had lost,
> God, I knew I had lost;
> O who am I? Who am I?
> I am the hoof that once
> Grazed in silence upon the grass
> But now rings like a bell on tarred streets.[28]

Ndebele's ingenious use of images, metaphors and similes demonstrate that the life of a black youth moves in a vicious circle. The youth starts off from the city where his subsistence is precarious; he then drifts into a "homeland" where his hopelessness reaches a nadir. At the end of the poem he is back in the city where he is forced to join a population afflicted by wholesale frustration.

In their fiction, R. R. R. Dhlomo and Modikwe Dikobe show that the conjuncture described above has prompted some blacks to resort to various compensatory, survival tactics. The "new" poets represent some of these survival tactics in a graphic and moving manner. Death, for instance, is portrayed as a reality that blacks have learned to flirt with:

Dying
has become
the mistress
with whom we
brazenly carry on
an illicit love affair
that ends only
in the grave

We rise
and kiss her
'Good morning my love'
and walk with her
hand in hand . . .[29]

Mtshali's usually indirect style is absent here; instead, direct, regretful protest is expressed in a non-militant manner. In the other poems of the period, death is treated with apparent casualness. The birth of a child is ironically regretted; the death of a newly-born child, before it experiences the sordid life of black South Africa, is depicted as desirable. In "Mother's Ode to a Stillborn Child", Mandlenkosi Langa attacks the death-like quality of the life led by blacks. Pretending to regret the stillbirth of the child, Langa writes:

I could feel your lust
to join the dead
living world
Your muted attempts
to burst like a Christmas chicken
into life.[30]

Njabulo Ndebele expresses the same death-in-life concept more concretely. In his poem, "Little Dudu", the body of a newly-born baby boy is metaphorically compared to that of a corpse, "O newly born coffin!"[31] The hands and actions of the elders nursing the baby are rendered in equally macabre terms: "Withered hands, mourning their own deaths/Would grope for the feel of his body . . .".[32]

In "Mother's Ode to a Stillborn Child", however, Langa's cynicism reaches its height in the second and last stanza where he ironically implies that still-birth is preferable to live birth:

It is not my fault
that you did not live
to be a brother sister
or lover of some black child
that you did not experience pain
pleasure voluptuousness and salt
in the wound
that your head did not stop

a police truncheon
that you are not a permanent resident
of a prison island.[33]

Langa's approach here is more indirect than Mtshali's in the sense that the former employs no accusatory, political, rhetorical questions, but Langa's pervasive cynicism and satirical protest are immensely effective.

Sometimes the preference for premature death verges on apparent callousness. In his "An Abandoned Bundle", Oswald Mtshali provides one of the most gruesome[34] portraits of the brutish experiences black children undergo in South Africa. A young mother leaves a new-born baby abandoned on a rubbish heap and dogs tear it to pieces as they fight over it:

> Scavenging dogs
> draped in red bandanas of blood
> fought fiercely
> for the squirming bundle.
>
> I threw a brick;
> they bared fangs
> flicked velvet tongues of scarlet
> and scurried away,
> leaving a mutilated corpse –
> an infant dumped on a rubbish heap –
> "Oh! Baby in the Manger
> Sleep well
> on human dung."[35]

Like Mandlenkosi Langa, in his "Mother's Ode to a Stillborn Child", where a child's wish to be born is associated with the birth of Christ, Mtshali directly compares the circumstances of Christ's birth with those of the abandoned child. Both children are outcasts but Christ's outcast status in the manger is less deprived than the abandoned child's position on a dung hill. The other difference is that, whereas Mtshali's abandoned child dies, Christ is ultimately not abandoned and survives.

While Mtshali's attack on economic deprivation and its impact on blacks characterizes the entire poem, his sharpest criticism occurs in the last stanza. The quality of innocence which by logic should be associated with the abandoned child and with Christ is ironically attached to the remorseless mother who has left her child on the rubbish heap to die:

> Its mother
> had melted into the rays of the rising sun,
> her face glittering with innocence
> her heart as pure as untrampled dew.[36]

Mtshali's attack here is two-pronged. First, he criticizes a political system whose greed and selfish ideals encourage poverty and hence generate dehumanization and brutalization among blacks. The frequency with which senseless deaths occur in townships is such that one gets the impression that human life is cheap. Second, Mtshali criticizes blacks for "giving in" to dehumanization and brutalization. As Wally Serote has put it, "Oh you black boys/You thin shadows who emerge like a chill in the night/It's black women who are crying."[37] Indeed, there is obvious cynicism and sarcasm in the way Mtshali portrays the indifferent attitude of the remorseless mother in his "An Abandoned Bundle". The mother's indifference borders on cruelty, which Njabulo Ndebele has aptly described as, "Cruelty that shuts the mind/To the discernment of all goodness."[38]

The attitudes of Mtshali, Serote and Ndebele towards township criminal violence are by no means new. One only needs to recall Can Themba's account of the senseless murder of Henry Nxumalo in *The Will to Die*, Bloke Modisane's angry bemoaning of his father's cruel death in *Blame Me on History*, and Ezekiel Mphahlele's portrayal of murder in his short story, "In Corner B".

Both prose writers and poets, however, have unequivocally demonstrated that criminal violence does not help change the situation because it is invariably directed towards the wrong targets. Even if it were directed towards the oppressors themselves, it would still change little because the violence is inherently random, occurring outside any observable political programme. The violence is practised out of self-interest with the express objective of financial gain. What then are the other responses to the situation reflected by blacks who do not espouse criminal violence, particularly the "new" poets themselves?

By expressing their own attitudes to the situation, black writers have always inadvertently represented the feelings of different groups of their oppressed society. During the 1950s, for example, the responses of prose writers varied from writer to writer. Can Themba has summarized the responses thus:

. . . Nat's was such a voice . . . Sobukwe's is that of protest and resistance. Casey Motsisi's that of derisive laughter. Bloke Modisane's that of implacable hatred. Ezekiel Mphahlele's that of intellectual contempt. Nimirod Mkele's that of patient explanation to be patient. Mine that of self-corrosive cynicism.[39]

Among poets, Dennis Brutus's attitude has been discussed in the second chapter. His attitude is one of endurance and hope predicated on the acceptance of suffering. As he himself has put it in his poem "Cold":

steel ourselves into fortitude
or accept an image of ourselves
numb with resigned acceptance.[40]

This acceptance does not mean succumbing to the political oppressor but signifies determination.

The political attitudes of the "new" poets also vary from poet to poet. Of course, there are responses characteristic of the period that most of the poets share, but one may rightly argue that these responses are stylistic devices rather than political attitudes. The poets' real attitudes go beyond cynicism, sarcasm,

irony and satire. Oswald Mtshali, for instance, "is a poet who attempts a kind
of hope for the hopeless."[41]

In the last stanza of his poem "Men in Chains", this hopeful attitude comes
across quite clearly:

> One man with a head
> shaven clean as a potato
> whispered to the rising sun,
> a red eye wiped by a tattered
> handkerchief of clouds,
> 'Oh! Dear Sun!
> Won't you warm my heart
> with hope?'
> The train went on its way to nowhere.[42]

In the stanza above – as in the poems dealing with child characters discussed
earlier – Mtshali uses simile and metaphor to convey the suffering, humiliation
and poverty of the convict. The sentence, "a red eye wiped by a tattered
handkerchief of clouds", is particularly effective in its indirect, metaphorical
reference to the convict's poverty.

After painting this portrait of oppression, Mtshali implies his attitude to the
situation through the convict's response. Like the shepherd in "The Shepherd
and His Flock" who hopes to be guided into school by the "Sun above", the
convict also hopes that the same "Sun" will one day bring his suffering to an
end. There is a striking irony in the way Mtshali invokes the assistance of this
"Sun above", however.

Though the pun may refer to the Son of God, it is doubtful whether his hope
in future change is at all based on a belief in Christ's intervention. This is borne
out by the manner in which he ridicules the role of religion. In "This Kid is No
Goat", Mtshali attacks the hypocritical and selfish promises of the church:

> . . . No more do I go to church
> where the priest has left me in the lurch
> His sermon is a withered leaf
> falling from the decaying pulpit tree
> to be swept away
> by violent gusts of doubt and scepticism.
>
> 'My wife and kids can worship there:
> they want to go to heaven when they die.
> I don't want to go to heaven when I'm dead.
> I want my heaven now,
> here on earth in Houghton and Parktown;
> a mansion
> two cars or more
> and smiling servants.
> Isn't that heaven?'[43]

Mtshali employs a series of assertive statements, images and metaphors to show the church's decadence. Towards the end of the concluding stanza, however, his characteristically ironical style creeps back as his philosophic and heavily sarcastic argument about the location of heaven completes what he considers to be the fallacious teaching of the church.

In "An Old Man in Church", the church is similarly satirized for what Mtshali views to be its exploitative attributes:

> I know an old man
> who during the week is a machine working at full
> throttle:
> productivity would stall,
> spoil the master's high profit estimate,
> if on Sunday he did not go to church
> to recharge his spiritual batteries.
>
> . . . He falls on raw knees
> that smudge the bare floor with his piety.
> He hits God's heart with screams as hard as stones
> flung from the slingshot of his soul.
>
> . . . The acolyte comes around with a
> brass collection plate
> the old man sneaks in a cent piece
> that raises a scowl on the collector's face
> whose puckered nose sneezes at such poor
> generosity.[44]

After exposing how the old man is exploited physically and financially, Mtshali closes the poem with the ironical beatitude: "Blessed are the meek for they shall inherit the earth."[45]

The hollowness of religious belief is further exposed in "The Washerwoman's Prayer". Like the old man in the church, the washerwoman has spent all her life working. One day, after overworking to the point of break-down, she prays for God's intervention, but God responds:

> 'My child! Dear child,' she heard,
> 'Suffer for those who live in gilded sin,
> Toil for those who swim in a bowl of pink gin.'[46]

The response reveals the emptiness of conventional prayer in the South African situation, while the washerwoman's resignation suggests endurance and hope for possible change:

> 'Thank you Lord! Thank you Lord.
> Never again will I ask
> Why must I carry this task.'[47]

While Mtshali's criticism of the church sometimes becomes assertive, it is instructive to note that his style contrasts sharply with the impassioned attacks of Plaatje (attack on the Dutch Reformed Church in his *Mhudi* and *Native Life in South Africa*), and Modikwe Dikobe (attack on the white, exclusive church in *The Marabi Dance*).

Oswald Mtshali's hope for change is more clearly articulated in "Handcuffs", another poem dealing with the suffering of a convict. The poem sounds similar to Dennis Brutus's "Cold". Talking of the pain and restriction a convict experiences from handcuffs, Mtshali says:

Handcuffs
have steel fangs
whose bite is more painful
than a whole battalion
of fleas.

Though the itch in my heart
grows deeper and deeper
I cannot scratch.

How can I?
my wrists
are manacled.
My mind
is caged.
My soul
is shackled.[48]

In spite of this total lack of freedom, the convict does not surrender. Like Brutus in his prison poems, the convict is hopeful and determined to endure his suffering:

I can only grimace at the ethereal cloud,
a banner billowing in the sky, emblazoned,
'Have hope, brother,
despair is for the defeated.'[49]

While Mtshali's attitude is one of hope, Serote's is one of bitterness and anger. Serote's verse is generally more assertive. In his early poetry, however, Serote's rage does not lend itself to advocacy of any form of violence against the white regime. In his first collection of poetry, *Yakhal' Inkomo*, Serote gives the impression that negotiations between whites and blacks in order to bring about change are possible. But it is blacks who should spell out the terms of change while whites listen:

White people are white people,
They are burning the world.
Black people are black people,

They are the fuel.
White people are white people,
They must learn to listen.
Black people are black people,
They must learn to talk.[50]

His recent novel, *To Every Birth Its Blood*, "delves into the heart and soul of a nation heading for disaster and creates an awareness of why it is inevitable".[51] Like his predecessors of the 1950s Serote extensively examines the issues of economic deprivation and political oppression to illustrate this impending disaster.

"White People are white People", however, is one of the telling examples of Serote's attitude towards the system. He is not merely recording a simple process of talking and listening, but suggesting a turning of the tables in the political status quo. The poem is made up of assertive orders. Reconciliatory as some of the lines may sound, the curtness and repetitiveness of the style suggest an undertone of anger.

"What's in This Black 'Shit'", expresses Serote's anger in scatological terms. Even to themselves blacks can resemble vomit:

It is not the steaming little rot
In the toilet bucket,
It is the upheaval of the bowels
Bleeding and coming out through the mouth
And swallowed back,
Rolling in the mouth,
Feeling its taste and wondering what's next
like it.[52]

The plain statements in "Ofay-Watcher, Throbs-Phase XIII" have given way to concentrated metaphors and images. After defining the "shitlike" character of blacks, Serote goes on to illustrate how this negative portrait is promoted by the regime. He gives examples of black people's social, political and economic problems – problems that prompt Serote's defiance towards white authority:

I'm learning to pronounce this "Shit" well,
Since the other day,
At the pass office,
When I went to get employment,
The officer there endorsed me to Middleburg,
So I said, hard and with all my might, "Shit"!
I felt a little better;
But what's good, is, I said it in his face,
A thing my father wouldn't dare do.
That's what's in this black "Shit".[53]

This stanza contrasts with the opening one in that it contains no other metaphor or image except the word "Shit". Serote sets out to recreate an incident and hence uses simple explanation throughout. He portrays the development of his character's defiance.[54] The word "Shit", usually used by some white officials to refer to blacks or their actions, is now being used by the black character to curse the whites. The cathartic effect of this turning of the tables is graphically expressed. For all its rage, "What's in This Black 'Shit'" is devoid of the militant tone that characterizes the work of poets such as Don Mattera and other new poets who wrote after the Soweto uprising.

Indeed, though "hate is conjured up in Serote's work, ". . . he himself is not free to hate":[55]

> To talk for myself,
> I hate to hate,
> But how often has it been
> I could not hate enough.[56]

The perennial, hateful situation of blacks is so understated that the reader may easily forget that Serote is a poet who usually reflects a great deal of sadness and anger. In "Waking Up, The Sun, The Body", Serote's tendency to experience anger without necessarily hating is reinforced:

> For what do you do when, again and again,
> Things around and in you beg you with a painful
> embrace to hate,
> And you respond with a rage and you know,
> That you can never hate.
> This is a waking deep as the distance of the sun,
> Mind-defying as the knowledge of God.[57]

Ultimately, Serote's reluctance to hate boils down to "patient" waiting for possible change:

> I have tasted, ever so often,
> Hunger like sand on my tongue
> And tears like flames have licked my eye-lids
> Blurring that which I want to see,
> I want to know,
> But Oh! often, now and then, everywhere where I
> have been,
> Joy, as real as paths,
> Has spread within me like pleasant scenery,
> Has run beneath my flesh like rivers glitteringly
> silver;
> And now I know:
> Having been so flooded and so dry,
> I wait.[58]

Serote's waiting is probably synonymous with Mtshali's espousal of hope for the hopeless.

Anger and Beyond: The Poetry of James Matthews

Among the poets who wrote before the 1976 Soweto uprising, James Matthews is probably the angriest. His anger goes far beyond that of poets like Wally Serote in that Matthews is not content just to be angry against a system that oppresses blacks – he openly advocates hatred. This hatred is not, however, characteristic of his poetry alone. During the 1950s and the early 1960s, Matthews wrote short stories such as "The Party", "The Park" and "The Portable Radio" (which appeared in Richard Rive's *Quartet*), which reflected a similar mood of satirical rage. His subsequent collection of poems, co-authored with Gladys Thomas, is perhaps most representative of his style.

The collection is appropriately entitled *Cry Rage*, and the poetry abounds with what James Matthews himself has referred to as "declarations" of those who have learned how to hate enough and to survive.[60] While the title poem encapsulates the mood that runs through most of the poems, the one that opens the collection best represents Matthews's method:

It is said
that poets write of beauty
of form, of flowers and of love
but the words I write
are of pain and of rage

I am no minstrel
who sings songs of joy
mine a lament
I wail of a land
hideous with open graves
waiting for the slaughtered ones

Balladeers strum their lutes and sing
tunes of happy times
I cannot join in their merriment
my heart drowned in bitterness
with the agony of what white
man's law has done.[61]

These protestations are later reinforced when Matthews again asserts that his poetry records ". . . the anguish of the persecuted/whose words are whimpers of woe/wrung from them by bestial laws."[62] One reason why Matthews's poetry is so assertive is the influence of Black Consciousness;[63] while it can also be detected in the works of Mtshali, Serote, Langa and Ndebele, it is most obvious in Matthews's poetry.

Like Solomon Plaatje in his novel, *Mhudi*, Modikwe Dikobe in his recent collection of poetry, *Dispossessed*, and a great many of the Black Consciousness writers, Matthews partly views the oppression of blacks in its historical context. The apparent innocence of the white man's arrival in South Africa is portrayed as an event that was quickly followed by the dispossession and exploitation of blacks:

> We watched the white man's arrival
> in strange-shaped ships we did not know
> now we have become trespassers
> on the shores of our land
>
> . . . the fields that were ours
> our cattle can no longer graze
> and like the cattle we are herded
> to starve on barren soil
>
> we die in the earth's depth
> to fill his coffer with gold
> his lust for the shiny pebbles
> outweighs his concern for our lives
>
> . . . in his house our mothers
> and sisters soothe his young
> tendering them the love they need
> only to be rejected in later years[64]

The directness and querulousness of these lines are more pronounced than in the work of the poets discussed earlier. For instance, whereas Casey Motsisi employs a humorous, but at the same time satirical, anecdote to illustrate the inevitability of Sally's social position as nanny in his poem, "The Efficacy of Prayer", in the final stanza of "We Watched the White Man's Arrival", Matthews directly complains about the menial nature of the job and the apartheid associations that go with it.

In "Democracy", Matthews demonstrates that the manner that characterizes the colonial settlers' arrival is akin to the hypocritical political system they have evolved. His anger with the system leads him to make wholesale condemnation of the Western interpretation of democracy:

> democracy
> has been turned
> into a whore
> her body ravished
> by those who
> pervert her
> in the bordello
> bandied from crotch to hand
> her breasts smeared
> with their seed
> and for us
> denied the delight
> of her body
> in our bordello
> democracy has turned
> syphilitic[65]

Matthews's rare use of sexual symbolism unmasks what he deems to be the spuriousness of Western democracy. As Nadine Gordimer has observed, the contrast Matthews makes "between political catchwords and brutal sexual imagery carries . . . immediacy."[66] In another poem, "The Basis of Democracy Rests Upon", Matthews shows how some of the basic tenets of democracy such as "fraternity" and "equality" are hypocritically invoked in liberal circles.

In "In This Land of Sunshine", he is convinced that the hypocrisy of his oppressors is partly the result of self-interest. Matthews contrasts the disadvantaged position of blacks with the privileged and well-to-do lives of whites:

> In this land of sunshine
> Love has been termed a crime
> And to the protectors of white civilization
> An obscene thing if carried across the colour line
> The brotherhood of man a mockery
> When man lets his brother starve in a shanty
> While he and his are settled in splendour
> Pockets and larder filled with plenty
> One brother to live must carry a pass
> Another brother's life turned into a sham
> When asked if he is his brother's keeper
> The remaining brother replied; bloody hell, I am.[67]

The portrayal of blacks starving while whites wallow in plenty is reminiscent of Breyten Breytenbach's exposure of the racist and unequal manner in which food is distributed in South African prisons. In Matthews's poem, the sense of white nonchalance in the face of the suffering of blacks is clearly conveyed by the exclamation, "bloody hell, I am."

As long as the minority political system continues, the physical hunger depicted in "In This Land of Sunshine" remains inseparable from the blacks' political hunger:

> We have been offered
> pie in the sky
> but never smelled it
> neither will it appease
> our hunger for rights
> that are rightfully ours
> we watch through the window
> as they sit feasting
> at a table loaded with equality
> and grow frantic at its flavour.[68]

Matthews is ridiculing the government's establishment of sham "independent states" for blacks. The ironic depiction of a "table loaded with equality" alludes to the meetings between the government and leaders of the puppet "states".

Although Matthews predominantly writes about the oppression and suffering of the downtrodden in his own country, his outlook is partly international. In "I Thought", he equates his position with that of the incarcerated people of the Eastern Bloc countries:

> I thought
> that I was the only one
> whispering our rage and pain
> then it
> came aclamouring in my ears
> there in the darkness of night
> other voices
> voices from the sealed tombs of
> Hungary, Poland and Moscow underground
> not whispering but loudly shouting
> the things that I whispered to myself
> . . . our voices
> would reach out one for the other
> making us brothers united in our protest.[69]

The comparison that Matthews makes is predicated on different political arrangements. His own suffering is perpetrated by a colonial regime that seeks to perpetuate a racial hegemony, whereas the suffering of the other peoples in the poem is a result of ideological differences within societies that are polarized between socialist and capitalist values.

Matthews's comparison of the "rage and pain" of a black South African with the suffering of a black American is based on common experiences of racial inequality. A black American in a Harlem ghetto is to him as politically and economically disadvantaged as a black person in the South African township of Soweto:

> I share the pain of my black brother
> and a mother in a Harlem ghetto
> with that of a soul brother in Notting Hill
> as I am moved from the land I own
> because of the colour of my skin
>
> Our pain has linked us
> from Manenberg to Soweto
> to the land of the not so free
> and britannia across the sea[70]

The author's solidarity with black Americans is prompted by the influence of Black Consciousness which, as the succeeding chapter will demonstrate, has affinity with the Black Power movement active in America in the 1960s. This is illustrated by the last stanza of his poem:

> Now our pain unites us
> into burning brands of rage

that will melt our fetters
and sear the flesh of the mockers
of our blackness and our heritage[71]

Black Americans who are oblivious of this unity and solidarity are portrayed as opportunists and collaborators with oppressors. Matthews severely criticizes Percy Sledge[72] for singing for a whites-only audience during the latter's visit to South Africa:

Say, Percy dad,
You run out of bread that you've got to
come to sunny south africa to sing soul
in the land of your fore-fathers?

Well, Percy dad,
You're not doing me a favour by
performing for the "black is beautiful" scene
when other soul brothers, pinky
have to stand in the rain outside

Say, Percy dad,
will you tell nina simone back home
that you, a soul singer, did a segregated act
or will you sit back flashing silver dollar smiles
as they cart the loot from your Judas role to the
bank.[73]

This portrayal in the last stanza makes Percy's singing to a segregated audience, in the penultimate stanza, sound more revolting.

Matthews fervently argues that only force can change South Africa. A number of his poems intimate the need for blacks to resort to armed confrontation. In "To Label My Utterings Poetry", one of his prison characters impatiently asks, "will it never be the fire next time?",[74] and in "We Have Been Offered" he asks, "how long can we contain the rumble of hunger in our belly?"[75]

In "Lord, How Long Lord, How Long", Matthews openly accepts the need to take a stand against white oppression:

Lord, how long Lord, how long
must we suffer the iniquities
of the ruling class
their strength rested in a rifle
and a law perverted
to enforce their might

. . . Lord, how long Lord, how long
must we contain ourselves and turn the other cheek
and endure the harshness they display
to turn us into eunuchs and not men
who dare to take a stand

and wreak vengeance for what they had done
Lord, how long Lord, how long?[76]

Matthews's resolve to take revenge is expressed more forcefully and uncompromisingly in "You Have Taught Us":

You have taught us
that you have no reason
so reason not with us
when our rage will find you

rage sharp as a blade
to cut and slash
and spill blood
for only blood can appease
the blood spilled
over three hundred years[77]

Matthews's anger is probably at its most intense in this poem. Shunning the possibility of negotiation with the oppressors, he feels that he is already killing them off. Through the use of terms such as "cut", "slash", "blood" and "spill", he demonstrates zest in violent retribution.

Later, in "They Have Driven Us Hard, Lord", he expresses confident optimism akin to that of Alex La Guma (in *In the Fog of the Season's End*) by predicting the inevitable collapse of the apartheid system. Matthews makes effective use of the parallel of the violent fall of Jericho:

they have driven us hard, Lord
stripped us of our land
lash us with their laws
but the walls of Jericho will fall

. . . terrifying like thunder will be
the trumpet roar of our rage
that will rent prison cages asunder
as the walls of Jericho fall.[78]

The metaphors, similes and images of destruction in the second stanza indicate that the system would fall through violent revolution. The reprise of the "fall of Jericho" emphasizes the inevitability of the collapse.

In all his poems that address the necessity of armed struggle, Matthews is closer to the younger poets who wrote after the Soweto uprising than to the poets writing in the late 1960s and early 1970s when *Cry Rage* appeared. In terms of detail, his poetry as a whole is among the most informative about the condition of blacks. In terms of style, however, his intense desire to provide this information prompts him to "use cliches of politics, tracts and popular journalism"[79] which cause his detractors to dismiss his work as propaganda. Because of this strong political element, Matthews's collection of poetry, *Cry Rage* (co-authored with Gladys Thomas) was banned in South Africa in 1973, only a year after its publication. Similar collections succeeding *Cry Rage*, such as *Black Voices Shout* and *Pass Me the Meatballs, Jones*, have also been banned.

Although the indirect style of writing survived briefly, its most representative exponents like Oswald Mtshali, Wally Serote, Mandlenkosi Langa and Ndebele succeeded in filling the literary gap created by the repressive laws of the early 1960s. As their own political situation became difficult, like their predecessors, they too were forced to leave the country. Their position was immediately taken by younger, militant writers, mainly of poetry and drama, whose literary fire had been kindled by the spirit of Black Consciousness and the Soweto uprising of 1976. The style of these "new" writers was, of course, qualitatively different from that of Oswald Mtshali and his contemporaries.

Notes

1. N. W. Visser, "South Africa: The Renaissance that Failed", *Journal of Commonwealth Literature*, Vol. 11, No. 1 (1976) p. 42. Robert Royston also talks of the same hope for some kind of literary revival in his *Black Poets in South Africa*.

2. Nadine Gordimer, "Writers in South Africa: The New Black Poets", *Exile and Tradition*, (ed.) Rowland Smith, p. 134.

3. Oswald Mtshali, interview with Ursula A. Barnett, *World Literature Written in English*, Vol. 12, No. 1 (1973) p. 30.

4. Ibid., p. 42.

5. Ursula A. Barnett, *A Vision of Order*, p. 52.

6. Oswald Mtshali, *Sounds of a Cowhide Drum*, p. 1.

7. John Povey, "Three South African Poets: Dennis Brutus, Keorapetse Kgositsile and Oswald Mbuyiseni Mtshali, *World Literature Written in English*, Vol. 16, No. 2. (1977) p. 274.

8. Mtshali, *Sounds of a Cowhide Drum*, p. 1.

9. Ibid.

10. Ibid.

11. Mbulelo Mzamane's criticism of what he considers to be Mtshali's "borrowed" style cited in Barnett, *A Vision of Order*, p. 51.

12. Gordimer, "Writers in South Africa", p. 135.

13. Mtshali, *Sounds of a Cowhide Drum*, p. 3.

14. John Povey, "South Africa", *Literature of the World in English* (ed.) Bruce King, p. 170.

15. Mtshali, *Sounds of a Cowhide Drum*, p. 3.

16. James Matthews, "To Label My Utterings Poetry", in James Matthews and Gladys Thomas, *Cry Rage*, p. 70.

17. Matthews, "Two Little Black Boys", *Cry Rage*, p. 60.

18. Ibid.

19. Ibid.

20. Casey Motsisi, "The Efficacy of Prayer", *Black Poets in South Africa*, (ed.) Robert Royston, p. 10.

21. Ibid.

22. Lewis Nkosi, *Home and Exile*, p. 7.

23. Mongane Wally Serote, "Her Name is 'Dooti'", *Yakhal' Inkomo*, p. 14.

24. Serote, "Burning Cigarette", *Yakhal' Inkomo*, p. 12.

25. Mtshali, *Sounds of a Cowhide Drum*, p. 24.

26. Njabulo Ndebele, *Black Poets in South Africa*, p. 45.

27. James Matthews and Gladys Thomas give an extended portrayal of life in a "homeland" in their collection of poetry, *Cry Rage*.

28. Ndebele, p. 46.

29. Mtshali, *Sounds of a Cowhide Drum*, p. 61.

30. Mandlenkosi Langa, *Black Poets in South Africa*, p. 31.

31. Ndebele, *Black Poets in South Africa*, p. 37.

32. Ibid.

33. Langa, p. 31.

34. In her introduction to Oswald Mtshali's *Sounds of a Cowhide Drum*, Nadine Gordimer has appropriately referred to the poem as a "ghastly vision" and as "one of the most shocking poems ever written".

35. Mtshali, *Sounds of a Cowhide Drum*, p. 60.

36. Ibid.

37. Serote, *Yakhal' Inkomo*, p. 19.

38. Ndebele, *Black Poets in South Africa*, p. 39.

39. Can Themba, *The Will to Die*, p. 101.

40. Dennis Brutus, *A Simple Lust*, p. 52.

41. Povey, "Three South African Poets: Denis Brutus, Keoraptse Kgositsile and Oswald Mtshali", p. 277.

42. Mtshali, *Sounds of a Cowhide Drum*, p. 8.

43. Ibid., p. 25.

44. Ibid., p. 20.

45. Ibid.

46. Ibid., p. 5.

47. Ibid.

48. Ibid., p. 57.

49. Ibid.

50. Serote, "Ofay – Watcher, Throbs – Phase XIII", *Yakhal' Inkomo*, pp. 50–51.

51. Publisher's (backcover) note, Serote, *To Every Birth Its Blood*.

52. Serote, *Yakhal' Inkomo*, p. 8.

53. Ibid.

54. The development of this defiance is usually attributed to the influence of the Black Consciousness Movement (BCM), which started in the late 1960s and reached its climax in the first half of the 1970s. The Movement's central objective was to promote political consciousness among the discriminated against and exploited peoples of South Africa regarding their identity, dignity, group cohesion and solidarity, self-reliance and denunciation of all oppressive arrangements.

55. Gordimer, "Writers in South Africa", p. 145.

56. Serote, *Yakhal' Inkomo*, p. 31.

57. Ibid., p. 27.

58. Ibid., p. 36.

59. Matthews, quoted in Gordimer, "Writers in South Africa", p. 146.

60. Ibid.

61. Matthews, *Cry Rage*, p. 1.

62. Ibid., p. 70.

63. In their introduction to *The Return of the Amasi Bird*, Tim Couzens and Essop Patel point to the emergence of James Matthews as a black consciousness poet declaring black assertiveness in the early seventies.

64. Matthews, *Cry Rage*, p. 5.
65. Ibid., p. 2.
66. Gordimer, p. 150.
67. Matthews, *Cry Rage*, p. 37.
68. Ibid., p. 4.
69. Ibid., p. 66.
70. Ibid., p. 12.
71. Ibid.
72. A black American soul singer who toured Malawi, Rhodesia and South Africa in 1972.
73. Matthews, *Cry Rage*, p. 49.
74. Ibid., p. 70.
75. Ibid., p. 4.
76. Ibid., p. 63.
77. Ibid., p. 65.
78. Ibid., p. 13.
79. Gordimer, p. 74. She believes that the overt political content of Matthews's poetry "deadens and debases" the poetry.

5.   Black is Beautiful

Black Consciousness and the Poetry of Affirmation in the 1970s

The repressive atmosphere of the early 1960s stifled political activity among blacks. While the political activists who went into exile resorted to armed struggle, those who remained inside the country found themselves "caught in an extremely frustrating political situation where virtually all channels for the expression of anti-apartheid sentiment were closed."[1] Silence, akin to the literary silence broken by Oswald Mtshali and his contemporaries, descended over the black political scene.

Political Alternatives after Sharpeville

There were, however, liberal organizations such as the Liberal and Progressive Parties and the National Union of South African Students (NUSAS), a non-racial organization, which claimed to be sympathetic to the situation of blacks. Blacks were free to join these organizations but police repression still prevented them from airing their grievances freely. Hence, as Gail Gerhart has argued, "it was whites in these organizations who, for the most part, took on the task of articulating African grievances and demands."[2] By the late 1960s, however, a "new generation" of black youth who had escaped the demoralization of seeing their nationalist organizations almost totally destroyed,[3] felt the need to re-establish an internal organization through which the black people could express their political views independent of liberal spokesmanship. This need was keenly felt among students, especially those in so-called "tribal" universities.

NUSAS and the Failure of Liberal Politics

Owing to its non-racial nature and international accreditation, black students were initially attracted towards NUSAS.[4] As time passed, however, the students became disenchanted with the organization's limitations. Despite its purported non-racialism, NUSAS was unable to shield blacks from the system's discriminatory and segregatory laws. Clive Nettleton states the organization's dilemma as follows:

The major problem facing NUSAS as a non-racial organization existing in a society based on discrimination and racialism is that, while preaching the ideal of non-racialism, the members of the organization are unable to live out their ideals: these remain ideals and, for the vast majority of students, unreal. The fact is that; while it is still possible for White and Black students to hold joint congresses and seminars, and to meet occasionally at social events, they live in different worlds.[5]

Even at the congresses, seminars and social events that Nettleton mentions, this racial dilemma was manifest. A typical case occurred when Rhodes University "prohibited mixed accommodation or eating facilities at the conference site"[6] in July 1967. This incident, Nettleton argues, was the turning point leading to the formation of an independent, black student organization.

Black students also complained about NUSAS's conservative approach and composition which, they believed, "had a built-in white majority who consistently favoured caution and moderation in their advocacy of liberal reform, and a minority who sought no reform at all."[7] The pervasive conservatism of NUSAS reached its peak in July 1964 when most of its white members openly dissociated themselves from the pleas of Jonty Driver, the president of the organization, that students should "turn from protest politics to real action for liberation."[8] To militant black students, white students' refusal to accept Driver's suggestion was accommodationist and ineffective.

Whereas most white students felt comfortable with this conservatism, black students strongly identified with the aspirations of the black people and felt, in a forum such as a NUSAS congress, that they were representing not only the black students but all black people.[9] The thrust of the black students' approach was to initiate a radical, broad-based political awakening to be realized by organizing and politicizing the people. In an interview with Gerhart, Steve Biko underlined the importance of this approach:

> Now, my attitude all the time had been, whilst I was in NUSAS, that the people feel that blacks should operate on their own, that people must organize. Within NUSAS I am merely expressing my own attitude or my own opinion, and I'll do nothing by way of organizing.[10]

Although Biko's point is not very clear, he objected to the individualistic nature of NUSAS as opposed to the communal approach espoused by the black students in the organization.

The Emergence of the Black Consciousness Movement

It was in these circumstances that black students in NUSAS formed the South African Student's Organization (SASO), to express the grievances and demands of black students. Together with subsidiary organizations such as the Black People's Convention (BPC), the South African Students' Movement (SASM) and others, SASO developed into the Black Consciousness Movement

(BCM) which became a political mouthpiece not only of students but of all the downtrodden groups of the South African population.[11] It should be borne in mind, however, that at its inception, the BCM did not pretend to take over the role of the banned ANC and PAC. As Sam C. Nolutshungu has argued:

> SASO itself was not a political party, had no well defined ideology, programme of action or code of internal discipline. Having arisen as a secession from the white-dominated National Union of South African Students, it was primarily a students' organization (with bloc affiliation through students' representative councils) . . . Its attitude to other political organizations among blacks, especially the banned and exiled African National Congress and Pan Africanist Congress, shows how limited were its own pretensions to becoming or creating a national political organization: it neither sought to replace them or seriously attempted, before 1974, to establish a formal relationship with them. On the contrary, it saw them as the legitimate spokesmen of "the people" and the leaders of the liberation struggle, SASO's own role being defined narrowly as complementary to their efforts. While this did not imply an uncritical attitude, there was a widely shared, strongly held belief among SASO militants that black consciousness organizations should not, or could not, set themselves up as an alternative force.[12]

By the time it was banned in 1977, however, the BCM had become such an influential national political organization that it could easily have rivalled the influence of the banned nationalist parties. The BCM had mobilized the majority of all the politically, economically and socially disadvantaged ethnic groups in the country. Even the white community itself had been alarmed by the Movement's widespread support.

Black Consciousness itself is a hybrid political philosphy whose basic tenets seem to be informed by various ideologies. Its meaning has been extensively defined by Steve Biko:

> Black Consciousness is an attitude of mind and a way of life . . . Its essence is the realization by the black man of the need to rally together with his brothers around the cause of their oppression – the blackness of their skin – and to operate as a group to rid themselves of the shackles that bind them to perpetual servitude. It is based on a self-examination which has ultimately led them to believe that by seeking to run away from themselves and emulate the white man, they are insulting the intelligence of whoever created them black. The philosophy of Black Consciousness therefore expresses group pride and the determination of the black to rise and attain the envisaged self . . . Hence thinking along lines of Black Consciousness makes the black man see himself as a being complete in himself. It makes him less dependent and more free to express his manhood. At the end of it all he cannot tolerate attempts by anybody to dwarf the significance of his manhood.[13]

The concepts contained in this definition are by no means new to the experiences of blacks in most parts of Africa and those in the diaspora. The

BCM's emphasis on the acceptance of one's blackness, black pride, black solidarity and unity remind one of some of the objectives of the American Black Power movement[14] of the 1960s. There is striking similarity between what Steve Biko outlines in his definition and what Stokely Carmichael and Charles V. Hamilton expected of black American people:

> Black people must redefine themselves, and only *they* can do that. Throughout this country, vast segments of the black communities are beginning to recognize the need to assert their own definitions, to reclaim their history, their culture; to create their own sense of community and togetherness . . . When we begin to define our own image, the stereotypes – that is, lies – that our oppressor has developed will begin in the white community and end there. The black community will have a positive image of itself that *it* has created. This means we will no longer call ourselves lazy, apathetic, dumb, good-timers, shiftless, etc. Those are words used by white America to define us. If we accept these adjectives, as some of us have in the past, then we see ourselves only in a negative way, precisely the way white America wants us to see ourselves. Our incentive is broken and our will to fight is surrendered. From now on we shall view ourselves as African–Americans and as black people who are in fact energetic, determined, intelligent, beautiful and peace-loving.[15]

In both cases, black history and culture are positively asserted. There is a strong belief that the way to political nationalism is through cultural nationalism.[16] White standards of judging the identity and behaviour of black people are repudiated.

The BCM's outlook was also heavily influenced by other political ideologies inside and outside Africa. "Frantz Fanon's analysis of settler colonialism and its psychological consequences for rulers and ruled, the writings of Leopold Senghor on Negritude, Kenneth Kaunda on African humanism, and, most importantly, Julius Nyerere on self-reliance and *ujamaa* or African Socialism",[17] all informed the Movement's philosophy, of which the centrepiece was the BCM's persistent stress on fostering political consciousness among black people. But the aim was not to trigger in the masses a spontaneous eruption into violent action, but rather to rebuild and recondition the mind of the oppressed in such a way that eventually they would be ready to demand forcefully what was rightfully theirs.[18] Although the notion of "conscientizing" the masses was borrowed from the American Black Power,[19] it was carefully applied to the realities of the black South African situation.

The BCM and the Literature of Assertion

Because of the BCM's consciousness-raising objective, the literature that has emerged as a result of the Movement's influence has generally tended to be assertive, didactic, exhortatory and overtly political. The literature ranges from direct political statement to township poetry and theatre that focus on various aspects of what Tim Couzens and Essop Patel have appropriately termed, "the black experience".[20] Though some of the writers who depict this "black experience" are accomplished, a great many of them are not really writers. They are political activists whose primary objective is to register their grievances and demands. As James Matthews has aggressively argued:

> I wrote. It was not prose. Critics hyena-howled. It was not poetry, they exclaimed. I never said it was. I was writing expressions of feelings. I would find it extremely difficult to write poems of love or praise of nature. Neither would I produce lines so finely polished or use metaphors and metre-art for art's sake. I would feel like a pimp using words as decoration for my whoring . . . I am not a poet, neither am I a "writer" in the academic sense.[21]

Much writing of the period reflects the style espoused by Matthews. Steve Biko, for instance, has written a political manifesto (*I Write What I Like*), not a literary work. The book will be used only as a reference point in the following discussion of Black Consciousness poetry.

As mentioned earlier, the BCM, like American Black Power, inculcated a sense of racial pride in the minds of black people. In common with most black writers of this period, poets wrote for black people and they wrote about their blackness, and out of their blackness, rejecting anyone and anything that stood in the way of self-knowledge and self-celebration.[22]

In his poem, "I am Black", James Matthews asserts his blackness in a manner most characteristic of the mood of the period:

> my Blackness fills me to the brim
> like a beaker of well-seasoned wine
> that sends my senses reeling with pride.[23]

The mode in this poem is borrowed. There are obvious echoes of Keats's "Ode to a Nightingale". Nevertheless, the imagery emphasizes the poet's blackness and the pleasure he derives from it. In "Look Upon the Blackness of My Woman", blackness becomes not only a source of confidence and delight, but a celebration of beauty:

> Look upon the blackness of my woman
> and be filled with the delight of it
> her blackness a beacon among the insipid
> faces around her
> proudly she walks, a sensuous, black lily
> swaying in the wind
> This daughter of Sheba.[24]

There are similarities between this poem and Leopold Senghor's poem, "Black Woman". In both poems, the black woman is praised in unstinting terms. Matthews's comparison of his blackness with "well-seasoned wine" in "I am Black" is also similar to Senghor's comparison of the beauty of his woman with "black wine":

Naked woman, dark woman!
Firm-fleshed ripefruit, dark raptures of black
   wine, mouth making lyric my mouth

Naked woman, black woman!
I sing your passing beauty, form that I fix
   in the eternal
Before jealous destiny burns you to ashes
   to nourish the roots of life.[25]

While this kind of writing may accomplish its political purpose, to some critics, the style lacks poetic forcefulness. Henry C. Lacey argues that similar poetry by Amiri Baraka (Le Roi Jones), a black American poet of the 1960s, is insipid and flat. Lacey cites Baraka's poem, "Sterling Street September (for Sylvia)" as an example:

I CAN BE THE BEAUTIFUL BLACK MAN
because I am
the beautiful black man, and you, girl, child
nightlove,
you are beautiful
too.

We are something, the two of us
the people love us for being
though they call us out our
name.

What Lacey finds insipid is the repetitious and doctrinaire nature of the poem. These characteristics are, however, meant to meet the didactic intentions of the poet.

   Don Mattera, like Matthews, derives unbridled pleasure from his blackness. In his poem, "Black Plum . . .", Mattera compares himself to a fruit in a beautiful garden. On a large scale, the garden symbolizes the African continent whose people and products have been abused by the colonial experience:

This land
This soil so stiff-necked and proud,
This beautiful earth is a garden
And I am the fruit
Squeezed of energy
Drained of love
Dried of hope:

   a garden watered by anguish,
   fertilized by the tears
   of my people,
   strewn with the seeds
   of their lives . . .

I am the black plum

Fruit of mama africa
Spirit that cries out beyond the horizon
The soul seeking emancipation.

I am africa.[27]

Mattera's symbolism specifically applies to South Africa and her suffering black population. The assertive tone in the last two stanzas emphasizes the need for freedom, and the statement, "I am Africa", gives the impression that Africa belongs to no other group of people except blacks. The similarities in the work of Mattera and Matthews are clearly their use of an assertive style and their preoccupation with the anguish of blacks.

Besides being depicted as beautiful, blackness is also portrayed as a reassuring symbol of a bright future for blacks. The darkness and suffering that open Mattera's poem, "Blackness Blooms . . .", soon give way to images of new beginnings, light and sweetness:

Come morning
Come glorious light
Return justice
Heal my broken sight.

And now black sunbeams fall on the slope
Bringing new light to fulfil my hope
Conscious of their sacred duty
Sweet, sweetly my blackness blooms
And becomes my beauty.[28]

Although the tone is assertive, the images in this poem do express the political statement intended. The "blooming" refers to the gradual unfolding of a political consciousness that ultimately initiates change. The same blackness that is the scapegoat for the oppression and exploitation of blacks, becomes beautiful when black people liberate themselves. The implicit portrayal of united opposition against the oppressor in Mattera's poem may be contrasted with Baraka's bemoaning the absence of unity and fellow-feeling among black Americans in his poem, "Cold Term":

Why can't we love each other and be beautiful? Why do the beautiful corner each other and spit poison? Why do the beautiful not hangout together and learn to do away with evil? Why are the beautiful not living together and feeling each other's trials? Why are the beautiful not walking with their arms around each other laughing softly the soft laughter of black beauty?[29]

The rhetorical approach here is similar to Matthews's style in "Can the White Man Speak for ME?". While the series of questions may compel the reader to re-examine its value as poetry, the questions are too banal and repetitious. Although the form differs, the political purpose of the poems of Mattera and Baraka is similar. The liberatory beauty that Mattera depicts is, of course, somewhat different from the personal beauty Matthews and Senghor celebrate in their poems, ("Look Upon the Blackness of My Woman" and "Black Woman", respectively). Generally, however, all the poets employ the concept of black beauty in a militant manner.

Blacks who attempt to escape from their blackness by imitating the style of whites are condemned for opportunism, alienation and artificiality:

> My sister has become a schemer and
> a scene-stealer
> her free-swinging breasts strangled
> by a bra
> face smeared with astra [sic] cream
> skin paled for white man's society
> songs of the village
> traded in for tin pan alley
> 'black is beautiful' has become
> as artificial as the wig she wears.[30]

Oswald Mtshali attacks similar qualities to ridicule the values of a detribalized woman:

> She's very sophisticated,
> uses Artra, Hi-Lite
> skin lightening cream,
> hair straightened,
> wears lipstick
> a wig, nail polish:
> she can dance
> the latest 'Monkey'.[31]

While the content of Matthews's and Mtshali's jibes are similar, the manner of the two poets is rather different. The tone of Mtshali's poem differs from that of the genuine BCM poets; it exudes the values of Black Consciousness but is not written as a political statement. Whereas Mtshali pokes fun at the alienated woman in his poem, Matthews hurls angry accusations at his sister; hence, the mood of the latter's poem is serious while that of the former's relaxed and humorous. It is instructive to note that the values Matthews and Mtshali attack in their poems are also criticized in some of the black American writings of the 1960s:

> Look around today, in every small town and big city, from two-bit catfish and sodapop joints into the 'integrated' lobby of the Waldorf-Astoria, and you'll see conks on black men. And you'll see black women wearing these green and pink and purple and red and platinum-blonde wigs. They're all more ridiculous than a slapstick comedy. It makes you wonder if the Negro has completely lost his sense of identity, lost touch with himself.[32]

Malcolm X's style is direct and heavily accusatory, closer to that of James Matthews.

The BCM's concern with the past of black people is closely connected with the BCM's emphasis on the pride and dignity blacks ought to feel from being black. As mentioned earlier, stress is put on the need for a new and incisive redefinition, reidentification and reappraisal of black life through cultural reaffirmation.[33] "Our culture must be defined in concrete terms . . . It is through the evolution of our genuine culture that our identity can be fully rediscovered",[34] Steve Biko asserts. In the writings which deal with these concerns, the exploitative materialism and individualism of white, capitalist culture are contrasted with black people's cultural respect for others, their sharing of property and their general sense of communalism.

Exploring a people's past in literature may be a tricky undertaking however. A frequent criticism levelled against this kind of writing is that it usually fails to give a balanced and convincing portrait of that past:

> The question is how does a writer re-create this past? Quite clearly there is a strong temptation to idealize it – to extol its good points and pretend that the bad never existed.
>
> This is where the writer's integrity comes in. Will he be strong enough to overcome the temptation to select only those facts which flatter him? If he succumbs he will have branded himself as an untrustworthy witness. But it is not only his personal integrity as an artist which is involved. The credibility of the world he is attempting to re-create will be called to question and he will defeat his own purpose if he is suspected of glossing over inconvenient facts. We can not pretend that our past was one long, technicolour idyll. We have to admit that like other people's pasts ours had its good as well as its bad sides.[35]

Some of the BCM writers who deal with this theme seem to be free from the problem Achebe has expatiated upon above. The writers endeavour to give an unrhetorical portrayal of how black South African culture used to be and how the culture has been disrupted by the colonizer's imposition of Western beliefs and values.

The preoccupation with an eroded black culture is not unique to the poets of the early 1970s. Plaatje's novel, *Mhudi*, partly decries the obliteration of a culture his people used to cherish. The novel opens with the picture of an idyllic pre-colonial, well-ordered society. The division of labour between men and women is clearly defined. The society is governed by uncomplicated laws of land ownership, hunting, bartering, marriage and religious rituals. Food supplies are plentiful and the people own numerous cattle. Above all, a distinct sense of mutual respect and communalism prevails. This eudaemonic life, however, is not without its internal contradictions. Plaatje gives a vivid account of the expansionist activities of the Matabele, and later, the cultural disruption initiated by the Matabele incursions reaches its peak when the Boers arrive and impose their rule.

Poets of the BCM examine the past from a similar perspective. In his poem, "Time Immemorial Part I", Modikwe Dikobe replicates what Plaatje records in his novel:

On the slope of this mountain
Happily lived my forefathers
    In affluence.
Happily they lived on this mountain.
Festivals, weddings not in want.

Afar field crops, they harvested.
They organized hunting: in letsolo or singles.
Afar field beyond those hills
They herded their cattle
Herdboys moulding cattle,
Hunting games,
Never was there a day of dearth.[36]

This harmonious life is again described in Dikobe's longer poem, "Dispossessed":

You were born in affluence
Land as vast as sea
Pegging, pegging each seasonal year
A plot for ploughing
Hundreds of livestock you possessed
Your dwelling a fortress
Your wives as many as your fingers
Each night, a different woman
Not a word of grouse.[37]

The style in both poems is "quiet, clear and unrhetorical".[38] Though Dikobe betrays some nostalgia for the idyllic early life he is recording, the quality of that life is neither exaggerated nor romanticized. This manner of portrayal differs from that of Mafika Pascal Gwala. Gwala "reveals the past of Africa as a glorious one, and tries to make all Africa's children aware of 'the black giant/that always had been/even yesterday.'"[39]

Although not a member of the BCM, Credo Mutwa has written a play that deals with the primary, cultural concerns of the Movement. The play, entitled *uNosilimela*, dramatizes traditional issues such as the origin and destiny of man, love of one's neighbour, love and respect for the laws and religion of the black peoples' forefathers. The characters involved are both animal and human, giving the play the aura of an immemorial, folkloric past. Credo Mutwa's preoccupation with the beliefs and values of this past at the expense of contemporary values and political problems has, however, been criticized:

. . . though Mutwa's reverence for the African past and its values is part of what contemporary Black Consciousness is about, Mutwa's rejection of the modern city, its technology and its children in favour of a mystical paradise presided over by a religious hierarchy, stamps him as both a romantic visionary and a conservative.[40]

Criticism and dislike of Mutwa have been deepened by his denigration of the

Soweto uprising and its participants. According to Kavanagh, in 1976, Credo Mutwa wrote an unsolicited letter to the Minister of Justice, Jimmy Kruger, in which he compared Black Consciousness to Nazism and urged the government to suppress the June uprising by sending in the army. In retaliation the people of Soweto burnt his house down.[41]

Oswald Mtshali's portrayal of traditional life is more immediate than Mutwa's. His vision is less remote. In his poem, "Inside My Zulu Hut", Mtshali celebrates the life in a manner familiar to most black people:

> It is a hive
> without any bees
> to build the walls
> with golden bricks of honey.
> A cave cluttered
> with a millstone,
> calabashes of sour milk
> claypots of foaming beer
> sleeping grass mats
> wooden head rests
> tied with *riempies*
> to wattle rafters
> blackened by the smoke
> of kneaded cow dung
> burning under
> the three-legged pot
> on the earthen floor
> to cook my porridge.[42]

The images of food, housing, housing equipment and the language that Mtshali employs all capture an easily recognizable traditional ethos.

The need to rewrite black history is taken as integral to the revival of black culture. In his autobiography, *Blame Me on History*, Bloke Modisane has given a critique of what he believes to be the distorted perspective of South African historiography:

> South African history was amusing, we sat motionless, angelically attentive, whilst the history teacher recounted – as documented – the wars of the Boers against the "savage and barbaric black hordes" for the dark interior of Africa; the ancestral heroes of our fathers, the great chiefs whom our parents told stories about, were in class described as blood-thirsty animal brutes. Tshaka, the brilliant general who welded the Mnguni Tribelets into a unified and powerful Zulu nation, the greatest war machine in South African history, was described as a psychopath.[43]

Poets of the BCM consistently reject this negative and racist image of black ethnic groups, chiefs and heroes. In opposition to the prejudiced white portrayal of Tshaka as a "psychopath", Mtshali depicts him as a strong, invincible, larger than life, political leader:

His baby cry
was of a cub
tearing the neck
of the lioness
because he was fatherless

The gods
boiled his blood
in a clay pot of passion
to course in his veins

His heart was shaped into an ox shield
to foil every foe

Ancestors forged
his muscles into
thongs as tough
as wattle bark
and nerves
as sharp as
syringa thorns.[44]

This poem is among Mtshali's best. The images reflect a traditional milieu in that they allude to black religious practices, the role of ancestors, inter-ethnic fights, weapons of war, and vegetation found in the South African veld. The Africanness of these images captures the cultural practices of blacks more graphically than writing about blackness in a mere rhetorical fashion.

In the concluding stanza, Tshaka comes across as a shrewd patriot whose far-sighted vision anticipates colonial conquest:

His eyes were lanterns
that shone from the dark valleys of Zululand
to see white swallows
coming across the sea
His cry to two assassin brothers:

"Lo! you can kill me
but you'll never rule this land!"[45]

Black Consciousness writers search out past heroes in their work. The respect Mtshali gives to Tshaka is similar to that accorded to Bambatha, a political figure who led his people against white rule in 1906.[46] In his elegy, "The Spirit of Bambatha", A.N.C. Kumalo compares Bambatha's courage and determination with the boldness of such contemporary but deceased political figures as John Dube, who used to be an ANC representative in Lusaka, and Abraham Tiro, a young BCM activist who fled to Botswana in 1974[47] but was subsequently killed by a letter bomb:

Dube and Tiro
warriors in an impi

the spirit of Bambatha
beat in their breast.[48]

The almost automatic inclusion of traditional warrior trappings is designed to produce a stock response. Later, in a style similar to that of Yeats's "In Memory of Major Robert Gregory", Kumalo invokes the memory of other political and historical heroes such as Hintsa, Makanda, Luthuli, Sikhukhuni, Saloojee, Nkosi and Ngudle.[49] The poem ends on a note of appeal to blacks to derive inspiration from the courage of these heroes and to struggle for freedom.

The BCM's emphasis on the pride and dignity which blacks derive from their blackness, and on the need to reaffirm black culture has also led to a rejection of government-created institutions. The most abhorred and widely debated are the "bantustans". Steve Biko has given a detailed enumeration of what he considers to be the social, political and economic intentions of the bantustan policy:

> To create a false sense of hope amongst the black people so that any further attempt by blacks to collectively enunciate their aspirations should be dampened.
> To offer a new but false direction in the struggle of the Black people. By making it difficult to get even the 13% of the land the powers that be are separating our "struggles" into eight different struggles for eight false freedoms that were prescribed long ago. This has also the overall effect of making us forget about the 87% of land that is in white hands.
> To cheat the outside world into believing that there is some validity in the multinational theory so that South Africa can now go back into international sport, trade, politics, etc. with a soothed conscience.
> To boost up as much as possible the intertribal competition and hostility that is bound to come up so that the collective strength and resistance of the black can be fragmented.[50]

Conceived as part of the political theory of the BCM, Biko's point by point denunciation of the bantustan policy has the tone of a public speech delivered at a political rally. Although there are differences in form, the earnestness of the passage is similar to that of the poetry of James Matthews and Don Mattera.

While an Afrikaner scholar like D. A. Kotzé argues that the blacks who have accepted the bantustan policy are "pragmatists", who have "come to terms with the realities of separate development",[51] Steve Biko denounces bantustan leaders for "subconsciously aiding and abetting in the total subjugation of the black people . . .".[52] In a poem referred to earlier, Matthews exposes this collaboration between the government and bantustan leaders:

> We watch through the window
> as they sit feasting
> at a table loaded with equality
> and grow frantic at its flavour.[53]

In "Dialogue", to intensify his sense of the gullibility of bantustan leaders,

Matthews compares the attraction of the pseudo-independence of the "homelands" with the tantalizing glitter of "fool's gold":

> Dialogue
> the bribe offered by the oppressor
> glitters like fool's gold
> dazzling the eyes of the oppressed
> as they sit around the council table
> listening to empty discourse promising
>   empty promises
> beguiled by meaningless talk
> they do not realize ointment-smeared words
> will not heal their open wounds
> the oppressor sits seared with his spoils
> with no desire to share equality
> leaving the oppressed seeking warmth
> at the cold fire of
> Dialogue.[54]

The image of the oppressor as a selfish trickster and hypocrite comes across forcefully. Matthews's other poems on the bantustan question deal with stock issues, such as impoverished soil, unemployment, poverty and overcrowded living conditions. All these issues have been discussed in earlier chapters.

The opportunism of bantustan leaders has been a target of frequent attack from outside. For instance, Chief Gatsha Buthelezi's recent argument that white South Africans will be forced to initiate reform because of "self-interest", has led some critics to accuse him "of opportunism, of trying to ensure a stake in a post-apartheid system for himself and his organization, *Inkatha ye Nkululeko ye Sizwe* (National Cultural Liberation Movement)."[55] Perhaps what is more important in the discussion of the bantustan policy is the realization that the policy itself is inherently ephemeral. With the escalating armed struggle and the mounting international criticism of the entire apartheid system, the future of both the government and the bantustans is bleak indeed. Roger Southall has summarized this bleakness well:

> The prospect is that the bantustan policy is beset by its own limitations. Far from being possible way stations on the road to a restructured South Africa, those bantustans which opt for or are cajoled into independence are likely to enjoy only a finite existence as separate political entities. As grossly dependent regimes with minimal popular support, their very existence would seem to be predicated upon the continuance of white power.[56]

To counter the divisive politics of the government bantustan policy, the BCM encourages unity among black people:

> Another significant aspect of Black Consciousness is the call for cohesive group solidarity, i.e. black solidarity. Thus the quintessence of Black Consciousness is the realization and acceptance of blacks in South Africa

that, in order to play a positive role in the struggle of liberation and emancipation, they must effectively employ the concept of group power and thereby build a strong base, from which to counter the oppressor's policy of divide and rule.[57]

The emphasis on black unity in the 1970s has created a new political development. Earlier chapters have demonstrated that, in the 1950s and early 1960s, white liberals played a significant role in black politics. By the end of the 1960s, however, liberal politics began to be questioned. The quarrel that has ensued between the BCM and liberals is bitter.

The first and foremost objection to the liberals' approach to South African politics is the liberals' "insistence that the problems of the country can only be solved by a bilateral approach involving both black and white."[58] To the BCM, this position is hypocritical and it does not enable black people to free themselves from white domination, physically and psychologically. As Steve Biko has argued:

> The integration they talk about is first of all artificial in that it is a response to conscious manoeuvre rather than to the dictates of the inner soul. In other words the people forming the integrated complex have been extracted from various segregated societies with their inbuilt complexes of superiority and inferiority and these continue to manifest themselves even in the "non-racial" set-up of the integrated complex. As a result the integration so achieved is a one-way course, with the whites doing all the talking and the blacks the listening.[59]

Steve Biko's interpretation of "integration" concurs with that of Stokely Carmichael and Charles V. Hamilton. Because the goals of integrationists are middle-class, articulated primarily by a small group of blacks with middle-class aspirations or status (Biko sarcastically calls them "intelligent and articulate"[60] blacks), Carmichael and Hamilton argue that the politics of "integration" are individualistic and unrealistic.[61] "Black people have not suffered as individuals but as members of a group",[62] Carmichael and Hamilton assert. Worse than that, Carmichael and Hamilton maintain that "integration means that black people must give up their identity, deny their heritage."[63] To the BCM, as to the American Black Power, this parochial and alienating approach does not bring about any significant political change. Hence, Steve Biko reduces South African integrationist circles to mere tea-parties where hackneyed questions such as "how can we bring about change in South Africa"[64] are consistently asked.

In the poetry of the 1970s, the liberals' hypocritical approach is viciously exposed. In his poem, "Paper Curtains", Mafika Pascal Gwala dismisses the approach by comparing multiracialism with capitalist, tattered rags:

> If you say
> Black, White and Yellow
> can make or break the walls that surround them

then you shall not shame yourself
by clothing them
Black, White and Yellow
in tattered rags
picked up from the gutters
of the Stock Exchange.[65]

Gwala's style is direct and descriptive. "Integration" itself is ridiculed.

In James Matthews's "Liberal Student Crap", liberalism is portrayed as shallow, patronizing and paternalistic:

You just don't understand
There's no-one as liberal as me
Some of my best friends are
Kaffirs, Coolies and Coons
Forgive me, I mean other ethnic groups
How could it be otherwise?
I'm Jewish. I know discrimination
From the ghetto to Belsen
So, don't get me all wrong
'Cause I know just how you feel
Come and see me sometime
My folks are out of town.[66]

Matthews's success in exposing the speaker's false sense of identity and solidarity lies in his use of a cool, ironical approach. His characteristic anger, however, manifests itself when he points a finger at liberals and "religious" whites who show hypocritical concern for the plight of blacks. "White man/who needs your double-faced morality?"[67] Matthews angrily asks. The "double-faced morality" he refers to is expanded upon in his poem, "They Speak So Sorrowfully":

they speak so sorrowfully about the
children dying of hunger in Biafra
but sleep unconcerned about the rib-thin
children of Dimbaza
they spend their rands to ease the plight
Of the suffering in Bangladesh
but not the thought of a cent to send
to relieve the agony of Ilinge . . .[68]

With its pervasive mood of rage, the poem is probably one of Matthews's most caustic indictments of the white community, and is certainly one of the closest in style to that of poets like Wally Serote and Mandlenkosi Langa.

In "Paper Curtains", Mafika Gwala's attack is aggressive. The liberals' "firm moral rejection of violence as a way of initiating political change"[69] is angrily dismissed as fraudulent and hypocritical:

And if you cry change

You shall not shrink
at the slightest shaking
of the speedneedle
as it races across the meter of our lives
to register the pace of the motor
that drives home freedom. Sacrifice.

For if you shout:
You're going too far!
YOU'RE severing peaceful relations!
If you cry: You're overhasty!
You're running too fast!
Then my friend you are a hypocrite
Then you're a stuntist fraud in a dead and mighty fall.[70]

The language in this poem is purple and abusive, the style conversational and
querulous. The political message comes across clearly, but as poetry, it does not
work on its own. Gwala's method differs significantly from that of other
politically committed black poets such as the Martinique poet, Aimé Césaire.
Césaire's criticism of the indifferent and apolitical nature of his Martinique
fellow blacks is certainly political, but his poem transcends the merely
rhetorical:

> And in this town a clamouring crowd, a stranger to its own cry as the town,
> inert, is a stranger to its own movement and meaning, a crowd without
> concern, disowning its own true cry, the cry you'd like to hear because only
> that cry belongs to it, because that cry you know lives deep in some lair of
> darkness and pride in this disowning town, in this crowd deaf to its own cry
> of hunger and misery, revolt and hatred, in this crowd so strangely garrulous
> and dumb.
>
> In this disowning town, this strange crowd which does not gather, does
> not mingle: this crowd that can so easily disengage itself, make off, slip
> away. This crowd which doesn't know how to crowd, this crowd so perfectly
> alone beneath the sun: this crowd like a woman whose lyrical walk you have
> noticed but who suddenly calls upon a hypothetical rain and commands it
> not to fall; or makes the sign of the cross without visible reason; or assumes
> the sudden grave animality of a peasant woman urinating on her feet, stiff
> legs apart.[71]

Disparaging as Césaire's portrayal sounds, the politics and the poetry in his
poem are the same thing. The poetry is in the political and social images that he
uses. Hence, whereas Césaire writes poetry that is political, Gwala and most of
his fellow BCM poets write political statements using verse form and
metaphorical expressions.

The BCM's disenchantment with liberal politics has generated a virulent
rejection of liberal dominance in black politics. The spirit of group solidarity
promoted by the Movement has given rise to an aggressive form of self-
reliance. Blacks are now encouraged to believe that they are their own

liberators. In his poem, "Who Wants To Be Mothered?", Basil Somhlahlo angrily rejects liberal patronage in the black people's struggle for freedom:

> Do not do things for me, let me do them.
> Think no thoughts for me, let me think them.
> You bore me with your thoughts;
> Who wants to be mothered?
>
> . . . Show me the way, do not walk the way for me.
> My legs are strong, my head not closed, O please not closed.
> I know my goal so
> Do not mother me.[72]

Like that of Mafika Pascal Gwala, Somhlahlo's style is conversational and uncomplicated. Somhlahlo's poem consists merely of direct complaints against the self-styled leadership of liberals. Matthews employs a similar technique in "Can the White Man Speak For Me?", in which he uses a series of accusatory and rhetorical questions to show that liberals are not socially, politically and economically qualified to speak for black people:

> Can the white man speak for me?
>
> Can he feel my pain when his laws
> tear wife and child from my side
> and I am forced to work a thousand miles away?
>
> does he know my anguish
> as I walk his streets at night
> my hand fearfully clasping my pass?
>
> is he with me in the loneliness
> of my bed in the bachelor barracks
> with my longing driving me to mount my brother?
>
> will he soothe my despair
> as I am driven insane
> by scraps of paper permitting me to live?
>
> Can the white man speak for me?[73]

Matthews's complaint against liberals is that, despite their pity, they can never truly put themselves in the situation of blacks. Like the other whites, liberals are not oppressed by restrictive laws, they are not expected to carry passes neither do they leave their families in bantustans to work in mines as blacks do. In that case, liberals cannot pretend to understand the black people's suffering because they lack inside experience. Steve Biko believes that one reason liberals lack inside knowledge is that they deliberately evade the experience of blacks:

> A game at which the liberals have become masters is that of deliberate evasiveness. The question often comes up "what can I do?" If you ask him to do something like stopping to use segregated facilities or dropping out of varsity to work at menial jobs like all blacks or defying and denouncing all

provisions that make him privileged, you always get the answer – "but that's unrealistic!". While this may be true, it only serves to illustrate the fact that no matter what a white man does, the colour of his skin – his passport to privilege – will always put him miles ahead of the black man. Thus in the ultimate analysis no white person can escape being part of the oppressor camp.[74]

Liberals are, therefore, viewed as hypocrites, pretending to sympathize with the suffering of blacks and yet, deep in their hearts, wishing to uphold white racism or at least unwilling to part with its privileges.

The BCM's withdrawal from multiracial organizations, its pride in blackness, its encouragement of black solidarity and its rejection of the Westernization of blacks and of liberal spokesmanship in black politics, have prompted the Movement's detractors to accuse it of racism.[75] The charge has come from all quarters of the white community, particularly from liberals, who have borne the brunt of the Movement's political onslaughts. D. A. Kotzé, for instance, confidently argues that the BCM is partly guided by a racist ideology:

> . . . the refusal to acknowledge the good will of at least certain Whites, and cynicism and suspicion regarding Whites' motives towards Blacks testify to a racist bias.[76]

Even Alan Paton believes that the philosophy of the BCM has racist overtones. Paton places the origin of the "racism" in a political and racial context, however:

> Black consciousness is the direct creation of white arrogance. Pride in having a white skin I find an inexcusable vulgarity. I am unable to say the same about pride in having a black skin. I understand the spiritual and psychological necessity for black people to be proud of black skin, even though I regret the reasons for it. Pride in white skin and pride in black skin are for me both vulgarities . . . How long will the young zealots be satisfied with a mush of culture, mysticism, and going round saying haven't I a lovely skin?[77]

Paton argues that one cannot win freedom merely by asserting one's colour. One needs "power"[78] to change the order of things. Given the liberals' rejection of armed struggle, however, one wonders how Paton expects an oppressed and repressed group of people to acquire "power" in a police state. Biko has refuted the charge that the BCM is racist:

> Those who know,[79] define racism as discrimination by a group against another for the purposes of subjugation or maintaining subjugation. In other words one cannot be a racist unless he has the power to subjugate. What blacks are doing is merely to respond to a situation in which they find themselves the objects of white racism. We are in the position in which we are because of our skin. We are collectively segregated against – what can be more logical than for us to respond as a group?[80]

Paton's disappointment and frustration with the BCM's attacks on liberals has led him to ask "whether the White liberal should leave South Africa, keep silent for ever, go north and be trained as a guerrilla fighter or just lie down and die."[81] The BCM's answer to Paton's question is that liberals should educate their white community against racism and in favour of an inevitable black rule. As Steve Biko has vividly put it: "the liberal must serve as a lubricating material so that as we change the gears in trying to find a better direction for South Africa, there should be no grinding noises of metal against metal but a free and easy flowing movement which will be characteristic of a well-looked-after vehicle."[82]

Other white writers have unwittingly answered Paton's question. Nadine Gordimer, for instance, believes that liberalism is on the decline because it "has proved itself hopelessly inadequate to an historical situation".[83] What the South African situation needs, Gordimer implies, is not a solution based on a sterile and hypocritical multiracialism, but a solution predicated on a thorough understanding and appreciation of "the economic connections with race oppression".[84]

Pierre L. van den Berghe's critique of liberal politics is, probably, more direct and uncompromising. To him, the politics of non-violence and pity, in the South African situation, are inappropriate and untenable:

> Nothing, I fear, short of violent revolution and guerrilla warfare with outside support has realistic prospects of destroying apartheid.
>
> The prognosis for violent change has become increasingly convincing over the years, while the scenarios for evolutionary change seem increasingly implausible. Consequently, moral commitment to non-violence in a situation such as that of South Africa almost inevitably relegates one to the role of a cheering spectator in the revolutionary struggle.[85]

Given the inevitability of revolution and the subsequent black rule, van den Berghe suggests that white South Africans have only two options: to stay on terms of equality with blacks, or to emigrate to Europe, North America, Australia or New Zealand.[86] Heribert Adam implies that this emigration may be unnecessary, however, because liberalism is still viable enough to bring about change agreeable to all ethnic groups: ". . . in the end the accumulation of small-scale reforms at the micro-level may well account for more change than the advocates of an instant revolution will ever admit. In this respect, liberals have not failed."[87] Adam does not indicate how long his gradualist approach would take.

The revolution that van den Berghe so forcefully advocates is a favourite theme in much of the poetry of the 1970s. Although not as theoretically militant as some of the writings discussed in the chapter on revolutionary fiction, the poetry clearly espouses armed struggle. As demonstrated earlier, Matthews is the dean of the poets who write poetry of this kind. His poems, "Lord, How Long Lord, How Long?", "Rage Sharp As A Blade", "We Have Been Offered", and "They Have Driven Us Hard Lord", discussed earlier, all advocate violent retribution. Don Mattera, too, writes in favour of applying force to change the order of things in South Africa.

In "No time, Black Man . . .", Mattera angrily encourages confidence and defiance and urges the need to dismantle oppression:

Stand Black man,
Put that cap back
On your beaten head

Look him in the eye
Cold and blue
Like the devil's fire
Tell him enough,

Three centuries is more
Than you take
     Enough . . .

Let him hear it
if he turns his face and sneers
Spit and tell him shit
It's all or nothing
He's got all
And you have nothing.[88]

Again, a poem of this nature cannot work outside its political context. The poem has no poetic figures of speech except angry directives and political statements. Mattera's manner of calling his fellow blacks to action differs vastly from Aimé Césaire's poetic and controlled complaint against the cowardice of his Martinique fellow blacks:

My cowardice rediscovered!
I bow to the three centuries which support my civil
rights and my minimized blood.
My heroism, what a joke!
This town suits me to perfection.
My soul is supine. Like this town, supine in the
dirt and mud.
I demand for my face the dazzling prize of being
spat upon!
Being such as we are, can the rush of virility, the
limb of victory, the large-clodded plain of the
future, belong to us?
I prefer to admit that I have babbled generously,
my heart in my brain like a drunken knee.[89]

Césaire is actually writing about the necessity of resistance without being shrill about it; this coolness is absent in Mattera's poem. In the last stanza of his poem, Mattera's frustration and impatience become more uncompromising:

Don't bargain with oppression
There's no time man,
Just no more time
For the Black man
To fool around.[90]

There is obvious black American infuence in Mattera's language. The political anger in the poem is similar to the "nihilist joy"[91] in a black American poem like Imamu Amiri Baraka's "Black Dada nihilismus":

Come up, black dada

nihilismus. Rape the white girls. Rape their
    fathers.
Cut the mothers' throats.
May a lost god damballah, rest or save us
against the murders we intend
against his lost white children
black dada nihilismus.[92]

Baraka sounds more attracted to violence than does Mattera. The urgency in the last stanza of Mattera's poem, however, implies that only armed struggle, not negotiation, can liberate the black people. People who fear the struggle are encouraged to respect those who are courageous enough to undertake it:

If we seek to be free
    yet fear to die,
Let us at least,
    honour those who serve
And ask not why . . .[93]

The poet's respect for courage and fearlessness is further expressed in an elegiac celebration of the sacrifice of a dead guerrilla:

You whose AKs are ballpens,
Write of his courage
And of the gift of his love
Laid on the altar of sacrifice;
Cover him with tender words
To soothe the longing heart
That pines for the native earth

Build him a stout barricade
With your firm phrases,
Bathe his wounds in the healing flow of tears.[94]

Mattera's language and depiction of the deceased guerrilla are rhetorical. The dead combatant is unquestionably a hero who should be immortalized. Mattera's automatic attribution of heroism is further evidenced in other places by his impassioned depiction of the roles of such political figures as Walter

Sisulu, Robert Sobukwe and Nelson Mandela.

Like James Matthews, Mattera has an internationalized view of the struggle for freedom. This is probably because of the influence of Pan Africanism in the BCM. Mattera's poem, "Elegy for Beirut . . ." shows solidarity with the Palestinian people, expressed rhetorically:

> Where was I
> On that grim night
> When the gun-mongers
> Danced in the blood
> of Palestinian exiles
>
> Where was I
> If only to fling
> A handful of stones
> At those killers.[95]

In the second stanza of the poem, Mattera becomes a Che Guevara of South Africa, an international revolutionary who is prepared to participate directly in the Palestinian struggle. The poem itself is plain, consisting of only rhetorical questions and regrets. In the last stanza, Mattera gives orders like an army general preparing to avenge the death of some of his soldiers:

> Blow loud the ramshorn
> Snuff out the unholy candles
> The dying
> Is not over yet
> Palestine shall be avenged![96]

In Mazisi Kunene's poem, "Vengeance", the threat of retribution takes on an ever-growing and engulfing form:

> We did not forget them.
> Day after day we kindled the fire,
> Spreading the flame of our anger
> Round your cities,
> Round your children,
> Who will remain the ash-monuments
> Witnessing the explosions of our revenge.[97]

Although one has the impression that the revolution Kunene is portraying is more organized, more broad-based and, perhaps, likely to be more effective, the tone of his poem is as threatening as that of the last stanza of Mattera's "Elegy For Beirut".

Mattera's spirit of solidarity is also applied to other countries within Africa undergoing revolutionary activity. The people of Namibia are encouraged to die for freedom:

> Lift up your dreams
> On the wings of desert winds

Freedom is a cactus flower
Nourished by the juice
of Namibian lives
Sprouting anew
On dry riverbeds.[98]

Despite the earnest and rhetorical nature of this stanza, the sense of revolutionary death yielding regenerative benefits comes across forcefully. Mattera's use of images is effective. In "Zimbabwean Love Song", the fruition of revolutionary activity into freedom is portrayed as something commendable. As in the case of "Namibian Love Song . . .", the bitter-sweet experiences of revolution are celebrated:

Nana Zimbabwe,
It was your dance
Of daring feet
Which set the bush on fire,
Made the dying sweet[99]

Unlike most of Mattera's poems, this stanza has been conceived as poetry. The stanza has a lyrical quality and the urgency Mattera has depicted in his other poems is portrayed as fulfilled.

Despite its artistic weaknesses, the militant poetry of the 1970s fulfilled the political objective that prompted its emergence. Committed poetry organizations such as Medupe brought their poetry to schools and public halls in Soweto[100] and oral performances by these organizations distinguished poetry as one of the most effective political weapons. As Tony Emmett has rightly argued:

Although the Medupe poets were members of a literate society, they placed considerable emphasis on the oral aspects of their writing . . . An oral rendition . . . demands a greater degree of participation and involvement from an audience than a printed poem does of a reader. Even more important, perhaps, in terms of the Black Consciousness movement, is the fact that while reading is largely an individual occupation, recitation of poems within the oral framework has to involve a group, or audience, and this sort of structure is more conducive to feelings of group solidarity. The 1977 banning of the Medupe group, along with seventeen other Black Consciousness organizations, was unlikely to lead to the demise of the type of political poetry practised by its members. Poems could be retained in memory and continue to be recited rather than written and read. They could be recalled when opportunities presented themselves rather than within formalized contexts like scheduled poetry readings; they could be taught to a variety of intermediaries to facilitate widespread transmission, and remain covert by the use of local dialects, images or associations, or indigenous languages.[101]

The effectiveness of the poetry of the 1970s was achieved by combining recitation with dramatization. The recitation was made lively and memorable by the performers' dramatization[102] and by drumming.

Partly because of this "conscientizing" role of poetry, by the time the Soweto uprising occurred, a whole generation of politically-conscious students had arisen. Gail Gerhart has observed that:

> . . . by the end of 1972 [there] was an upsurge in political consciousness among high school students, leading to the formation of a welter of political youth organizations across the country. The most notable of these, and the ones which were to provide the impetus behind the township youth uprisings of 1976, were the South African Students' Movement, formed in Soweto high schools, and the National Youth Organizations, a federation of youth groups in Natal, the Transvaal, and the eastern and western Cape.[103]

The BCM's solidarity with the banned ANC and PAC and revolutionary groups in countries like Mozambique became obvious. This mounting attraction to revolution made the BCM vulnerable to police repression. In March 1973, "banning orders were issued to Steve Biko, Pityana, and six other SASO and BPC leaders, and when new individuals came forward to take leadership positions, they too were banned."[104] These leaders were subsequently detained on Robben Island in December 1976. In 1977, Steve Biko died mysteriously[105] in police custody.

The year 1976 was, however, one in which South Africa witnessed one of the most defiant and bloody mass uprisings in its political history. "What presented itself initially as a protest against the use of Afrikaans in African schools took on ever new dimensions as its social base widened and deepened. The struggle culminated in September in a disciplined stay-at-home by large sections of the black working class . . ."[106] Despite the killings and arrests that occurred during the uprising, the spirit of defiance among black youth never died. The mood of the BCM still lingers on in South African politics. The Azanian People's Organization (AZAPO), for instance, is a latter-day version of the Black Consciousness Movement. AZAPO's rejection of Senator Edward Kennedy's recent visit to South Africa provides a good example of the anti-liberal sentiments the Organization has inherited from the BCM. As Michael Valpy has reported:

> AZAPO, the smaller and more militant of the two main anti-Government black groups, labelled the Kennedy visit a hypocritical sham. It said the senator had done nothing to eliminate the economic and social inequality of blacks in his own country and accused him of trying to further his own political ambitions on the backs of South Africa's blacks.[107]

Notes

1. Gail M. Gerhart, *Black Power in South Africa*, p. 252. See also, Ranwedzi Nengwekhulu, "The Meaning of Black Consciousness in the Struggle for Liberation in South Africa", *Political Economy of Africa*, (eds.) Dennis L. Cohen and John Daniel, pp. 201–203.

2. Gerhart, *Black Power*, p. 257.

3. Editorial Briefings, *Review of African Political Economy*, No. 7 (1976), p. 109.

4. The overt racism and ethnocentrism of the Afrikaanse Studentebond (ASB) prevented black students from joining the organization. Unlike NUSAS, ASB had no international accreditation.

5. Clive Nettleton, "Racial Cleavage on the Student Left", *Student Perspectives on South Africa*, (eds.) Hendrik W. Van Der Merwe and David Welsh, p. 125.

6. Gerhart, p. 260.

7. Sam C. Nolutshungu, *Changing South Africa*, p. 166.

8. Gerhart, p. 258.

9. Nettleton, "Racial Cleavage", p. 126.

10. Steve Biko, interview with Gail M. Gerhart, quoted in Gerhart, *Black Power in South Africa*, p. 168.

11. According to the SASO Newsletter, Vol. 5, No. 1 (May/June 1975), "Black people are those who are by law or tradition, politically, socially and economically discriminated against as a group in the South African society of their aspirations".

12. Nolutshungu, *Changing South Africa*, p. 149.

13. Steve Biko, "The Quest For a True Humanity", *I Write What I Like*, (ed.) Aelred Stubbs C. R., pp. 91–2.

14. Black Power itself was an integral part of the political climate that emerged in the late 1950s. This climate was occasioned by the emergence of the Civil Rights Movement which, like the black South African political parties of the same period, was non-violent and multi-racial. By the 1960s, the Civil Rights Movement had had such an impact that protest against racial injustice and the Vietnam War, and the overall way people treated each other, came not only from political activists but from socially and politically conscious artists (who sang both folk and rock music) such as Bob Dylan. According to John Panter (interview, 9 April 1985), Dylan's music (e.g. "Blowin' in the Wind" and "Subterranean Homesick Blues") expressed the general discontent of the period. Black Power, however, was characterized by its violent, separatist and, sometimes, leftist nature. For a detailed study of the development of black resistance against racial injustice in America, see Thomas T. Lyons, *Black Leadership in American History* (Menlo Park: Addison-Wesley Publishing Company, 1971); Herbert Hill, *Anger and Beyond* (New York: Harper and Row, Publishers, 1966); and Stokely Carmichael and Charles V. Hamilton, *Black Power* (New York: Random House, 1967). For connections between black American thought and African political attitudes, see Abdul R. M. Babu, "Black American Influence on Africa", *Africa Now*, No. 46 (Feb., 1985), p. 45, and A. P. Walshe, "Black American Thought and African Political Attitudes in South Africa", *The Review of Politics*, Vol. 32, No. 1 (January 1970) pp. 51–77.

15. Stokely Carmichael and Charles V. Hamilton, *Black Power*, pp. 37–8.

16. Ian Steadman, "Alternative Politics, Alternative Performance: 1976 and Black South African Theatre", *Momentum*, (eds.) M. J. Daymond, J. U. Jacobs and Margaret Lenta, p. 218.

17. Gerhart, p. 274.

18. Ibid., pp. 285–6.

19. In *Black Power*, Carmichael and Hamilton emphasize the importance of politicizing black people: "We aim to define and encourage a new consciousness among black people ... This consciousness ... might be called a sense of peoplehood: pride, rather than shame, in blackness, and an attitude of brotherly communal responsibility among all black people for one another."

20. Tim Couzens and Essop Patel, (eds.), *The Return of the Amasi Bird*.

21. James Matthews's statement, *Momentum*, (eds.) M. J. Daymond, J. U. Jacobs and Margaret Lenta, pp. 73–4.

22. Stephen Henderson, "Survival Motion", Mercer Cook and Stephen E. Henderson, *The Militant Black Writer*, p. 65.

23. James Matthews, "I am Black", quoted in Ursula A. Barnett, *A Vision of Order*, p. 68.

24. James Matthews, "Look Upon the Blackness of My Woman", James Matthews and Gladys Thomas, *Cry Rage*, p. 69.

25. Leopold Senghor, "Black Woman", *300 Years of Black Poetry*, (eds.) Alan Lomax and Raoul Abdul, p. 135.

26. Imamu Amiri Baraka, "Stirling Street September (for Sylvia)", Henry C. Lacey, *To Raise, Destroy and Create*, p. 121.

27. Don Mattera, "Black Plum . . .", *Azanian Love Song*, p. 18.

28. Don Mattera, *Azanian Love Song*, p. 18.

29. Imamu Amiri Baraka, "Cold Term", Henry C. Lacey, *To Raise, Destroy and Create*, p. 121.

30. James Matthews, *Cry Rage*, p. 48.

31. Oswald Mbuyiseni Mtshali, "The Detribalized", *Sounds of a Cowhide Drum*, p. 48.

32. Malcolm X (with the assistance of Alex Haley), *The Autobiography of Malcolm X*, p. 138.

33. Nengwekhulu, "The Meaning of Black Consciousness", *Political Economy of Africa*, p. 198.

34. Steve Biko, "White Racism and Black Consciousness", *I Write What I like*, (ed.) Aelred Stubbs C. R., p. 70.

35. Chinua Achebe, "The Role of the Writer in a New Nation", *African Writers on African Writing*, (ed.) G. D. Killam, p. 9. Achebe argues that he finds Camara Laye's *The Dark Child* "a little too sweet" in its portrayal of the African past.

36. Modikwe Dikobe, *Dispossessed*, p. 2.

37. Ibid., p. 5.

38. Editorial (backcover) note, Modikwe Dikobe, *Dispossessed*.

39. Barnett, p. 65.

40. Robert Mshengu Kavanagh, ed., introduction, *South African People's Plays*, pp. xix–xx.

41. Ibid., p. xviii.

42. Mtshali, *Sounds of a Cowhide Drum*, p. 9.

43. Bloke Modisane, *Blame Me On History*, p. 41.

44. Mtshali, *Sounds of a Cowhide Drum*, p. 12.

45. Ibid.

46. A. N. C. Kumalo, "The Spirit of Bambatha", *Poets to the People*, (ed.) Barry Feinberg, p. 63.

47. Ibid.

48. Ibid., p. 62.

49. Ibid., p. 63.
50. Steve Biko, "Let's Talk About Bantustans", *I Write What I Like*, pp. 83-4. For a detailed analysis of the bantustan policy, see Roger Southall, *South Africa's Transkei*.
51. D. A. Kotzé, *African Politics in South Africa*, p. 77.
52. Biko, "Let's Talk About Bantustans", p. 85.
53. Matthews, *Cry Rage*, p. 4.
54. Ibid., p. 3.
55. Paul Knox, "Visiting Chief Seeks Aid For Zulu People", *The Globe and Mail* (26 February 1985), p. 8.
56. Southall, *South Africa's Transkei*, p. 304.
57. Nengwekhulu, "The Meaning of Black Consciousness", p. 198.
58. Biko, "Black Souls in White Skins?", p. 20.
59. Ibid.
60. Ibid., p. 22.
61. Carmichael and Hamilton, p. 53.
62. Ibid., p. 54.
63. Ibid., p. 55.
64. Biko, p. 22.
65. Mafika Pascal Gwala, "Paper Curtains", *Black Poets in South Africa*, (ed.) Robert Royston, p. 66.
66. Matthews, *Cry Rage*, p. 33.
67. Ibid., p. 14.
68. Ibid., p. 6.
69. Pierre L. van den Berghe, introduction, *The Liberal Dilemma in South Africa*, (ed.) Pierre L. van den Berghe, p. 12.
70. Gwala, p. 66.
71. Aimé Césaire, *Return to My Native Land*, pp. 38-9. Emile Snyder has also quoted the first section of this passage in his article, "Aimé Césaire: The Reclaiming of the land", *Exile and Tradition*, (ed.) Rowland Smith, p. 32.
72. Basil Somhlahlo, "Who Wants to Be Mothered?" *Black Poets in South Africa*, p. 90.
73. Matthews, *Cry Rage*, p. 9.
74. Biko, pp. 22-3.
75. According to Carmichael and Hamilton, a similar charge was levelled against American Black Power in the 1970s. See *Black Power*, p. 47.
76. Kotzé, *African Politics in South Africa*, p. 84.
77. Alan Paton, "Black Consciousness", *Reality*, Vol. 4, No. 1 (March 1972), p. 9.
78. Ibid.
79. Although he does not mention their names, Biko is probably referring to Carmichael and Hamilton. The way Biko defines "racism" sounds too similar to their definition. See *Black Power*, p. 47.
80. Biko, p. 25.
81. Paton's newspaper article, quoted in Kotzé, *African Politics in South Africa*, p. 85.
82. Biko, pp. 25-6.
83. Nadine Gordimer, "The Novel and the Nation in South Africa", *African Writers on African Writing*, (ed.) G. D. Killam, p. 51.
84. Gordimer, "South Africa's Daughter", interview with Anne Collins, *City Woman* (December 1982), p. 26.

85. van den Berghe, *The Liberal Dilemma in South Africa*, p. 13.

86. Ibid., p. 62.

87. Heribert Adam, "The Failure of Political Liberalism", Heribert Adam and Hermann Giliomme, *Ethnic Power Mobilized: Can South Africa Change?*, pp. 283–4.

88. Mattera, *Azanian Love Song*, p. 46.

89. Césaire, *Return to My Native Land*, p. 70.

90. Mattera, *Azanian Love Song*, p. 46.

91. Werner Sollors, *Amiri Baraka/Le Roi Jones: The Quest For a "Populist Modernism"*, p. 92.

92. Sollors, pp. 92 and 93.

93. Mattera, *Azanian Love Song*, p. 74.

94. Ibid., p. 105.

95. Ibid., p. 104.

96. Ibid.

97. Mazisi Kunene, *Poets to the People*, p. 77.

98. Mattera, *Azanian Love Song*, p. 106.

99. Ibid., p. 95.

100. Mbulelo Mzamane, "Literature and Politics among Blacks in Southern Africa", *PULA*, Vol. 1, No. 2 (1979), p. 7.

101. Tony Emmett, "Oral, Political and Communal Aspects of Township Poetry in the Mid-Seventies", *Soweto Poetry*, (ed.) Michael Chapman, pp. 177–8.

102. Emmett, p. 177.

103. Gerhart, *Black Power*, p. 297.

104. Ibid., p. 298.

105. See Donald Woods, *Biko*, pp. 159–260.

106. Editorial Briefings, *Review of African Political Economy*, No. 7 (June 1976), p. 108.

107. Michael Valpy, "Kennedy's Visit Widens the Gaps in Already Divided South Africa", *The Globe and Mail*, No. 25 (January 1985), p. 8.

6. The People's Cause

Popular Theatre and the Political Ferment of the 1970s

The political milieu that produced assertive poetry in the early 1970s was also responsible for the emergence of radical theatre during the same period. The specific reasons for the rise of drama have been well summarized by Robert Mshengu Kavanagh.

> The reasons why theatre became a crucial area of political activity in the 1970s are self-evident. Conventional political action was illegal and dangerous. The press and radio were in the hands of the white establishment. Publishing was a white monopoly and vulnerable to censorship. Film was obviously beyond the reach of the political artist. Theatre on the other hand had many advantages: it was cheap, mobile, simple to present, and difficult to supervise, censor, or outlaw. Clearly it was the one medium left to the people to use to conscientize, educate, unify and mobilize both cadres and rank and file.[1]

While Kavanagh emphasizes the convenience of using drama alone, it should also be stressed that the roles of poetry and drama as instruments of politicization were, sometimes, inseparable. Both genres constituted the main vehicles for the artistic and cultural assertion of the period and, often, the two were combined in mixed media shows incorporating drama, poetry and music.[2] This combination characterized some of the shows of the Theatre Council of Natal (TECON):

> Because of lack of facilities in many of these places [townships and the black section of Natal University], the shows produced incorporated a range of simple pieces not requiring scenery or props. TECON called these pieces "choric verse": some were based on poems, others were dialogues for several voices. In most cases black poetry was used to express Black Consciousness, and the distinction between "drama" and "poetry" became blurred.[3]

This interdependence did not, however, necessarily mean that poetry and drama were always inextricable from each other. There were many shows in which either genre was performed or read independently of the other.

Political theatre in South Africa developed in the 1950s and 1960s. The flimsy veneer of multiracialism in the 1950s gave rise to plays that portrayed the political theme of racial co-existence. Athol Fugard's *The Blood Knot*, for example, deals with the relationship between two brothers, one dark- and the other light-skinned ("coloured") who, despite the government's segregatory Group Areas' Act, live under the same roof. Though published in 1964, Lewis Nkosi's *The Rhythm of Violence* handles a similar theme. A black boy dies in an attempt to save the life of the father of his white girlfriend from a bomb explosion. As the 1960s progressed, political plays of this nature became few and far between.

Non-radical Musical Drama

In the same decade, musicals became the predominant form of drama. Musical plays were "created and performed in the townships, rarely emerging from them (though some of them were later designed for white only audiences) . . .".[4] The drama came to be known as township theatre. The essence of this theatre has been clearly defined by Kavanagh:

> By definition, . . . the first characteristic of township theatre is that it is urban. The second is that it is commercial. Although many of the plays project an apolitical message and propose non-radical solutions to society's ills, the issues they deal with are, however, an accurate reflection of the quality of life led by the urban majority.
>
> Township theatre . . . is about education, sex (adultery, promiscuity, rape) religion, crime, drink, the corruption and cruelty of the authorities.[5]

With music and dance at its centre, township theatre was box-office drama, mainly calculated to entertain and to raise money. The political content mentioned in Kavanagh's definition was totally subordinated to these objectives.

Owing to their non-intellectual and non-committed nature, "the plays of township theatre were only slightly, if at all – scripted. They were largely improvised by the actors themselves, who usually worked during the day and performed or rehearsed at night."[6] My discussion of musical plays, therefore, will not be based on texts but on summaries and articles written by journalists and literary scholars who either had the opportunity to carry out research inside South Africa, or saw the plays performed live, within or outside the country.

One of the first box-office black musical plays was the production of *King Kong* in 1959. Todd Matshikiza composed the music, Pat Williams wrote the lyrics, Harry Bloom wrote the book, Arthur Goldreich designed sets and costumes and Leon Gluckman produced the play.[7] Unlike the musical plays that succeeded it, *King Kong* was a non-exploitative, musical version of township fiction. The play dramatized the pathos of township life, focusing upon the life story of a boxer-cum-gangster, Ezekiel Dhlamini (who called himself King Kong), who was convicted of killing his girlfriend. *King Kong* also celebrated shebeen life in the black shanty town. The performers were all black, including celebrated musicians such as Todd Matshikiza and Miriam Makeba. Writing about the effectiveness of the play's performance, Harry Bloom says:

> The actors were not so much acting, as living out their normal lives on the stage. *King Kong* is about African life in shanty town. And a whole town with all its characters, noises, scenes, and problems comes miraculously to life on a few square feet of stage surrounded by canvas scenery. There was a fearful sense of reality about Lucky and his Prowlers Gang, about their gloating viciousness and their power to terrorize the whole town. The reason is that in real life every township dweller lives in constant dread of gangsters.[8]

Putting African life into musicals was successful because whites were sympathetic to the life thus revealed to them. The play had a strong impact on whites because it was produced at the height of liberalism in South African politics. With the advent of the Sharpeville emergency soon after the play's production, however, *King Kong* represented the end of the era of liberalism.

The enormous success of *King Kong*, both at home and abroad, produced a plethora of theatre groups in major cities such as Johannesburg, Port Elizabeth, Cape Town, Durban, Grahamstown, East London[9] and others. Black producers like Gibson Kente (who was working for Union Artists of Southern Africa which had produced *King Kong*) exploited the "basic form"[10] of *King Kong* and produced musicals such as *Sikalo*, *Lifa* and *Zwi* that dramatized happy aspects of township life.

As time passed, however, white producers were seen as exploiting[11] the vogue of black musicals. Although the actors and actresses who took part in white-created plays remained black, the plays themselves were aimed at whites. In addition, the plays deliberately presented a distorted view of the social, cultural and political life of black people. This warped portrayal provoked bitter criticism from radical blacks and white sympathizers:

> The Westernized black musical was something that really began in 1957 [sic], when the success of *King Kong* suggested its potential as a lucrative South African export. *King Kong* had much to recommend it, especially Miriam Makeba's performance and Todd Matshikiza's music, but it gave rise to a sequel of undistinguished commercial ventures. Song and dance, traditional forms of cultural expansion in Africa, were viewed through racist eyes as "inherent characteristics". This theory is still subscribed to and "innate rhythm" presents itself as raw material from which profit can be made.[12]

Anthony Akerman's critique is specifically based on the content and implications of two plays, *Kwa Zulu* (named after one of the bantustans) and *Ipi Tombi* (Where Are the Girls). The plot of the first play has been summarized by *Plays and Players*:

> A proud chief with his four beautiful wives is witnessing the courting of his eldest daughter by a young man . . . . Initiation enforced, the marriage

proceeds. But there is jealousy of another beautiful maiden . . . and this impossible desire escalates into an evil that precipitates a famine. The witch-doctor enacts his ritual and discovers her as the evil-doer; she is cast out, begs readmission, persuades the chief's first wife to propitiate God through prayers, and the community prospers.[13]

While the portrayal of the role of chiefs, traditional doctors, the invocation of spirits, the banishment of evil-doers and the propitiation of gods seem indigenous enough, one never ceases to wonder what this cultural "assertion" is meant to achieve. *Kwa Zulu* is mute on the political policy of bantustans implied by the play's title. Characters are depicted as though they are completely oblivious to their political predicament. To that extent, the play is escapist and employed for purposes of promoting apartheid:

> This world of 'chiefs', 'beautiful maidens' and 'witch-doctors' has more to do with the fairy-tale unreality of escapist musicals than the reality of life in South Africa. The material has nothing to do with the problems facing either urban blacks, or those people the South African Government is trying to retribalize in the impoverished Bantustans. *Kwa Zulu* . . . is little more than pro-Bantustan propaganda.[14]

The excessive exploitation in *Ipi Tombi* is the subject of Akerman's complaints. Though the play opened in Johannesburg in 1974, *Ipi Tombi* resembles the escapist musicals of the 1960s. In common with *Kwa Zulu*, characters range from "witch-doctors" to "beautiful maidens", but the symbolism of the characters is more clearly defined. Russell Vandenbroucke has given a detailed summary of the play.

There are, on the one hand, the "evil", "primitive" and "diabolical" ways of the traditional doctor and the black culture he represents, and on the other, the virginal purity, beauty and hope of "civilized" Christianity. The narrator decides to go to the city to find work to support his family. In Johannesburg and its outlying townships, the chorus is composed equally of men and women with each man having his mate. Becoming disillusioned with urban life the narrator returns to the countryside.[15]

Ipi Tombi is obviously a play that seeks to reinforce the stereotypes of unthinking whites. Black actors and actresses are used to perpetuate their own debasement. The symbolism equating black with evil, primitivism and diabolism, and white with purity, beauty and hope is represented by the clash between traditional religion and Christianity. This portrayal of the clash of cultures differs from that of black writers, whether South African or non-South African. Chinua Achebe (*Things Fall Apart*) and Ngugi wa Thiong'o (*The River Between*) for instance, stress the disruptive effects of the colonial imposition of Christianity on black culture. In *Ipi Tombi*, however, traditional culture is viewed in contradictory terms: some aspects of the culture, such as the practice of traditional medicine, are vilified, other forms of the culture such as songs and dances are considered "good". The songs and dances, which are normally employed to express various aspects of black culture, are presented in a social vacuum as entertainment for white audiences:

A dance called Orgy was added, looking like it came from the Caribbean. Highly provocative. What was the idea? Is this what goes on in the average village in Msinga as family entertainment? The beauty of black dance was at times reduced to a sexy and suggestive rotation forward of the pelvis called 'ukufenda'. This, I was told by a cast member, was the choreographer's favourite movement. I wonder why.[16]

Commercial black musicals capitalized on the prurience described above. This sexually titillating dance involves dancers who have bare breasts, bare thighs[17] and are ever-smiling. The stereotype meant to be perpetuated here is that of "smiling natives" with "innate rhythm".

Ipi Tombi strengthens the white South African misconception that blacks belong to nowhere else except bantustans. The narrator of the play is a "good Bantu". He has become disillusioned with the (presumably) alien ways of the white man's urban world, a world that can never be his. He eagerly and happily returns to his rural home where he belongs, it is implied, where he can live simply and contentedly in proximity to the land.[18] *Ipi Tombi*'s stress on music and dance, its glossing over the oppression of blacks and its portrayal of bantustans as "hospitable" landscapes to which blacks can conveniently return and resume their "simple, rustic life", obscure the politico-economic realities of black people. Like most plays of its nature, *Ipi Tombi* is economically and physically exploitative, presumptuous, paternalistic, condescending and misleading.

Radical Drama

Although commercial musical plays flourished till the early 1970s, it was between 1972 and 1975 that township theatre became radical. The commercialism and escapism of the previous decade gave way to a committed theatre which Jacques Alvarez-Pereyre has described as "theatre at the grass roots".[19] This theatre dealt with such topical issues as cultural assertion, defiance and black solidarity. A number of factors were responsible for the emergence of the radical theatre:

> Political plays by groups such as the Serpent Players and Workshop '71 suggested the possibility of theatre that not only reflected the exploitation of the people but protested against it. The Black Consciousness Movement's efforts to popularize the ideas of black self-respect and self-reliance began to take effect and its theatre caught the imagination of the students. These years also saw a wave of strikes throughout the urban area. Inflation spiralled and unemployment became chronic.[20]

The Serpent Players (led by Athol Fugard), Phoenix Players and Workshop '71 were based in town (as opposed to black townships) and the theatre they produced was known as town theatre.[21] Both blacks and whites were involved and mostly concerned with political rather than commercial plays. In the

TEACHING AREAS

— (20ᵇˡᵏ) S. African writing

— Anglophone African (with a special emphasis on poetry)

— Blk diaspora (esp U.K. & U.S.)

— (20) African Am.

— (20) British (eg. postwar)

— (20) Xcano

— Postcolonial theory / materialist theory / Feminist theory
       Resistance theory

■ History & Lit / Anthropology & Lit.

PUBLISHABLE MATERIAL

— Essay on Chipasula & Gwala

— Train chapter — RIAL

— Ndebele chapter — WLE

— Boerak / Ornin chapter — WLT

— Granniosaw paper — Afr. Am R

— Pringle paper — EinA

— Essay on Ireland & Gib

38

②

The two things which he emphasized most
as poet + practical man were sees.
+ the princess 7 the vehi-life.

1960s, Serpent Players, for example, had started producing political plays such as *The Blood Knot* and *Boesman and Lena*. Between 1973 and 1974, Serpent Players (Athol Fugard, John Kani and Winston Ntshona) produced and subsequently published *Sizwe Bansi Is Dead*, a political play, which partly led to the demise of white-created musicals.

The political concerns that were stifled in musicals found expression in a variety of radical plays that followed the footsteps of *Sizwe Bansi Is Dead*. Among these Credo Mutwa's *uNosilimela*, produced by Workshop '71 in 1973 and 1974, gave a rich and complex treatment of the theme of cultural assertion. With the play's emphasis on black culture and history, Workshop '71 was probably the most qualified theatre group to undertake the production of *uNosilimela*. The cultural concerns of the group have been spelled out by one of its most eloquent members, Kavanagh:

> Workshop '71 attempts to create South African theatre out of a composite culture of all South Africans at a time when there is not a meeting of cultures but a confrontation of cultures . . . Workshop '71 wants to bring together people from different cultures and involve them in work that brings understanding of those differences and a way to go beyond them. Its plays deal with the differences of its members and are performed before audiences whose responses are often conditioned by those differences.[22]

uNosilimela is precisely a play that dramatizes these cultural differences. Traditional, black culture and Western culture are dealt with in a plot that ranges from precolonial times to the present. The first quarter of the play portrays an immemorial black past. An old world of gods, traditional doctors, spirits, myths, legends and custom is invoked by the storyteller:

> In the name of the great gods of our fathers, in the name of Dumakade, the far thunderer, and Somnganise, the friendly one, god of peace, and also in the name of Mvelingangi, firstborn of the *almighty* and the great mother of creation, we must this night do something so beautiful it will delight the ancestral spirits in the village and bring fear into the hearts of evil wizards that prowl in the bush![23]

The traditional inhabitants of this world, the amaQuashi, share knowledge of the origin and destiny of man, the rise and fall of stone-built empires and heavenly bodies like stars. Human and animal characters mingle and sometimes reproduce, giving birth to characters like uNosilimela, the heroine of the play. Inter-ethnic fighting is characterized by potent magic that is capable of making the opponents' houses and cattle disappear. Misunderstandings can be resolved only by appealing to traditional doctors, gods and goddesses, who would prescribe the appropriate way of bringing about a reconciliation.

Failure to abide by the society's standards of living results in immediate self-exile or banishment. Solemamba, one of King Magadlemzini's sons, fails to cope with the rigid discipline of his people and decides to leave for Johannesburg declaring: "I'm leaving the land of the amaQuashi to return on

the day the sun falls out of the sky and the hens peck at it with their beaks."[24]
Solemamba's apocalyptic proclamation is a vivid rejection of the ways of his
society. The removal of his bracelet (a traditional ornament) from his wrist,
and his symbolic hurling of the bracelet to the ground, reinforce this rejection.

When uNosilimela strikes her mother, Namdozolwana, in disrespect, she is
immediately banished by the Earth Mother:

> The hand that strikes the mother is cursed throughout the land! Expel that
> child from your household. She must wander and suffer, never settle, be
> driven like a leaf before the wind. Expel her or I shall desert you! The cattle
> will die, the crops be burnt by the sun.[25]

As in Solemamba's case, when uNosilimela is about to leave her people, she
reflects on how "oppressive" traditional life can be and she embraces the
possibility of freedom with careless abandon:

> A dark cloud of shame hangs over my head. But it has bright silver edges! I
> am now free, free to live, to learn and free to love! Farewell, tribal stuffiness
> and restriction! And welcome life and endless joy![26]

uNosilimela's preoccupation is not to denigrate black culture, however, but to
reassert it. Solemamba's and uNosilimela's decision to go to Johannesburg
enables the author to give a critique of Western culture. Johannesburg is
portrayed, not as a centre for commercial benefit as musical plays imply, but as
a breeding ground for the disorientation of black people. The reader is brought
face to face with the seamy world of shebeens, urban thugs, violence,
prostitution and passes. Solemamba is transformed by the roughness of this life
and becomes the deadliest and most feared urban thug: "When I got to
Johannesburg I turned into a thief, a robber and a killer! The people called me
the Green Python."[27] The violence of city life is further represented by Alpheus
Mafuza's callous wish to have uNosilimela die at the hands of her own brother,
Solemamba (a professional murderer hired, paid by the rich to liquidate their
enemies). Probably Mutwa's aim is to demonstrate the disorder and violence of
urban life – a life-style that, of course, contrasts with what he considers to be the
well-ordered nature of traditional life.

uNosilimela's own cultural and moral degeneration, Mutwa believes, is as
serious as that of Solemamba. Initially the neglected wife of an urban egoist
and bigamist, Alpheus Mafuza, she ends as a whore. Between these two phases
of her life, instances of poverty, homelessness and rape occur with amazing
regularity. But the most important event that occurs to uNosilimela is her
contact with Christianity. Mutwa uses this to further attack Western culture by
pointing to what he considers to be the disruptive nature of Christianity. The
Old Woman who uNosilimela meets outside the church talks about this
disruption:

> My child, you are not the only one who's being torn apart between the old
> faith of our fathers and the new faith of the whiteman. Many find they
> cannot, no matter how hard they try, completely turn their backs on their

ancestors and upon the ways of the old ones and yet at the same time feel forced to follow the faith of the whiteman for reasons you well know.[28]

Although uNosilimela is baptized as a Christian, the author has uMvelingangi, the traditional God, lecture her on the nature of the Supreme Being:

> There is no such thing as a true God or a false one. God is one. Throughout the universe. It is only Man in his wickedness, Man in his weakness who gives God a race, a colour and a shape. God is one even on the farthest shores of Creation.[29]

The traditional God purifies uNosilimela of all her sickness and disease, and this purification symbolizes her parting with city life and Western culture; once purified she returns to her people. It is easy here to accuse Mutwa of inadvertently reinforcing the racist misconception that blacks belong to homelands, as is done in white-created musical plays. But, the return of Mutwa's heroine to the rural areas has a different purpose. A prophecy that revolves around her is to be fulfilled. Because of her purgatorial suffering in Johannesburg and the opportunity she has to talk directly to the traditional God of her own people, uNosilimela becomes in effect a sacrificial lamb whose suffering saves the amaQuashi from the nuclear holocaust which obliterates Johannesburg. An ultra-traditional society, devoid of hate and war, subsequently emerges from the ashes of the wiped out white world.

Mutwa's belief that traditional society can be devoid of hate and war is unrealistic and misleading. Prose writers such as Plaatje and Abrahams are much more subtle in demonstrating that traditional societies were also bedevilled by ethnic disputes and wars. Even more unconvincing is the way Mutwa's rural characters so easily survive a nuclear explosion. With all its technological advancement, Johannesburg fails to cope with the explosion, but black people in the rural areas do. No matter how strong a society's spirits and gods may be, it is straining credulity to suggest that the society can be spared from the disaster of a nuclear holocaust merely by hiding in a mountain tunnel. Above all, Mutwa's substitution of pure, unadulterated traditional life for urban life is backward-looking and utopian. Contemporary black society has become so proletarianized and urbanized that the return to the past that Mutwa postulates is impracticable and defeatist. Blacks need to grapple with the problems of present-day industrial South Africa in the light of how the past has contributed in shaping those problems. This reciprocity between past and present has been well articulated by T. S. Eliot: ". . . the past should be altered by the present as much as the present is directed by the past."[30] The reciprocity – Eliot argues – constitutes a balanced "historical sense".[31] Mutwa's rigid belief in the virtues and self-containment of traditional life has been challenged by some of his fellow black people:

> The new generation, though, is relearning the past and consciously and proudly claiming its culture and history. This is not simply a return to the past, but a step forward to meet the problems of the future with the strength of the past.

The new theatre takes cognizance of the early African theatre described by Credo Mutwa, but reflects a changed society. It takes account of the experiences of the urbanized and exploited industrial workers whose sensitivity has been changed forever by a polyglot and variegated society and its technology, films, records, international music and culture, and western theatrical conventions and staging. Above all, the new theatre must be conscious of the powerful forces mobilized to inhibit and repress this great accumulation of knowledge and power.[32]

The advocacy of a total return to the past at the expense of the present is, therefore, not only romantic but a negation of the future.

Perhaps one reason why Athol Fugard's city play, *Sizwe Bansi Is Dead*, was so influential in radicalizing township theatre and political thought of the 1970s was because it addressed itself to immediate social concerns. While its primary preoccupation is the dehumanizing effect of pass laws, *Sizwe Bansi Is Dead* examines other political and economic issues. Familiar as these may sound, the effectiveness of Fugard's theatre lies in the vivid manner in which he portrays the issues:

Athol Fugard's choice of a small number of characters and emphasis on actors 'staking' their 'personal truths', derives in part from the influence of Jerzy Grotowski's 'theatre laboratory'. In both cases, the method is one whereby the characters reveal themselves to the audience. *Sizwe Bansi Is Dead* is a play based on the elaboration of personal biography. A small number of case histories, situated in appropriate social contexts, serve as social commentary.[33]

Fugard's choice of a small number of characters (usually two or three in each cast) is similar to the number of characters in some of the plays of the absurdist school such as Samuel Beckett's and Harold Pinter's. The revelation of "personal truths" (by characters) and the mood of dehumanization that characterize Fugard's *Sizwe Bansi Is Dead* are also typical of the plays of Beckett and Pinter. To that extent, Fugard's *Sizwe Bansi Is Dead* has absurdist characteristics. The personal biography, case histories and the revealing actions of the characters in the play all contribute to expose the exploitation and oppression of the system.

Sizwe Bansi Is Dead begins with the self-revelation of Styles, one of the two characters in the play. His monologue, which is roughly as long as Lucky's gibberish speech in Beckett's *Waiting for Godot*, is a caustic attack on American investment and multinationals in general. As Styles reads a newspaper, he comes across an item that deals with the Ford motor factory; this immediately reminds him of his experiences as an employee at the factory, especially the visit of Henry Ford II. Through irony, paradox and carefully chosen descriptions which highlight the absurdities characteristic of working conditions in the factory, Styles achieves a skilful and indirect verbal indictment of industrial relations[34]:

"Styles, tell the boys that when Mr Henry Ford comes into the plant I want them all to look happy. We will slow down the speed of the line so that they can sing and smile while they are working."

Gentlemen, he says that when the door opens and his grandmother walks in you must see to it that you are wearing a mask of smiles. Hide your true feelings, brothers. You must sing. The joyous songs of the days of old before we had fools like this one next to me to worry about . . .[35]

The word "smile", that Styles constantly uses in the play, signifies the endemic hypocrisy the system has given rise to.

Although it is the local authorities themselves who slow down production because of Henry Ford's visit, immediately after his departure, the black workers are overworked to compensate for the lost production:

He [Henry Ford II] didn't even look at the plant! And what did I see when those three Galaxies disappeared? The white staff at the main switchboard.

"Double speed on the line! Make up for production lost!" It ended up with us working harder that bloody day than ever before.[36]

The extra labour is not, however, remunerated. It is this kind of exploitation that ultimately prompts Styles to leave the factory and establish his own business as a photographer. This represents a clear decision to survive in a harsh environment, and this theme of survival pervades the play. As Derek Cohen has rightly put it, *Sizwe Bansi Is Dead*

is a drama primeordinately [sic] about survival under a system which seeks to deprive individual human beings of the right to affront their own destinies or to define their own existences: the passbook proves that you are who *they* say you are; and the play comes to grips with the question of survival and this condition.[37]

Styles's method of grappling with the system has, however, been criticized:

Styles's response to his heightened awareness of the exploitative nature of the multinationals remains fundamentally individual and individualized. Thus the devisers of the play do not explore the potential of the material they have only sketched into space and silence. There remains an evasion of underlying and fundamental issues. Styles does not develop his skills as potential spokesman and intermediary between local white management and black employees. On the contrary, he chooses to withdraw from the situation and to assert his 'manhood'. He chooses personal assertion, not public commitment, in the interests of maintaining the family of which he is the head and chief breadwinner.[38]

Hilary Seymour is a critic whose literary approach and political beliefs are similar to those of Alex La Guma. Like La Guma, Seymour's perspective is proletarian and hence, revolutionary. The perspective emphasizes the role of the collective at the expense of that of the individual. Seymour's criticism of Styles's withdrawal from the Ford motor factory is predicated on the fact that, given his political awareness as a worker, Styles could have ended up a trade union leader galvanizing his fellow-workers against the system's exploitation. But his withdrawal, Seymour argues, alienates him from the workers, making his struggle with the system individualistic and self-serving. Seymour goes on to argue that, because of his extreme self-interest, Styles ends up exploiting his fellow black people, and his commercial success depends "on the gullibility, sentimentality and good-natured naivety of his customers . . ."[39] whom he cheats when they visit his studio.

Seymour's criticisms are all valid but, as he himself is aware, Fugard is not a revolutionary playwright. Fugard is a liberal dramatist whose major concern is merely to expose the exploitativeness and oppression of the system by dramatizing them. This method has been well described by Winston Ntshona, one of the writers and actors of *Sizwe Bansi Is Dead*:

> Whether you talk in terms of the content or whether you view the work from the artistic point of view, the three of us, we view both the artistry and the content. These are the things that incorporate life as we see it through art. And then the three of us, in sweating it out, working it out, you know picking up situations, because I believe this is how an artist should do, every sensible artist. Whenever one is involved in all he is doing, he is selecting from life, from his immediate surroundings, the themes that affect his life, because in the overall end of it all, what you're going to see on stage is never no ghosts, no apparitions; those are human beings talking about their lives, their immediate surroundings. And then the three of us were satisfied with the output and the input into the work. Now somebody coming along to see the show; sits there, watches, comes out, either satisfied or dissatisfied.[40]

Ntshona's argument shows that the method employed in *Sizwe Bansi Is Dead* is that of a liberal, critical realist; the system is criticized without grappling with ways of changing it. This approach is at odds with that of a critic like Seymour who argues that, "the vision of society in this kind of literature is static and pessimistic with regard to material conditions and progress."[41]

Despite the liberal limitation of the play, Fugard succeeds in exposing the depersonalizing dimensions of the will to survive among black people. Styles's advocacy of survival reaches its peak when Sizwe Bansi appears on the scene. Again, as in the case of characterization in some of the plays of Beckett and Pinter, Styles and Sizwe Bansi play the roles of different characters. Styles appears as Buntu and Sizwe Bansi as the Man. Sizwe Bansi himself is looking for a job but he has neither a pass nor a job permit. Hence, he faces the risk of being arrested and sent back to the homelands. On their way back from a shebeen, however, Sizwe Bansi and Styles discover the body of a murdered man (killed by urban thugs) who happens to have a pass-book with a valid worker's permit in his pocket. Styles quickly suggests that Sizwe Bansi take the pass-book and use it for his own job-hunting purposes. But possession of the book means that Sizwe Bansi loses his identity and adopts the dead man's name, Robert Zwelinzima.

Initially, Sizwe Bansi is unwilling to accept this suggestion. He asks: "I don't want to lose my name, how do I get used to Robert? and how do I live as another man's ghost?"[42] This concern with the need to preserve one's identity must have greatly appealed to the Black Consciousness Movement, one of whose objectives was to re-establish the identity and dignity of black people. In the play, however, Styles's witty pragmatism prevails. He persuades Sizwe Bansi to adopt the dead man's identity by harping on the social and economic benefits that could accrue from using the pass-book. The benefits include averting police harassment, securing a job, being able to maintain a family and leading a "luxurious" life. These are, of course, the benefits Sizwe Bansi anticipates. Even more persuasively, Styles comes up with the philosophic argument that, because of economic deprivation and political oppression, black South Africans are just as good as dead people:

> Wasn't Sizwe Bansi a ghost? . . . When the white man looked at you at the Labour Bureau what did he see? A man with dignity or a bloody passbook with an N. I. number? Isn't that a ghost? When the white man sees you walk down the street and calls out, 'Hey, John! come here' . . . to you, 'Sizwe Bansi' . . . isn't that a ghost? Or when his little child calls you 'Boy' . . . you a man, circumcised with a wife and four children . . . isn't that a ghost? Stop fooling yourself. All I'm saying is be a real ghost, if that is what they want, what they've turned us into. Spook them into hell, man![43]

Given the way whites view blacks in South Africa, this equation of anonymity with ghostliness is appropriate. La Guma first used this idea of ghostliness when one of his characters proclaims: "That's us, us, Michael, my boy. Just ghosts, doomed to walk the night."[44] But, while La Guma's Shakespearean allusion is clearly critical of any ghostly existence, Styles's advice that Sizwe Bansi become "a real ghost" may easily be misconstrued as an acceptance of the situation. Despite his rage with the system, Styles has become a ghost that haunts his own people. His will to survive is informed by the law of the jungle, the survival of the fittest. Baffled by Sizwe Bansi's reluctance to capitalize on the death of Robert Zwelinzima, Styles selfishly argues: "Look, if someone was to offer me the things I wanted most in life, the things that would make me, my wife, and my child happy, in exchange for the name Bantu . . . you think I wouldn't swop?"[45]

In its ruthlessness and self-centredness, Styles's exploitative philosophy may be compared to the blunt and brutal confessions of Ngugi wa Thiong'o's Wanja, in his novel, *Petals of Blood*:

> As for me, it's a game . . . of money . . . You eat or you are eaten . . . And now I can go anywhere . . . even to their most expensive clubs . . . they are proud to be seen with me . . . even for one night . . . and they pay for it . . . I have had to be hard . . . It is the only way . . . the only way . . . Look at Abdulla . . . reduced to a fruit seller . . . oranges . . . sheepskins . . . No, I will never return to the herd of victims . . . Never . . . Never . . .[46]

Wanja's proclamation is that of a typical and uncaring prostitute. Her behaviour is inconsiderate, brutal and exploitative. As in the case of Styles,

Wanja has been hardened by the evil nature of the system (in Wanja's case, the system is neocolonial). Wanja's retaliatory exploitation is predominantly directed towards the system's upholders however. Even more important, by the end of the novel, her politics of exploitation has been overtaken by political awareness. Wanja's closeness to enlightened political activists such as Karega (a trade union leader) and Abdulla (a former Mau Mau guerrilla) transforms her and she becomes part of the collective opposition that threatens to bring down the Kenyan neocolonial regime. Styles, however, remains a political individualist, and his vigorous proselytizing produces more individualists. At the end of the play, Sizwe Bansi agrees to enter Styles's rat race. The agreement reveals one of the most dehumanizing ironies in black South African life. As Patrick O'Sheel has argued:

> In content the play turns on the ironies of Sizwe Bansi's 'death', a death that opens the prospect of a job, and hence a life, for a black family. It is a life that costs the sacrifice of name and honour; a life bearing the ghostly identity of a real dead man, whose death epitomizes the lawless violence of the black townships, themselves ironically creations of South African law.[47]

On the level of revolutionary action, *Sizwe Bansi Is Dead* is not "committed", but it should be appreciated that, given the repressive aftermath of Sharpeville, the play's bold exposure of the effects of the system's exploitation and oppression is radical. As mentioned above, Fugard's preoccupation with political issues partly encouraged black playwrights to turn from non-radical musical plays to committed drama, but much of the impetus behind this movement was as a result of the influence of the Black Consciousness Movement. Theatre groups such as the Theatre Council of Natal (TECON), The People's Experimental Theatre (PET), Workshop '71 (not a BCM theatre group) and individual producers such as Gibson Kente (who had established his own theatre company in the mid-1960s) began to produce politically committed theatre. The radicalism of this theatre goes beyond that of Fugard in the sense that the theatre not only registers protest but also advocates change.

The theme of survival in Fugard's *Sizwe Bansi Is Dead* is portrayed in a more revolutionary manner in the Workshop '71 play, *Survival*, although the subject matter of the play is not new. Like Fugard's *The Island*, *Survival* deals with the harrowing experiences of political prisoners on Robben Island. The stock themes of confinement, inedible food, sordid living conditions, and the comparison of the oppressive nature of prison life with what obtains on the mainland are graphically portrayed through the technique of reports delivered by various prisoners. The intention of the reports may be compared to the political purpose of *Antigone*, a play-within-a-play in Fugard's *The Island*. What concerns us here, however, is *Survival*'s emphasis on black people's sense of survival in life-destroying circumstances.

While Fugard's Styles advocates survival in selfish terms, the question of survival in radical black writing has been associated with the courage and determination of the whole black society in the face of oppression. Some of Dennis Brutus's poetry vividly records this defiant endurance:

> Somehow we survive
> and tenderness, frustrated, does not wither.

> Investigating search lights rake
> our naked unprotected contours:

> But somehow we survive
> severance, deprivation, loss.
> most cruel, all our land is scarred with terror,
> rendered unlovely and unlovable;
> sundered are we and all our passionate surrender

> but somehow tenderness survives.[48]

Brutus's tone is bitter and melancholic but the black people's resolve to continue struggling for freedom is effectively stressed.

In *Survival*, the will to survive is portrayed more defiantly. As in Brendan Behan's *The Quare Fellow*, *Survival* opens with prisoners singing. In both cases, the singing itself is both "an affirmation of man's vitality in the face of" oppressive systems[49] and a registration of the political protest of the prisoners. While Behan's prisoner sings about hunger and the mice that squeak in his cell, the prisoners in *Survival* sing about the necessity of immediate revolutionary change:

> The people are living in our world
> the people are watching in our world
> the people are waiting in our world

> move, man!
> Don't take your time.
> Now is the right time.
> The iron is red hot!

> Strike now, my man, strike now and don't drag your feet
>   now's the time.
> Strike now, my man, strike now and never fear the heat
>   it's going to be fine.
> And sweet and free the time's a-coming, coming
> In jails and slums the drums are drumming, drumming.

> Brother, strike that drum
>   while the drum is taut
> Brothers, strike the iron
>   while the iron is hot.[50]

The cocky, defiant confidence and the use of black Americanisms such as "man", "my man", and "brothers" in this song betray the influence of American Black Power. Extremely aggressive in its revolutionary approach to political change, the song sounds like Don Mattera's assertive poetry, especially, "No Time Black Man . . .". It also offers a good example of the blurred distinction between the drama and the poetry of the 1970s, pointed out at the beginning of the chapter. If Fugard's protest in *Sizwe Bansi Is Dead* is criticized for being too soft, the protest in this song may also be criticized for being too shrill and authoritative.

The theme of survival is addressed more directly in the last section of the play:

> Prison destroys, If no one can say which is the more destructive prison – jail or the system – then the whole nation should perish, the people should buckle, there should be chaos. The spirit should die.[51]

The dialogue that follows Themba's argument demonstrates that, despite their suffering, black people continue to resist oppression:

> Fana: But it doesn't.
> Dan: The people are not destroyed.
> Seth: They go on.
> All (together): They survive!
> Themba: What's more . . .
> Fana: They grow in numbers and self-sufficiency.
> Seth: The spirit lives even more fiercely.
> Dan: In short . . .
> All (together): . . . they triumph![52]

This dialogue is completely undeveloped. There is no discussion but rather successive pronouncements of how blacks survive their situation. And, although the words of a chant like "They survive" or ". . . they triumph" may appear stylistically "crude" on a page, the dramatic effect of chanting such political slogans in unison is far from "crude".

In Themba's concluding explanation, the spirit of survival is directly connected with the struggle for freedom. The inevitable role of the masses in the struggle, and the certainty of victory, are pointed out:

> A people survive by grimly holding on. But at the same time they achieve what their oppressors cannot help envying them for. The strength lies with the people, who carry with them in their lives the justification for the struggle – the victory that is . . .[53]

The directness of this passage is similar to the political nature of various passages in Alex La Guma's novel, *In the Fog of the Season's End*. In the passage above, survival is explained in a way that sounds like revolutionary theory.

As its dialogue indicates, *Survival* is a play that sets out to protest against the suffering of black people and to advocate revolutionary change. The didacticism of the play and of other plays of its period was meant to concur with the BCM's objective of "conscientizing" the people.

The need for political change is the primary concern of Gibson Kente's *Too Late*. The form of the play is also "didactic and demonstrative".[54] Kente starts off by depicting a society of desperadoes. The township in which the play is set is infested with *majitas* (urban thugs who masquerade as religious people) who carry out acts of robbery and violence. The value of education has been debased by a system which does not pay salaries proportional to the professional qualifications blacks hold. Being a medical doctor, teacher or lawyer sound the same in terms of financial reward. Because of poverty and frustration, brilliant students abandon school and take to robbery; professional characters in the play, like the doctor, have become alcoholics. Black collaborators connive with the system's police to make underground methods of money-making (e.g., shebeen sales) impossible. Mufundisi, one of the characters in the play, rightly blames this state of affairs on the system:

> We all know that this young man [a drop-out from school] was God-loving, peace-loving and law-abiding. What's changed him? What's put hatred in him? From school children to the teachers, from the poor to the rich, the illiterate to the enlightened, the tsotsi to the law abiding, this hatred and resentment is rife. Tomorrow that poor young boy will be labelled dangerous and against the laws of the country. Forgetting that politics were forced on him. It's like being thrown into the rain and expected not to get wet, or food put into your hungry mouth yet still prohibited to eat.[55]

Mufundisi's accusation against the system is keen and to the point. The doctor, however, is not content with merely pointing out how the system supports the status quo; he advocates immediate change:

> Leaving the law, for now I am afraid unless something is done about this pettiness, the law is going to end up with a hot potato in its hands. Can't something be done to curb the bitterness in both young and old before it's TOO LATE?[56]

There is something desperate about the doctor's clarion call. The likelihood of the revolution is made obvious by Mufundisi's observation of a pervasive, political awareness among black people:

> Let us ask ourselves these burning questions. Can any force stop the prevalent bitterness in youth like Saduva? When even ordinary workers and labourers can organize massive strikes without influence or leadership? Are these not clear and vivid signs of saturation? That boy will never be the same again. Can't the powers that be do something?[57]

The awareness Mufundisi refers to is certainly a result of the politicizing mission of the BCM.

As theatre expressly intended to politicize the public, *Too Late* is as educative as *Survival*. Dealing with underpayment, poverty, robbery, police harassment and the overall frustration in townships, *Too Late* provides its audience with a political discussion of the issues they want to hear. The debasement of black education, in particular, is dramatized at a timely period, since that was one of the crucial grievances that led to the Soweto uprising of 1976; but *Too Late* is not without its limitation. Besides its earnest didacticism, the play's characterization is weak. For a play of its length (about 30 pages), *Too Late* has too many characters (about 30). In Fugard's *Sizwe Bansi Is Dead*, character development is accomplished through case histories and biographical flashback. In *Too Late*, characters appear and rapidly disappear before the reader or the audience has a clear idea of who they are, where they come from and when they are going to appear again. The characters are mere illustrations of the grievances with which the playwright is dealing. The incidents in which the characters take part are themselves so episodic as to confuse, and even bore, the reader or the audience. Gibson Kente is more concerned with the political grievances expressed or dramatized by the various characters than in convincing characterization and organization.

Drama is used as a tool of politicization most obviously in Mthuli Shezi's play, *Shanti*. The author himself was a top official of the BCM, "who had been elected vice-chairman of the Black People's Convention in 1972", but "died six months later after being pushed under a train following an argument with white railway officials over their treatment of some black women passengers."[58]

Shanti is a tendentious play whose concerns range from the assertion of blackness to a flirtation with revolution. The play opens with a rhetorical and querulous song:

> How long shall it be, Lord
> how long must we carry this burden
> how long must we yield?
>
> Will this pain ever cease
> will we ever be free
> will we ever enjoy life?
>
> How long must we bear this pain
> how long must we bear this suffering
> how long must we kneel in prayer?
>
> Do our prayers know the way
> are we praying and working
> are we working and praying
> are we sweating?
>
> But how long will this pain last
> HOW LONG . . . HOW LONG . . . HOW LONG?[59]

There is rage and impatience in this song. A discussion of this kind deals only with words, but the non-verbal elements such as dance and gesture are central to the play's impact. In live performances, a song such as this is intended not only to register protest but to arouse the audience's political emotions. As Kavanagh has put it, in black theatre "tears are brought by prayer and song".[60]

Shanti deals at length with such Black Consciousness issues as racism, black identity, pride and solidarity, but what distinguishes it from other plays of the period is its boldness in portraying a revolutionary situation. Because of the fear of censorship, *Survival* and *Too Late* merely advocate change. Though the black people's will to continue fighting for freedom is emphasized, the notion of revolution itself is never dramatized in those plays.

In *Shanti*, however, revolution is dramatized. Two of the chief characters, Thabo and Themba, escape from prison and head for Mozambique. They run into a group of guerrillas fighting for the liberation of Mozambique. Though Thabo's and Themba's arrival is viewed with suspicion, General Mobu (the guerrillas' leader) agrees to co-opt them into his guerrilla group. The agreement is in line with the BCM's belief in solidarity with other oppressed people, whether in South Africa, other parts of Africa or outside Africa. As General Mobu confidently proclaims after the death of Thabo:

> You all know our aim is to eliminate all prejudice, especially the evil called 'racism' . . . His struggle was our struggle.[61]

Despite the revolutionary zeal that swept South African townships in the 1970s, revolution itself is portrayed in abortive terms in this play. The characters associated with General Mobu and his guerrillas hardly come across as revolutionaries. Themba is a downright sell-out who subsequently defects and gives himself up to the South African police:

> One prisoner, Themba Kuboni, gave himself up to the police at the Messina police station this morning. He related the whole story of how he and a fellow convict, Thabo Mokgethi, came into contact with terrorists on the borders of Mozambique. Kuboni also warned of a notorious attack in the near future. Kuboni made it clear that he never sympathized with the bandits. Kuboni also told the police how he managed to escape pretending he was one of the corpses of the soldiers who were killed by the bandits. Kuboni was previously serving fifteen years for murder. The authorities are considering giving him remission for the valuable information he supplied.[62]

The manner of expression is typical of war communiqués. The guerrillas are pejoratively referred to as "bandits", and the government gives the impression that it is in control.

Unlike Themba, Thabo is portrayed as "committed" to the liberation of his country. The letter Thabo sends to his girlfriend, Shanti, reveals this "commitment":

> I am writing to say that I have since committed myself to the cause of fighting evil, and to make this my occupation. Although this comes as sheer coincidence, I feel it is one chance I cannot let lose. I have seen negotiations and roundtable talks fail. I am convinced that this decision is another way, much as you tend to question it . . . Keep well, my darling, and keep watching the gate for me, for one day I will come carrying a banner of liberation, when racism will be a thing of the past.[63]

Thabo's determination to fight the system sounds strong but his letter shows that the determination is not a result of free will. He became a guerrilla because of his unfavourable circumstances and not out of revolutionary commitment.

Even the much-written-about revolutionary zeal of the 1970s becomes questionable when Thabo suspects that his girlfriend may not approve of his decision. The girlfriend (Shanti) is portrayed as a radical. Because of the fear of censorship, there is throughout Shezi's portrayal of the revolution no connection made between Thabo and the ANC or PAC. These weaknesses and omissions make the revolutionary element in *Shanti* unconvincing and merely rhetorical.

In terms of style, the play is as weak as *Too Late*. It is episodic. Major incidents such as the convicts' escape from prison, the armed confrontation between the soldiers and the guerrillas and the death of Thabo are summarily narrated instead of being dramatized. Transitions from incident to incident are so abrupt as to make the plot of the play sound simplistic.

Drama as a Necessary Instrument of Politicization

Despite the criticisms levelled against the form of the radical theatre of the 1970s, the readers' and audiences' political expectations should be borne in mind. Kavanagh, who took part in the production of some of the plays, has observed that:

> Majority audiences in urban environments generally expect a play to teach, reveal, comment on either moral or political issues. They require a message. They expect the driving force of the play, its cohesion and its strongest channel of communication to be music and dance. They prefer large casts, many and varied narrative emphasis. Playmakers and actors attempt to create plays of this kind usually through a mixture of writing, public not private. Acting is passionate and committed, energetic and heightened.[64]

Because of this predominantly educative mission of radical drama, Kavanagh is of the opinion that the tendency "to dismiss the people's art as crude and unsophisticated . . . should be resisted."[65] This suggestion is directed to what Kavanagh refers to as intellectuals who have lost touch with their roots, the artists who have drifted away.[66] Whether Kavanagh's warning has been heeded or not is not important. In the 1970s radical drama became extremely popular among black people. Like the poetry of the Black Consciousness, the drama proved to be "a cultural weapon" that fostered "unity and solidarity."[67] This solidarity led to widespread political agitation and the students' celebration of the independence of Mozambique in 1974. As mentioned in the previous chapter, the celebration provided the opportunity for police intervention.

The effectiveness of radical drama was further indicated by the fact that a play like *Shanti*

> was considered significant enough to be used as one of the major documentary exhibits in the so-called 'Treason Trial' of 1975. The People's Experimental Theatre was listed as a subversive organization, the leading

practitioners of that theatre group were charged under the Terrorism Act, and one of the charges stated that the accused conspired '. . . to make, produce, publish, or distribute subversive and anti-white utterances, writings, plays, and dramas . . .'.[68]

By 1976, the Soweto uprising had occurred and, given the political role that radical theatre played prior to the uprising, it is only fair to conclude that, like the poetry of Black Consciousness, the theatre helped prepare the schoolchildren and workers for the uprising. In spite of its stylistic weaknesses:

> When evaluated within a broad cultural context this theatre attains significance as a radical counter-cultural theatre . . . Uninterested in finding an elitist audience, this theatre searched for theatrical images rather than literary complexities . . . Aesthetic considerations, at least as they were defined by white standards in literature and theatre were subordinated to political considerations . . . Its themes and techniques cannot be divorced from its function.[69]

The theatre, therefore, was a thoroughly utilitarian and mass-oriented art form whose effectiveness manifested itself in Soweto in 1976.

Notes

1. Robert Mshengu Kavanagh, "After Soweto: People's Theatre and the Political Struggle in South Africa", *Theatre Quarterly*, Vol. 9, No. 33 (Spring 1979) p. 36.
2. International Defence and Aid Fund, "A New Wave of Cultural Energy: Black Theatre in South Africa', *Theatre Quarterly*, Vol. 7, No. 28 (Winter 1977–78) p. 57.
3. Ibid., p. 59.
4. Robert Mshengu Kavanagh, ed., introduction, *South African People's Plays*, p. xiv.
5. Ibid., p. 33.
6. Ibid., p. xv.
7. Harry Bloom, foreword, *King Kong*, p. 14.
8. Ibid., p. 16.
9. Ursula A. Barnett, *A Vision of Order*, p. 234.
10. Kavanagh, *South African People's Plays*, p. xiv.
11. In some cases white producers were seen as taking over black musical plays. Todd Matshikiza, for instance, was afraid that white producers were taking over *King Kong*. See his *Chocolates For My Wife*.
12. Anthony Akerman, "Why Must These Shows Go On? A Critique of Black Musicals Made For White Audiences", *Theatre Quarterly*, Vol. 7, No. 28 (Winter 1977–78) p. 67.
13. *Plays and Players* Plot-Summary of *Kwa Zulu*, quoted in Akerman, p. 68.
14. Ibid.
15. Russell Vandenbroucke, "South African Blacksploitation", *Yale/Theatre*, Vol. 8, No. 1 (Fall 1976) pp. 68–9.
16. S'ketsh' on *Ipi Tombi*, quoted in Akerman, p. 68.

144   *The People's Cause*

17. Among whites, an entrée into sexual voyeurism was frequently offered by "native" life. Nude pictures invariably depicted black women. Ex-"protectorates", such as Botswana, Lesotho and Swaziland were visited by whites for sexual tourism. Lately, however, the casino, *Playboy*, X-rated movies have moved from the ex-"protectorates" to Sun City (the Las Vegas of South Africa) in Boputhatswana.

18. Vandenbroucke, "South African Blacksploitation", p. 69.

19. Jacques Alvarez-Pereyre, "Black Committed Theatre in South Africa", *Commonwealth*, Vol. 7, No. 1 (Autumn 1984) p. 81.

20. Kavanagh, "After Soweto: People's Theatre and the Political Struggle in South Africa", p. 34.

21. Kavanagh, ed., introduction, *South African People's Plays*, p. xiv.

22. Robert Mshengu Kavanagh, "Tradition and Innovation in the Theatre of Workshop '71", *Theatre Quarterly*, Vol. 7, No. 28 (Winter 77–78) p. 66.

23. Credo Mutwa, *uNosilimela*, *South African People's Plays*, (ed.) Robert Mshengu Kavanagh, p. 6.

24. Ibid.

25. Ibid., p. 24.

26. Ibid., p. 27.

27. Ibid., p. 57.

28. Ibid., p. 34.

29. Ibid., p. 51.

30. T. S. Eliot, "Tradition and the Individual Talent", *Selected Essays*, p. 15.

31. Ibid., p. 14.

32. Kavanagh, "Tradition and Innovation in the Theatre of Workshop '71", p. 64.

33. Hilary Seymour, "*Sizwe Bansi Is Dead*: A Study of Artistic Ambivalence", *Race and Class*, Vol. 21, No. 3 (Winter 1980) p. 277.

34. Seymour, p. 279.

35. Athol Fugard, *Sizwe Bansi Is Dead*, *Statements*, p. 7.

36. Ibid., p. 9.

37. Derek Cohen, "Drama and the Police State: Athol Fugard's South Africa", *Commonwealth Drama*, Vol. 6, No. 1 (Spring 1980) p. 159.

38. Seymour, p. 280.

39. Ibid.

40. Winston Ntshona, interview, "Art is Life, Life is Art", African Activist Association and Ufahamu, *Ufahamu*, Vol. 6, No. 2 (1976) p. 8.

41. Seymour, p. 287.

42. Fugard, pp. 36 and 38.

43. Ibid., p. 38.

44. Alex La Guma, *A Walk in the Night*, p. 28.

45. Fugard, p. 42.

46. Ngugi wa Thiong'o, *Petals of Blood*, p. 294.

47. Patrick O'Sheel, "Athol Fugard's 'Poor Theatre'", *Journal of Commonwealth Literature*, Vol. 12, No. 3 (1978), p. 72.

48. Dennis Brutus, *A Simple Lust*, p. 4.

49. Ted E. Boyle, *Brendan Behan*, p. 72.

50. Workshop '71, *Survival*, *South African People's Plays*, (ed.) Robert Mshengu Kavanagh, p. 131.

51. Ibid., p. 170.

52. Ibid.

53. Ibid.

54. Kavanagh, ed., introduction, *South African People's Plays*, p. xxvi.

55. Gibson Kente, *Too Late*, *South African People's Plays*, (ed.) Robert Mshengu Kavanagh, p. 123.

56. Ibid., p. 122.

57. Ibid., p. 123.

58. International Defence and Aid Fund, p. 61.

59. Mthuli Shezi, *Shanti*, *South African People's Plays*, (ed.) Robert Mshengu Kavanagh, p. 68.

60. Kavanagh, ed., introduction, *South African People's Plays*, p. xxx.

61. Shezi, p. 82.

62. Ibid., p. 83.

63. Ibid., pp. 82–3.

64. Kavanagh, ed., introduction, *South African People's Plays*, p. xxx.

65. Ibid.

66. Ibid.

67. Alvarez-Pereyre, "Black Committed Theatre in South Africa", p. 80.

68. Attorney-General's report and charge sheets, 1975, quoted in Ian Steadman, "Alternative Politics, Alternative Performance: 1976 and Black South African Theatre", *Momentum*, eds., M. J. Daymond, J. U. Jacobs, Margaret Lenta, p. 22.

69. Steadman, pp. 218 and 220.

7. Recent Trends in Black Writing

When asked what direction black South African poets would take in the 1980s, Mongane Serote answered: "What direction does the liberation struggle take in the 1980s? That is the direction of the black South African poet."[1] Besides demonstrating that black writing is seen as part of the struggle for freedom, Serote's response implies that protest in black writing varies from period to period depending on the changing political landscape. Serote's committed attitude may also be applicable to prose writers and playwrights.[2] From the times of Solomon T. Plaatje to the present, black writers have shown that the nature of the political demand in their writings is fundamentally the same, but its form varies from writer to writer.

While the political influence of literature was not particularly clear cut (in terms of action) in the 1950s and early 1960s, in the 1970s the correlation between writing and political action became obvious. The township poetry and drama that dominated the decade led to township uprising, and Soweto 1976 marked the climax of this continuing relationship between writing and politics. In this concluding chapter I propose to sketch briefly what has happened in literature since Soweto.

After Soweto: "New" Trends in Black Writing

Two dominant literary trends have determined the shape of black writing after Soweto. There is a continuing tradition of resistance poetry, drama and a little fiction growing out of the Soweto experience. The common elements are the rising itself, the role of the children in the vanguard of the resistance, and the affirmation of black people's unfaltering will to survive in the face of unrelieved suffering.

The other trend involves writers and critics who are seeking to create new insights[3] in black writing. These writers and critics feel that the descriptive protest against apartheid has become an overworked, and correspondingly less engaging, undertaking. They are asking for a kind of writing that transcends the advocacy of mass action and recording of mass suffering. Putting a higher premium on form rather than content, these writers and critics espouse symbolic and subtle political writing rather that direct, descriptive protest.

   In its portrayal of resistance, poetry has generally continued to be as direct as it was during the heyday of the Black Consciousness Movement. While the emphasis on issues such as black identity, pride and dignity has dwindled, contemporary poetry still displays anger, assertiveness, defiance and unflagging support for the political struggle. The poetry itself falls into certain stock conventions. Black people are generally seen as heroic. In some of the poems that portray the mood of the Soweto uprising, the motifs of schoolchildren as revolutionaries and as victims of the brutality of the system are common. In "Azanian Love Song", Don Mattera depicts the boldness and heroic defiance of the children:

> The Child has risen and walks defiantly
> towards the lion's lair undaunted,
> unafraid . . .[4]

   A similar heroic convention obtains in Mazisi Kunene's poem, "The Rise of the Angry Generation", where the children's courage and strength are praised in unstinting terms:

> . . . The once proud planet shrieks in terror
> Opening a vast space for the mysterious
>   young bird.
> For the merciless talons of the new generation
> They who are not deterred by false tears
> Who do not turn away from the fire
> They are the children of iron
> They are the fearless bees of the night
> They are the wrath of the volcanic mountains
> They are the abiding anger of the Ancestral
>   Forefathers.[5]

   The effects of the confrontation between the schoolchildren and the police are frequently discussed after Soweto. In Dennis Brutus's "There was a Girl", the thoughtless brutality of the police who butcher a little girl is made poignant by the poet's juxtaposition of the senseless murder with the girl's innocent participation in the uprising:

> There was a girl
> eight years old they say
> her hair in spiky braids
> her innocent fist raised in imitation
> Afterwards, there was a mass of red
> some torn pieces of meat
> and bright rags fluttering:
> a girl in a print dress, once, they say.[6]

Here, Brutus is lamenting human waste rather than merely praising the girl's "courage" in facing the police. The angry, defiant assertiveness in Mattera's

"Azanian Love Song" is missing in the poem and yet Brutus's gruesome and regretful depiction of the incident is a way of criticizing the system's callous and indiscriminate acts.

In Mattera's "No Children . . ." countless children have been killed, maimed and prematurely jailed. Instead of seeing children playing in the streets, one sees the state's symbols of repression, "hippos" (police armoured personnel carriers) and "guns" stalking "the silent streets":

> There are no children
>   Hippos, guns still stalk
>   The silent streets;
>   Blood, pain
>   Nurture an uncaring anger
> No children in Soweto,
>   Langa
>   Mannenberg,
> Not a child left in Sharpeville . . .
> Dead
> Jailed
> Crippled
> Blinded
> Tortured, yes
> The children have all become men.[7]

Heroic defiance has given way to pervasive vulnerability. Mattera's poem is angry. By bringing together the various places where blacks clashed with the police, he establishes the repressive trajectory of the system. Recent killings at Uitenhage and other townships indicate the seemingly inexhaustible growth of the list of massacre-locations.

Mongane Serote who, in his poetry of the late 1960s and early 1970s, advocated peaceful negotiation, writes in favour of revolution in the late 1970s and early 1980s. In his long poem, "Behold Mama, Flowers", Serote clearly anticipates his participation in a coming revolutionary storm:

> that my blood be cooked in the red blood of tigers
> that one day when the storm comes and tears my
> roots out you could say.
> he went because he had to go
> the African soil
> listen
> that this day
> held tight by a trembling dawn
> its sun held in a nightmare of birth
> like a woman sprawled leaving bloodstains on the
> sheet . . .[8]

The possibility of Serote dying in the anticipated struggle is rhetorically accepted. In "Time Has Run Out", his belief that the system's oppression and brutality can be countered only by fighting back is even more explicit:

> . . . my countrymen, can someone who understands that it is now too late,
> who knows that exploitation and oppression are brains which, being insane,
> only know how to make violence; can someone teach us how to mount the
> wound, the fight.[9]

Declamatory in tone, Serote's style in this poem is more prosaic than poetic.
Unlike Matthews and Mattera, Serote shows no zest for violent politics.
Political violence itself (as opposed to township thuggery) is portrayed as a
practice to which blacks are not accustomed; yet it is needed. Although the
poem betrays a sense of frustration and desperation, Serote is hopeful that one
day freedom may be achieved. Towards the end of "Behold Mama, Flowers",
this inevitable attainment of freedom is symbolized by flowers blooming.[10]

While he consistently advocates heroic resistance, Njabulo Ndebele does not
express belief in revolutionary politics. In "The Revolution of the Aged", his
protagonist condemns Soweto youths for revolutionary idealism and ill-timed
action:

> I have listened too
> to the condemnations of the young
> who burned with scorn,
> > loaded with revolutionary maxims
> > hot for quick results.
>
> . . . do not eat an unripe apple
> its bitterness is a tingling knife.
> suffer yourself to wait
> and the ripeness will come
> and the apple will fall down at your feet.[11]

These two stanzas are more forceful than the one quoted above. Ndebele's
"circumspect" but gradualist approach is clearer in the second part of his
poem:

> grey hair has placed on my brow
> the verdict of wisdom and the skin-folds of age
> bear tales wooled in the truth of proverbs:
> if you cannot master the wind,
> flow with it
> letting know all the time that you are resisting.
> that is how I have lived
> quietly
> swallowing both the fresh and foul
> from the mouth of my masters;
> yet I watched and listened.[12]

While this approach to the South African problem is part of an impassioned
reaction to pain and violence, one wonders how soon the "ripeness will come"

and when "the apple will fall down". Since Sharpeville, blacks have found a combination of the kind of resistance Ndebele advocates, and revolutionary activity to be more appealing. Bonisile Joshua Motaung, for example, vividly depicts the frustrating circumstances that prompts blacks to use violent means:

> So long we've been
> > friendly and patient
> > looking to the day when
> the trumpet of the Lord
> > shall sound
> > 'ABOUT TURN'
> > > and
> the first be the last
> > the bottom, the top
> > and lowly, the worldly.
> We, the silent majority
> > freedom disappears like a mirage
> > as we come.
> Our song is now hummed
> > for it's been sung too long.
> > We fail to cry
> > for tears we've lost
> > > we are guests to death
> > > strangers to life.[13]

Gradualist politics are shown to be ineffective in this poem. The last stanza could refer to death perpetrated by the system, or the acceptance of a bloody armed struggle by blacks themselves.

Much contemporary poetry, therefore, continues to be a vehicle of the struggle. As in the case of Black Consciousness poetry, much of this recent poetry is merely politics disguised as poetry. Despite its political preoccupations, however, poems by, for example, Njabulo Ndebele, Mongane Serote and Mandlenkosi Langa are conceived as poetry and not merely as political statement.

Fiction is, probably, the genre which has undergone the most significant stylistic shifts since Soweto. The direct style of the 1950s and early 1960s has become less pronounced. Among the works which demonstrate this stylistic change is Serote's novel, *To Every Birth Its Blood*. Set in Alexandra, outside white Johannesburg, the novel deals with the familiar themes of township life, political sabotage and exile. The content sounds similar to that of the short stories and autobiographies of the 1950s and 1960s, Peter Abrahams's novel, *A Night of Their Own* and Alex La Guma's *In the Fog of the Season's End*.

What distinguishes *To Every Birth Its Blood* from these early writings, however, is the novel's uniquely dispassionate portrayal of underground political activity and the harassment of blacks by the police. The revolution that Serote anticipates in his poem, "Behold Mama, Flowers" is realized in the second part of the novel. The suffering, frustration, desperation and despair that dominates the first part of the novel give way to the ever-growing influence of a political organization simply referred to as the Movement. Although the role of the collective is emphasized in relation to the activities of the Movement, Serote's method, unlike that of La Guma's *In the Fog*, is conventional:

> Like an old tree the Movement spread and spread its roots. It entrenches itself in the soil, issuing root after root, to spread and spread and spread. Some roots end up on rocks, baking in the sun. Some end up in sand. The roots spread and spread and spread. The tall tree, spreading its branches all around, gives shade to the weary.[14]

In other sections of the book, the extensive influence of the Movement is compared to the wind and the sea. This all-embracing imagery and symbolism has much to do with Serote's background as a poet. In Abrahams's *A Night of Their Own* and La Guma's *In the Fog*, language is descriptive rather than poetic.

Serote does not romanticize revolution. Death in the struggle is portrayed in a calm and humane manner. Two of the outstanding members of the Movement, Oupa (the protagonist's nephew) and Mandla, are captured and killed. The protagonist's attitude to their deaths, particularly to that of Oupa, is credible, moving and unsensationalized.

> I thought of Mary at the graveside. She held my mother's hand as she stood there, looking into the hole where her boy lay, now lifeless in a box, even in death hammering out a truth to us as we stood there, that a new chapter was finally being added to the history of our country. It was being written in the ink of life and death. It was being written that way because, as soon as they were born, the children died. They died before they could handle their cocks correctly for peeing. They died. They died, not having known that there was something called life.[15]

Towards the end of the novel, the protagonist leaves South Africa for Botswana. He has hope for the future of blacks inside South Africa although the Movement has been partly fragmented. The novel ends with the birth of a child, which – as in La Guma's *In the Fog* – symbolizes an optimistic future. Whereas La Guma's novel closes with an overt proclamation of impending, full-scale armed struggle, Serote's *To Every Birth Its Blood* ends with implied endorsement of the struggle.

The change from explicit, exhortatory protest to implicit criticism in the works of writers who are asking for something more than the advocacy of mass action and the recording of mass suffering is much more pronounced. The nature of the shift recalls Lewis Nkosi's complaint about the general method of black fiction writers in the 1950s and early 1960s:

> What we do get from South Africa – and what we get most frequently – is the journalistic fact parading outrageously as imaginative literature. We find here a type of fiction which exploits the ready-made plots of racial violence, social apartheid, interracial love affairs which are doomed from the beginning, without any attempt to transcend or transmute these given "social facts" into artistically persuasive works of fiction.[16]

The crux of Nkosi's argument is that black South African writers, instead of creating, tell, preach, chronicle and dwell too much on apartheid literature's well-worked themes. While Nkosi is concerned with the problem of how to write, a great number of black South African writers are concerned with what to write about. Recently, another black South African has advanced an argument similar to that of Nkosi. Njabulo Ndebele argues that to be intellectually engaging, contemporary black writing must go beyond mere description:

> It seems to me that a large part of the African resistance to the evil of apartheid has until recently, consisted of a largely descriptive documentation of suffering. And the bulk of the fiction, through an almost total concern with the political theme, has in following this tradition, largely documented rather than explained. Not that the political theme itself was not valid, on the contrary it is worth exploring almost as a duty. It was the manner of its treatment that became the subject of increasing dissatisfaction to me.
>
> I came to the realization, mainly through the actual grappling with the form of fiction, that our literature ought to seek to move away from an easy pre-occupation with demonstrating the obvious existence of oppression.[17]

While Ndebele's argument is cogent and instructive, it overlooks the fact that the descriptive writers of earlier decades, especially those of the 1960s and 1970s, were not satisfied with merely describing blacks' political situation; they expressly set out to teach both the common man and the intellectual. These writers proved to be extremely effective in creating both a changed mood and the political action that accompanied the change. The method that Ndebele advocates is what "literature" needs, but as long as blacks continue to expect literature to play a role in their struggle there will be controversy over what form writers should use.

Ndebele seems to have made his choice. His recent collection of stories, *Fools and Other Stories*, combines both explicit and implicit comment. The content of the stories, particularly that of "Fools", is similar to that of the short stories of the 1950s. Social, economic and political concerns are revealed through various forms of township experience.

In "Fools", the sections are explicit which deal with what Ndebele considers to be black writers' over-preoccupation with oppression. Talking to Zamani's wife about his experiences as a student outside the country, Zani says:

> But that was not all. Before we could be fully accepted, we had to "submit to Party discipline" by reading secret books which would make us committed scientists, so that we could appreciate even more who we were going to be working for. We started reading books about revolution. It was fascinating: Ghana, Russia, Cuba, China, Guinea, Algeria. And we ended up spending more and more time discussing politics and philosophy and less and less science. I look back now and say what a pity. Deep down in me I still want to be a scientist.
>
> But I learnt one lesson out of all this. It is that we should have stuck to our

science. You see, too much obsession with removing oppression in the political dimension, soon becomes in itself a form of oppression. Especially if everybody is expected to demonstrate his concern somehow. And then mostly all it calls for is that you thrust an angry fist into the air. Somewhere along the line, I feel, the varied richness of life is lost sight of and so is the fact that every aspect of life, if it can be creatively indulged in, is the weapon of life itself against the greatest tyranny.[18]

Ndebele's method here is not only critical of the way the black South African revolution is prosecuted, it is also heavily didactic. The second paragraph is the more revealing in its caveat against what Ndebele deems to be a political monomania among black people. Later, Ndebele's criticism assumes philosophical proportions:

The obviousness of analysis! A mind given completely to a preoccupation with an unyieldingly powerful, unabating negation, is soon debased by the repeated sameness of its findings. And in the absence of any other engaging mental challenges, its perceptions of viable alternatives become hopelessly constricted.[19]

Ndebele's subtle protest against the system appears towards the end of the story where the two protagonists, Zani and Zamani attempt to "break up a picnic on the Day of Convenant, Commemorating December 16, 1838, the day the Boers killed thousands of Black South Africans and dethroned their ruler, King Dingane."[20] As blacks enter the picnic grounds, a Boer appears and picks a quarrel with Zani. An ugly situation ensues in which the angry Boer lashes at any black person in his way with a whip. The symbolic significance of the episode is revealed when Zamani, the school teacher, shows typically heroic, unflinching endurance as the Boer madly lashes at him:

The Boer came at me again and again, his face so red that it seemed to have become the very blood he wanted to draw out of me. He did not look at me any more; he knew where I was. He looked only at the ground, at his feet, beating down the grass around him, to leave a small path of clearing as a sign of the futility of his battleground. He seemed to grow smaller and smaller the more he came at me. Then I felt totally numb. My mind had shut out all the pain. And, for the third time in about two weeks, I felt in the depths of me, the beginning of the kind of laughter that seemed to explain everything. And when the sound of laughter came out, it filled my ears, shutting out the pain ever further. It seemed to fill out the sky like a pounding drum. And that is when the Boer started weeping. And he seemed to weep louder, the fainter the power of his lashing became.

The blows stopped; and I knew I had crushed him. I had crushed him with the sheer force of my presence. I was there, and would be there to the end of time; a perpetual symbol of his failure to have a world without me. And he walked away to his car, a man without a shadow. The sun couldn't see him. And the sound of his car when he drove away seemed so irrelevant.[21]

Ndebele's calm portrayal of heroic and passive resistance in this episode is probably one of the most effective in black writing. Yet there is a built-in problem regarding his characters' level of political consciousness and the kind of resistance they embody. Zani who, of all Ndebele's "fools", is the most "politically aware", comes across as an incautious idealist. His attempts at politicizing Zamani's young, primary school pupils sounds naive and politically immature. Although his idea of breaking up the picnic is seen as noble, the act itself is ill-planned. Zamani, who hesitantly supports the idea, is a blind fellow-traveller. Despite the fact that he is the central character in the symbolic episode cited above, Zamani's politics are riddled with indecision and sometimes utter confusion. His decision to take part in breaking up the picnic is a result of compassion for Zani and not political commitment. The principal of Zamani's school (who has organized the picnic) is a shameless fifth-columnist, caring only about his own importance. The picnickers themselves are portrayed as a group of hedonists whose sole concerns are drinking, dancing and love-making rather than the political boycott Zani is advocating.

Since Ndebele is aware of the flaws of his characters, one can only conclude that, like his poem, "The Revolution of the Aged", "Fools" is a story that deliberately sets out to celebrate passive, anti-revolutionary resistance. "The veiled symbolism of this episode [the one quoted above] is clear: apartheid will wear itself out in the end",[22] M.N. concludes. But how long will that take? Fortitude alone can never make white South Africans relinquish political power. The society Ndebele depicts is in desperate need not only of political awakening, but also of a more effective form of resistance.

Indians have recently received unusual prominence in the politics and literature of South Africa. Together with "coloureds", the system has co-opted them into the political mainstream by offering them special "houses" in the parliament.[23] In the field of literature, a writer like Ahmed Essop has come to the forefront of black writing. As in the case of most of the writings discussed in this chapter, Essop's works appear after Soweto but they are not influenced by the experience and – except for *The Emperor* (1984) – reflect an earlier world.

Like Ndebele, Essop uses the implicit style in his writings. Essop's collection of short stories, *The Hajji and Other Stories*, and his novella, *The Visitation*, are set in a township of Johannesburg. The stories and the novella reflect the social, political, economic and religious life of an Indian community.

In "The Hajji", Essop portrays how the harmful influence of apartheid creates social divisions among the residents of the community. The protagonist of the story, Hassen, alienates himself from his brother Karim because the latter cohabits with a white woman: "When his brother had crossed the colour line, he had severed his family ties."[24] Hassen's fundamentalist respect for the purity of his religion at the expense of visiting his sick brother is made to look ridiculous. After Karim's death, Hassen suffers an immense sense of guilt, shame and loss as outsiders drive by on their way to bury his brother in his absence.

In "The Commandment", the disruptive effects of apartheid policies are dramatized in a more moving manner. Moses, an old black man who has worked among Indians for a long time, is suddenly driven almost insane by the threat of forced removal from the Indian community to a "homeland". When Moses begins to behave oddly the alienation between him and the Indian community hardens.

> During the final week Moses no longer slept but paced all night in the yard, talking, talking, and sometimes banging on a tin drum until our nerves became brittle. And then a queer thing happened to us. We began to hate him . . . Suddenly everyone avoided him and the children were sternly told not to go near him.[25]

Moses's desperation is graphically portrayed, and his rejection by the community is criticized in the most ironic terms. The fact that the same community liked Moses when he was a young and strong worker makes his expulsion from Fordsburg more demeaning to all.

At the end of the story, Moses accepts his predicament in a manner that shows Essop's mastery of irony:

> "I am going to my homeland", he went on and on. "I am going to see my chief and all my people. There are cities there! There are parks there! There are hospitals there! And there are no cemeteries there!"
>
> When the police arrived on the appointed day they found Moses – hanging from a roof-beam in a lavatory in the yard.[26]

On the worldly level, Essop's paradoxical representation of "homelands" intensifies their barrenness and tedious nature. Because of the ever-present poverty and disease, death is the order of the day. On a religious level, however, Moses's "homeland" may be taken to be a "heavenly homeland" where his spirit hopes to ascend after committing suicide. There, Moses believes, problems of racialism, suffering and death are non-existent.

A great deal of the content of Essop's writings has striking similarities with that of the black writings of the 1950s. As Rowland Smith has put it:

> The predominant flavour of the collection (*The Hajji and Other Stories*) is that of Fordsburg and Vrededorp, however, small oriental slums sandwiched between white working-class areas and coloured properties, all close to the city centre. Racial mixing both voluntary and involuntary is still possible in Essop's Fordsburg and the ebullience of its crowded courtyards, shops and fruit-filled cafes is part of the pre-Sharpeville aura of South African life. The mixture of gangsters, religious cranks, easy girls, roving males and the occasional white intellectual – all of whom are to be found in the stories – recalls the mood of black short fiction of the fifties, originating in *Drum* magazine and set in Sophiatown, the vibrant black slum close to downtown Johannesburg . . .[27]

While these concerns are introduced in the short stories, some of them are treated in greater detail in Essop's novella, *The Visitation*, which revolves around the misfortune of a gullible tycoon called Sufi. Sufi is an exploiter whose wealth mainly rests on the exorbitant rent he collects from his tenants. He has surrounded himself with several concubines whom he exploits sexually. The society in which Sufi lives has, however, been brutalized by the economic deprivation perpetrated by the system. The less privileged members of the society, particularly gangsters, live by sponging on the rich, and Sufi is their chief target. The leader of the gangsters is Gool, a determined and merciless leech.

Compared to the short stories, *The Visitation* is a less accomplished piece of writing. Both Gool's parasitic exploitation of Sufi and the latter's gullibility are overstated. The exaggeration is probably meant to achieve a satirical effect but ultimately the characters become incredible. Essop succeeds in exposing the corrupt nature of the residents of Fordsburg. Everybody in the novella (including gangsters, religious officials, journalists, sports people and lawyers) swindles Sufi at one time or another. The police and the entire legal leadership are portrayed as venal officials who collaborate with Gool in extracting money from Sufi: "'. . . the Captain expects a reward',," and "'We must remember he carries out orders', Gool said, 'There are others, his superiors. Even the magistrate'."[28]

Essop's treatment of the weaknesses of the legal personnel here is as funny as his depiction of Gool and Sufi. The decadence and degeneration in the novella are made more poignant by Essop's paradoxical and satirical use of the image of lamps. The lamps that Gool steals and gives to Sufi are supposed to provide the latter with light; instead, Sufi's life is fraught with darkness and frustration. In addition to his dwindling fortunes, Sufi's harem deserts him, and his daughter, Fawzia, is made pregnant and abandoned by Adil, a pseudo-journalist. Towards the end of the novella, Sufi's financial loss reaches a nadir. Through the power of Gool and the cunning of a lawyer, he is persuaded to sell his property in Fordsburg and buy land in Elysia, a segregated area to which Indians are to be moved. This section not only demonstrates Sufi's final financial collapse, but shows Gool's and the lawyer's lack of concern about the politics that affect their community; they capitalize on the imminent forced removal of their community. It is implied that part of the money from the sale of Sufi's property goes to Gool and the lawyer.

In style, *The Visitation* is less oblique than *The Hajji and Other Stories*. For instance, authorial commentary on the parallel between Sufi's exploitative attitude towards his tenants and concubines and the parasitical chicanery of Gool and his lackeys is direct. In most instances where Sufi is gulled, however, Essop's satiric humour is very effective. By the end of the novella, humour gives way to the serious and compassionate treatment of a family that has fallen victim to an opportunistic and corrupt world.

With the exception of politically explicit works such as Mbulelo Mzamane's *The Children of Soweto*, Miriam Tlali's *Amandla* and Sipho Sepamla's *A Ride on the Whirlwind*, much contemporary prose is oblique in its criticism of the system. In addition to the works already discussed, many of the short stories in Mothobi Mutloatse's *South Africa: Contemporary Writings* portray the black South African situation in an equally dispassionate manner. Since the politically active period of the 1970s, however, black South Africans have been accustomed to literature that expresses a direct political message and teaches. The indirect approach of recent prose writings has tended to make them less influential politically than poetry and drama; in addition prose fiction produced in the 1970s and early 1980s is minimal compared to the quantity of poetry and drama. Since the emergence of the BCM, poetry and drama have been deemed more effective media for politicization than have prose writings. This fact has recently been stressed by Oswald Mtshali:

> In the near future I do not foresee any novelist coming out of South Africa because the urgency of the situation does not allow time to sit down and pen a lengthy piece of writing as demanded by a novel. Another factor against a novel is that poetry, music and drama can be shared with many other people at the same time. But a novel can only be read alone.[29]

Although not new, Mtshali's argument is correct. With the exception of Mongane Serote's *To Every Birth Its Blood*, no significant novel by a black writer has appeared since Soweto.

Drama remains the most popular mode of political expression. Its message continues to be as direct as it was during the Black Consciousness days. The broad symbolism, passion, absurdity and satire that some of the plays employ seem to suit both the political situation and the revolutionary aims of theatre. Matsemela Manaka is one playwright who uses this method in *Egoli (City of Gold)*.

The city of gold is, of course, Johannesburg. The plot of the play hinges on the reminiscences and activities of two mine-workers, John and Hamilton. Both were prisoners in the same prison, escaped together and, as the play opens, are both mine-workers sharing a tiny room on the gold reef.

The mood of the play manifests itself as soon as it begins, with the room John and Hamilton share hung about with their helmets, gumboots, headlamps and webbing belts. The stage set is without walls and doors, and the small audience (about 200) sits around the acting area. This arrangement is probably intended to bring a sense of immediacy to the audience, enabling them to feel they too, are acting out the experiences of their daily lives.

Egoli deals with many issues discussed in earlier chapters, but its symbolic treatment of oppression warrants discussion. Like Athol Fugard's *Sizwe Bansi Is Dead*, *Egoli*'s most effective passages are reminiscences. John and Hamilton recall the time when they were prisoners. As the two characters appear on stage (in Act Two), they are chained together.

> In performance, the chain becomes a powerful metaphor: the condition of black workers in South Africa is tantamount to slave labour, the chain signifies the inextricable partnership of all blacks against the forces of oppression, and the breaking of the chain is the goal of all workers.[30]

As he attempts to break John's chain, Hamilton lectures his colleague on the need to be free:

You talk about 'care' as if you know how to look after your freedom. I am trying to cut these chains that curse your manhood. Chains that rust your brains. And you are busy talking about death. Stop telling me about killing you. God created man, but not for man to kill another man. Yet man suppresses man. He executes terrible laws that persecute and crucify another man.[31]

Hamilton's words express determination and confidence. The suppression about which he philosophizes applies not only in South Africa but throughout the world.

To break the chains of oppression in South Africa, *Egoli* endorses revolution:

> The work is great
> The work of liberation
> Mandela needs soldiers
> Soldiers of liberation.
>
> Soldiers, soldiers.[32]

At the end of the play, the revolutionary option is reiterated in an exhortatory and militant manner:

> For justice, freedom and peace to prevail in the country of our forefathers, we shall all have to stand up and face the enemy without fear. We shall all have to worship the spear and drink blood from the calabash until we all sing the same song.
> – 'Uhuru'.[33]

Although the message is overtly prescriptive, its impact is immense, and the accompaniment of political songs augments the electric atmosphere. The moment that Hamilton succeeds in breaking John's chain marks the climax of the play. As Ian Steadman has put it:

> In the central climactic scene of the play, when the chain is broken to the accompanying rhythms of a popular freedom song, Manaka's theatre succeeds in evoking from black members of the audience participating exclamations and salutes of recognition.[34]

In spite of its earnest didacticism, Manaka's *Egoli* is a powerful play. The images, flashbacks and revealing actions of the characters all contribute to the play's overall effect. *Egoli* was banned the same year that it was published, 1980.

Woza Albert is another comparatively recent play which, unlike *Egoli*, is still allowed to be performed inside the country. According to Akua Rugg who saw *Woza Albert* being performed:

> The play is short and deals with the basic economic, social and political structures of the system. There is much repetition of material, with characters and events rehearsing twin themes of repression and resistance. It

is comprehensive in scope; pass laws, the so-called black homelands, persecution of political dissidents and the continuous history of black rebellion from the days of the Zulu warrior kingdoms to the present are described in detail.[35]

The play also satirically exposes the hypocritical manner in which such issues as brotherhood and Christianity are viewed in South Africa. Mtwa and Ngema, who are the actors and co-authors of the play, incorporate the allegorical Second Coming of Jesus Christ (Morena) to demonstrate that, because of his advocacy of brotherhood and equality among people, "if Jesus Christ chose South Africa for his Second Coming, he would be arrested and taken to Robben Island".[36]

As in the case of Kumalo's poem, "The Spirit of Bambatha", *Woza Albert* ends with an invocation of the dead heroes of the South African struggle such as Albert Luthuli (after whom the play is named), Robert Sobukwe, Lilian Ngoyi, Steven Biko, Bram Fischer, Ruth First, Griffith Mxenge and Hector Peterson. The multiracial nature of the list shows that both black and white have died for the liberation of South Africa. The call for resurrection of the heroes has a direct bearing on the play's title, which means "Come Back Albert". Even more important, the resurrection is meant to provide the masses with the incentive to keep the revolution going.

Woza Albert is as politically charged as *Egoli*. White officials and values are ridiculed. Although parts of the play may sound inappropriately lighthearted, much of the humour comes from black people's endurance, the will to survive in a harsh environment.[37] *Woza Albert* fits into the category of contemporary drama in which symbolism, allegory and satire play a greater role in the criticism of the system than plain political statement (characteristic of the plays of the Black Consciousness period).

Stylistic and Thematic Parallels in Athol Fugard's Drama

Athol Fugard, whose play, *Sizwe Bansi Is Dead*, influenced radical black theatre in the early 1970s, must be referred to at this point. I shall briefly discuss two of his plays later to shed more light on the focus of my topic rather than deal with them as a topic in themselves. Although published in the early 1980s, Fugard's *"Master Harold" ... and the boys* (subsequently referred to as *"Master Harold"*) and *A Lesson from Aloes* deal respectively with the politics of the 1950s and the 1960s. Like *Egoli* and *Woza Albert*, both of Fugard's plays make extensive use of symbolism to convey their message.

"Master Harold" explores a racial theme whereby the possibility of a genuine relationship between Hally, a white character who plays the role of "Master Harold" and two black servants, Sam and Willie, is hinted at, destroyed and left an unrealized possibility at the end of the play. To demonstrate the lack of racial harmony, Fugard consistently employs the metaphor of ballroom dancing:

. . . we're bumping into each other all the time. Look at the three of us this afternoon: I've bumped into Willie, the two of us have bumped into you, you've bumped into your mother, she bumping into your Dad.

. . . None of us knows the steps and there's no music playing. And it doesn't stop with us. The whole world is doing it all the time. Open a newspaper and what do you read? America has bumped into Russia, England is bumping into India, rich man bumps into poor man. Those are big collisions, Hally. They make for a lot of bruises. People get hurt in all that bumping, and we're sick and tired of it now. It's been going on for too long. Are we never going to get it right? . . . Learn to dance life like champions instead of always being just a bunch of beginners at it?[38]

This passage is more explicatory and less optimistic than those in Fugard's former plays. The disharmony of which Sam complains exists not only in South Africa but throughout the world, and this disharmony is not only racial but also economic and ideological.

As the play progresses, the possibility of the harmony that Fugard advocates is bedevilled by the worsening domestic situation in Hally's family where Sam and Willie work. Hally and his crippled, sick father are not on good terms. Sam's attempt to persuade Hally to be more sympathetic and respectful towards his father leads to the final collapse of the possibility of inter-racial friendship between Hally and the two black servants. Sam's anger at Hally and the latter intentionally sitting on a "whites only" bench in the park, symbolize the continuing estrangement between black and white in the play. The possibility of improving the relationship is, however, left open and symbolized by Sam's anticipation of favourable "weather" in future.

A Lesson From Aloes deals with characters emerging from the Sharpeville emergency. Because of police repression and lack of mutual trust, the play's chief characters, Piet, Gladys (whites) and Steve (a "coloured") have been compelled to keep away from politics. Steve is about to leave for England, Piet has become a recluse with the strange hobby of keeping aloes, and Gladys is on her way to a mental hospital. In spite of the unfavourable circumstances, Fugard, in stressing the will to survive uses the image of aloes as a metaphor:

Aloes are distinguished above all else for their inordinate capacity for survival in the harshest of possible environments. In writing this play, I have at one level tried to examine and question the possibility and nature of survival in a country for which "drought", with its harsh and relentless resonances, is a very apt metaphor.[39]

The question of the white character surviving the situation is new to Fugard. Piet is as indigenous as the aloes. On a wider scale, however, the aloes symbolize the will to survive among the oppressed and repressed people of South Africa. To that extent, *A Lesson From Aloes* has affinities with Fugard's own play, *Sizwe Bansi Is Dead*, Mtwa's and Ngema's *Woza Albert* and Workshop '71's *Survival*, all of which, among other concerns, trace the theme of survival.

In its political message, *A Lesson From Aloes* is as direct as *"Master Harold"*. The flashbacks and biographical information that contribute to the oblique style in *Sizwe Bansi Is Dead* are not found in Fugard's latest plays. In their place, the metaphors he uses in both plays are suggestive and effective. Despite the political themes in plays such as *"Master Harold"* and *A Lesson From Aloes*, Fugard's reticence about writing mass-oriented theatre has been severely criticized by committed critics.[40]

Conclusion

With the increasing complexity of the South African political landscape, the correlation between writing and politics will continue to exist. Repressive phases similar to Sharpeville, Soweto and the recent state of emergency will always be there (if the political system remains unchanged) but all they can achieve is to prompt the banning of a few "politically sensitive" books and not halt black South African writing altogether. The repression that followed the Soweto uprising disrupted the BCM and its political projects but at present new political organizations like the UDF and AZAPO, which are as militant as the BCM, continue to spread their political message through direct statement and the performance of poetry and theatre. A politically charged play such as *Woza Albert*, for instance, may still be performed in South Africa.

Black writing has also been given a boost by the national recognition it has received from literary critics and scholars inside the country. Although South African literature in general continues to be discussed in terms of various racial rubrics ("white literature in English", "white literature in Afrikaans", "black literature in English" and "black literature in the vernacular"), literary critics and scholars have recently attempted to bring some of these different strands together in both conferences and publications. These attempts seem to have been most successful in the field of criticism where writing both by blacks and whites has either been discussed or printed side by side. As evidenced by some of the recent publications (Michael Chapman's *Soweto Poetry* and M. J. Daymond *et al's Momentum*) these discussions mainly focus on the issue of political commitment. Although black and white writers hold different views on this issue, such discussions enable the entire society to be aware of what black writers consider to be the relationship between writing and politics.

Despite the ever-present problem of banning, the future of black writing looks bright. More and more committed literature is coming out of South Africa and is read inside and outside the country. Examples are two radical plays, "Bopha" and "Sophiatown", recently produced by the Market Theatre. Even more important, black writers are interested not only in quantity, some of them are beginning to create qualitative insights that stress the relationship between form and content. But, whether implicit or explicit in style, black South African literature will continue to be politically committed and, as Mongane Serote rightly implies in the quotation which opened this chapter, this will persist until the liberation struggle is won.

Notes

1. Mongane Seote, "Interview With Mongane Serote", *Soweto Poetry*, (ed.) Michael Chapman, p. 115.
2. Mafika Gwala, "Writing As A Cultural Weapon", *Momentum*, (eds.) M. J. Daymond, J. U. Jacobs and Margaret Lenta, p. 53.
3. Njabulo Ndebele, "South African Writers Must Create New Insights", *Moto*, No. 28 (October 1984), p. 22.
4. Don Mattera, *Azanian Love Song*, p. 75.
5. Mazisi Kuene, "The Rise of the Angry Generation", *Poets To the People*, (ed.) Barry Feinberg, p. 79.
6. Dennis Brutus, *Poets To The People*, p. 10.
7. Mattera, *Azanian Love Song*, p. 76.
8. Serote, *Behold Mama, Flowers*, p. 50.
9. Serote, *The Return of the Amasi Bird*, (eds.) Tim Couzens and Essop Patel, pp. 385–6.
10. Serote, *Behold Mama, Flowers*, p. 61.
11. Njabulo Ndebele, *The Return of the Amasi Bird*, pp. 387 and 388.
12. Ibid., p. 386.
13. Bonisile Joshua Mataung, *The Return of the Amasi Bird*, p. 313.
14. Serote, *To Every Birth Its Blood*, pp. 182–3.
15. Ibid., p. 196.
16. Lewis Nkosi, *Home and Exile*, p. 126.
17. Ndebele, "South African Writers Must Create New Insights", p. 22.
18. Ndebele, *Fools and Other Stories*, p. 236.
19. Ibid., p. 262.
20. Review of *Fools and Other Stories*, by M. N., *Africa Now*, No. 45 (January 1985), p. 56.
21. Ndebele, *Fools and Other Stories*, pp. 275–6.
22. M. N., p. 56.
23. Rowland Smith, "Living on the Fringe: The World of Ahmed Essop", Unpublished Conference Paper on South African Literature, 25th Conference of the Association des Anglicistes de l'Enseignement Supérieur, Caen, 11 May 1985, p. 1.
24. Ahmed Essop, *The Hajji and Other Stories*, p. 2.
25. Ibid., p. 71.
26. Ibid.
27. Smith, pp. 2–3.
28. Ahmed Essop, *The Visitation*, p. 87.
29. Oswald Mtshali, "Black Poetry in Southern Africa: What it Means", *Aspects of South African Literature*, (ed.) Christopher Heywood, p. 127.
30. Ian Steadman, "Alternative Politics, Alternative Performance: 1976 and Black South African Theatre", *Momentum*, (eds.) M. J. Daymond, J. U. Jacobs and Margaret Lenta, p. 226.
31. Matsemela Manaka, *Egoli*, pp. 18–19.
32. Ibid., p. 21.
33. Ibid., p. 28.
34. Steadman, p. 226.
35. Akua Rugg, "Apartheid Without Tears", *Race Review*, Vol. 14, No. 5 (1983), p. 180.

36. Jacques Alvarez-Pereyre, "Black Committed Theatre in South Africa", *Commonwealth*, Vol. 7, No. 1 (1984), p. 84.

37. A hostile view of *Woza Albert* is found in Rugg's article where he argues that the play "is not an example of creation for liberation, but rather an act of collaboration with the South African authorities. It is a cultural artefact built to government specifications and suitable for export to promote an acceptable face of apartheid. Like the busy, laughing, dancing niggers on the plantations of old, the play serves to reassure the masters of South Africa that they face no immediate threat from their blacks and convince the visitor-audience that the situation in that country isn't as dread as her detractors claim."

38. Athol Fugard, *"Master Harold"* . . . *and the boys*, p. 46.

39. Fugard, introduction, *A Lesson From Aloes*, pp. xiii–xiv.

40. An anonymous critic quoted in M. J. Daymond *et al's Momentum* argues that, "although Fugard is hailed by liberal critics as a lonely St George emerging from a theatrical vacuum to attack the apartheid dragon, he is in fact insufficiently allied to the struggle that is being fought here and is not enough involved in the reality of South African majority theatre, which is anything but a vacuum. He cannot actually transcend his class position as a white South African artist paid by local and overseas liberal theatres and their audiences. He cannot understand the true nature of the experience, or the struggle of the majority in South Africa and has, in his plays of sole authorship, presented black characters as capable only of stoical perseverance."

Bibliography

Primary Sources

Published Books

Abrahams, P. *Song of a City* (Faber and Faber, London, 1945).
——— *Mine Boy* (Faber and Faber, London, 1946).
——— *Wild Conquest* (Faber and Faber, London, 1950).
——— *Tell Freedom* (Alfred A. Knopf, New York, 1961).
Bloom, H. *King Kong* (Collins, London, 1961).
Brutus, D. *Letters to Martha* (Heinemann, London, 1968).
——— *A Simple Lust* (Hill and Wang, New York, 1973).
——— *Stubborn Hope* (Heinemann, London, 1978).
Couzens, T. and Essop Patel (eds.) *The Return of the Amasi Bird* (Ravan Press, Johannesburg, 1982).
Dhlomo, R. R. R. *An African Tragedy* (Lovedale Institution Press, Johannesburg, 1928).
Dikobe, M. *The Marabi Dance* (Heinemann, London, 1973).
——— *Dispossessed* (Ravan Press, Johannesburg, 1983).
Driver, C. J. *Elegy For a Revolutionary* (Faber and Faber, London, 1969).
——— *Send War in Our Time, O Lord* (Faber and Faber, London, 1970).
Essop, A. *The Hajji and Other Stories* (Ravan Press, Johannesburg, 1978).
——— *The Visitation* (Ravan Press, Johannesburg, 1980).
——— *The Emperor* (Ravan Press, Johannesburg, 1984).
Feinberg, B. (ed.) *Poets to the People* (Heinemann, London, 1980).
Fugard, A. *The Blood Knot* (The Odyssey Press, New York, 1963).
——— *Boesman and Lena* (Samuel French, Inc., New York, 1971).
——— *Statements* (Oxford University Press, London, 1974).
——— *A Lesson From Aloes* (Random House, New York, 1981).
——— *"Master Harold" . . . and the boys* (Alfred A. Knopf, New York, 1982).
Gordimer, N. *Some Monday For Sure* (Heinemann, London, 1976).
——— *Something Out There* (Jonathan Cape Ltd., London, 1984).
Kavanagh, R. M. (ed.) *South African People's Plays* (Heinemann, London, 1981).
La Guma, A. *A Walk in the Night* (Heinemann, London, 1967).
——— *The Stone Country* (Seven Seas Publishers, Berlin, 1967).
——— *In the Fog of the Season's End* (Heinemann, London, 1972).
——— *Time of the Butcherbird* (Heinemann, London, 1979).
Manaka, M. *Egoli* (Ravan Press, Johannesburg, 1980).

Manganyi, N. *Exiles and Homecomings: A Biography of Es'kia Mphahlele* (Ravan Press, Johannesburg, 1983).

Matshikiza, T. *Chocolates For My Wife* (Hodder and Stoughton, London, 1961).

Mattera, D. *Azanian Love Song* (Skotaville Publishers, Johannesburg, 1983).

Matthews, J. and Gladys Thomas. *Cry Rage* (Spro-cas Publications, Johannesburg, 1972).

Modisane, B. *Blame Me On History* (E. P. Dutton and Co., Inc., New York, 1963).

Mphahlele, E. *Down Second Avenue* (Faber and Faber, London, 1959).

———— *In Corner B* (East African Publishing House, Nairobi, 1967).

———— *Chirundu* (Lawrence Hill and Co., Publishers, Inc., Westport, 1979).

Mtshali, O. M. *Sounds of a Cowhide Drum* (Oxford University Press, London, 1971).

Mutloatse, M. (ed.) *South Africa: Contemporary Writings* (Heinemann, London, 1980).

Ndebele, N. S. *Fools and Other Stories* (Ravan Press, Johannesburg, 1983).

Nkosi, L. *The Rhythm of Violence* (Oxford University Press, London, 1964).

———— *Home and Exile* (Longmans, London, 1965).

Pieterse, C. (ed.) *Seven South African Poets* (Heinemann, London, 1971).

Plaatje, S. T. *Native Life in South Africa* (Negro Universities, New York, 1969).

———— *Mhudi* (Heinemann, London, 1978).

Royston, R. (ed.) *Black Poets in South Africa* (Heinemann, London, 1973).

Serote, M. W. *Yakhal' Inkomo* (Renoster Books, Johannesburg, 1972).

———— *Behold Mama, Flowers* (Ad. Donker/Publisher, Johannesburg, 1978).

———— *To Every Birth Its Blood* (Heinemann, London, 1981).

———— *No Baby Must Weep* (Ad. Donker/Publisher, Johannesburg, 1985).

Stubbs, A. C. R. (ed.) *Steve Biko, I Write What I Like* (Heinemann, London, 1978).

Themba, C. *The Will To Die* (Heinemann, London, 1973).

Zwelonke, D. M. *Robben Island* (Heinemann, London, 1973).

Published Journal and Newspaper Articles

Caute, D. "New Directions in African Literature: Continuity and Change", *Times Literary Supplement*, No. 16, (November 1984) p. 1310.

Davies, W. "New Writing in Africa", *West Africa*, No. 3508 (November 1984) pp. 2266–69.

Gordimer, N. "Living in the Interregnum", *New York Times Book Review*, Vol. 29, Nos. 21–22, (January 1983) pp. 21–29.

Knox, P. "Visiting Chief Seeks Aid For Zulu People", *Globe and Mail* (26 February 1985) p. 8.

Uys, S. "The Laager Cannot Last Much Longer", *Manchester Guardian Weekly* (30 June 1985) p. 19.

Valpy, M. "Kennedy's Visit Widens the Gaps in Already Divided South Africa", *Globe and Mail* (25 January 1985) p. 8.

Wolfers, M. "A Harare Happening", *West Africa*, No. 3450, (September 1983), pp. 2232–34.

Unpublished Interviews

Chipeta, M. Personal Interview, 7 May 1985.

Klug, M. Personal Interview, 11 April 1985.

Segkouma, G. Personal Interview, 15 May 1985.

Panter, J. Telephone Interview, 9 April 1985.

Secondary Sources

Published Books

Achebe, C. *Things Fall Apart* (Heinemann, London, 1958).
———— *Morning Yet on Creation Day* (Heinemann, London, 1975).
Adam, H. and Hermann Giliomee. *Ethnic Power Mobilized: Can South Africa Change?* (Yale University Press, New Haven, 1979).
Arnold, M. (ed.) *Steve Biko: Black Consciousness in South Africa* (Random House, New York, 1978).
Barnett, U. A. *A Vision of Order* (Sinclair Browne, London, 1983).
Beckett, S. *Waiting For Godot* (Grove Press, New York, 1954).
Behan, B. *The Quare Fellow* (Methuen, London, 1956).
Berrian, A. H. and Richard A. Long (eds.) *Negritude: Essays and Studies* (Hampton Institute Press, Hampton, 1967).
Bisztray, G. *Marxist Models of Literary Realism* (Columbia University Press, New York, 1978).
Boggs, J. *Racism and the Class Struggle* (Monthly Review Press, New York, 1970).
Bozzoli, B. (ed.) *Town and Countryside in the Transvaal* (Ravan Press, Johannesburg, 1983).
Breytenbach, B. *The True Confessions of an Albino Terrorist* (Farrar Strauss Giroux, New York, 1983).
Burgess, A. *A Clockwork Orange* (Penguin Books, Harmondsworth, 1962).
Carmichael, S. and Charles V. Hamilton. *Black Power: The Politics of Liberation in America* (Random House, New York, 1967).
Césaire, A. *Return to My Native Land* (Penguin Books, Harmondsworth, 1969).
Chanaiwa, D. (ed.) *Profiles of Self-Determination* (California State University Foundation, Northridge, 1976).
Chapman, M. (ed.) *Soweto Poetry* (McGraw-Hill Book Company, Johannesburg, 1982).
Chinweizu, *et al. Toward the Decolonization of African Literature* (Howard University Press, Washington, 1983).
Cohen, *et al.*, (eds.) *The Militant Black Writer: In Africa and the United States* (The University of Wisconsin Press, Madison, 1969).
Craig, D. (ed.) *Marxists on Literature: An Anthology* (Penguin Books, Harmondsworth, 1975).
Davidson, B. *et al. Southern Africa: The New Politics of Revolution* (Penguin Books, Harmondsworth, 1976).
Day-Lewis, C. *The Mind in Chains* (Frederick Muller Ltd., London, 1937).
Daymond, M. J. *et al. Momentum* (University of Natal Press, Pietermaritzburg, 1984).
De Kiewiet, C. W. *A History of South Africa: Social and Economic* (Oxford University Press, London, 1941).
Eagleton, T. *Marxism and Literary Criticism* (Methuen and Co., Ltd., London, 1976).
Eliot, T. S. *Selected Essays* (Faber and Faber Ltd., London, 1932).
Esedebe, P. O. *Pan-Africanism: The Idea and Movement 1776–1963* (Howard University Press, Washington, 1982).
Fanon, F. *The Wretched of the Earth*, trans. Constance Farrington (Grove Press, Inc., New York, 1968).
February, V. A. *Mind Your Colour* (Kegan Paul International Ltd., London, 1981).

Feit, E. *African Opposition in South Africa: The Failure of Passive Resistance* (The Hoover Institution, Stanford, 1967).

Fiedler, L. A. and Baker A. Houston, Jr. (eds.) *English Literature* (The Johns Hopkins University Press, Baltimore, 1981).

Fischer, E. *The Necessity of Art*, trans. Anna Bostock (Penguin, Harmondsworth, 1959).

Gakwandi, S. A. *The Novel and Contemporary Experience in Africa* (Africana Publishing Company, New York, 1977).

Gerhart, G. M. *Black Power in South Africa* (University of California Press, Berkeley, 1978).

Glicksberg, C. I. *The Literature of Commitment* (Associated University Press, London, 1976).

Gray, S. *Southern African Literature* (Barnes and Noble Books, New York, 1979).

Grotowski, J. *Towards a Poor Theatre* (Simon and Schuster, New York, 1968).

Haley, A. *The Autobiography of Malcolm X* (Penguin Books, Harmondsworth, 1964).

Heywood, C. (ed.) *Perspectives on African Literature* (Heinemann, London, 1971).
——— *Aspects of South African Literature* (Heinemann, London, 1976).

Hill, C. R. *Bantustans: The Fragmentation of South Africa* (Oxford University Press, London, 1964).

Hill, H. (ed.) *Anger, and Beyond* (Harper and Row Publishers, New York, 1966).

Horrell, M. *Action, Reaction and Counteraction* (South African Institute of Race Relations, Johannesburg, 1963).

Huddleston, Father T. *Naught For Your Comfort* (Collins, London, 1956).

Jabavu, D. D. T. *The Black Problem* (Lovedale Press, Alice, 1920).

Jahn, J. *Muntu* (Faber and Faber, Ltd., London, 1961).
——— *A History of Neo-African Literature* (Faber and Faber, London, 1966). 1966).

Johnson, R. W. *How Long Will South Africa Survive?* (Oxford University Press, New York, 1977).

Johnstone, F. A. *Class, Race and Gold* (Routledge and Kegan Paul, London 1976).

Jones, E. D. (ed.) *African Literature Today* (Heinemann, London, 1973).

Jordan, A. C. *Towards an African Literature* (University of California Press, Berkeley, 1973).

Killam, G. D. (ed.) *African Writers on African Writing* (Northwestern University Press, Evanston, 1973).

King, B. (ed.) *Literature of the World* (Routledge and Kegan Paul, London, 1974).

King, B. *et al.* (eds.) *A Celebration of Black and African Writing* (Ahmadu Bello University Press and Oxford University Press, Zaria, 1975).

Klima, V. *et al.* *Black Africa: Literature and Language* (D. Reidel Publishing Company, Dordrecht, 1976).

Kotze, D. A. *African Politics in South Africa 1964–1974* (C. Hurst and Company, London, 1975).

Lacey, H. C. *To Raise, Destroy, and Create: The Poetry, Drama and Fiction of Imamu Amiri Baraka (Le Roi Jones)* (The Whitson Publishing Company, New York, 1981).

Legum, C. and Margaret. *The Bitter Choice* (The World Publishing Company, New York, 1968).

Lenin, V. I. *On Literature and Art*, trans. Institute of Marxism–Leninism (Progress Publishers, Central Committee of the C.P.S.U., Moscow, 1970).

Lomax, A. and Raol Abdul. *300 Years of Black Poetry* (Dodd, Mead and Company, New York, 1970).

Lukacs, G. *The Meaning of Contemporary Realism*, trans. John and Necke Mander (Merlin Press, London, 1962).

Luthuli, A. *Let My People Go* (Collins, London, 1962).

Maes-Jelinek, H. (ed.) *Commonwealth Literature and the Modern World* (Librairie Marcel Didier S.A., Bruxelles, 1975).

Magubane, B. M. *The Political Economy of Race and Class in South Africa* (Monthly Review Press, New York, 1979).

Mandela, N. *No Easy Walk to Freedom* (Heinemann, London, 1965).

Mander, J. *The Writer and Commitment* (Secker and Warburg, London, 1961).

Margolies, D. N. *The Function of Literature* (International Publishers, New York, 1969).

Marquard, L. *Liberalism in South Africa* (South African Institute of Race Relations, Johannesburg, 1965).

Marx, K. *Economic and Philosophic Manuscripts of 1844*, trans. Martin Milligan (Lawrence and Wishart, London, 1959).

Mezu, S. O. (ed.) *The Philosophy of Pan-Africanism* (Georgetown University Press, Washington, 1965).

Moore, G. *Seven African Writers* (Oxford University Press, London, 1962).

———— *African Literature* (Ibadan University Press, Ibadan, 1965).

Mphahlele, E. *Voices in the Whirlwind and Other Essays* (Hill and Wang, New York, 1967).

Mugomba, A. and Mougo Nyaggah. *Independence Without Freedom* (Abc-Clio, Santa Barbara, 1980).

Nazareth, P. *Literature and Society in Modern Africa* (East African Literature Bureau, Nairobi, 1972).

Niven, A. (ed.) *The Commonwealth Writer Overseas* (Librairie Marcel Didier S.A., Bruxelles, 1976).

Nkosi, L. *Tasks and Masks: Themes and Styles of African Literature* (Longman, Harlow, 1981).

Nolutshungu, S. C. *Changing South Africa* (David Philip, Publisher, Cape Town, 1982).

Nyerere, J. K. *Freedom and Socialism* (Oxford University Press, London, 1968).

Ollman, B. *Alienation* (Cambridge University Press, Cambridge, 1976).

Olney, J. *Tell Me Africa: An Approach to African Literature* (Princeton University Press, Princeton, 1973).

Omer-Cooper *The Zulu Aftermath: A Nineteenth Century Revolution in Bantu Africa* (Northwestern University Press, Evanston, 1966).

Owomoyela, O. *African Literatures: An Introduction* (African Studies Association, Brandeis University, Waltham, 1979).

Palmer, E. *The Growth of the African Novel* (Heinemann, London, 1979).

Parker, K. (ed.) *The South African Novel in English* (The Macmillan Press, Ltd., London, 1978).

Pinter, H. *The Birthday Party*, (Methuen, London, 1965).

———— *The Caretaker* (Methuen, London, 1966).

Sartre, J.-Paul *What is Literature?* trans. Berhard Frechtman (Methuen and Co., Ltd., London, 1950).

Sembene, O. *God's Bits of Wood* (Heinemann, London, 1970).

Slote, B. (ed.) *Literature and Society* (University of Nebraska Press, Lincoln, 1964).

Smith, R. (ed.) *Exile and Tradition* (Longman and Dalhousie University Press, London, 1976).

Southall, R. *South Africa's Transkei: The Political Economy of an "Independent" Bantustan* (Monthly Review Press, New York, 1983).

Tabata, I. B. *The Awakening of a People* (Russell Press, Nottingham, 1974).

Trotsky, L. *Literature and Revolution*, trans. Rose Strunsky (The University of Michigan Press, Ann Arbor, 1960).

Tucker, M. *Africa in Modern Literature* (Frederick Ungar Publishing Co., New York, 1967).

van den Berghe, P. *South Africa: A Study in Conflict* (University of California Press, Berkeley, 1967).

——— (ed.) *The Liberal Dilemma in South Africa* (St. Martin's Press, New York, 1979).

van der Merwe, H. W. and David Welsh (eds.) *Student Perspectives on South Africa* (David Philip, Publisher, Cape Town, 1972).

Wade, M. *Peter Abrahams* (Evans Brothers Ltd., London, 1972).

Wastberg, P. (ed.) *The Writer in Modern Africa* (The Scandinavian Institute of African Studies, Uppsala, 1968).

wa Thiong'o, N. *The River Between* (Heinemann, London, 1965).

——— *Petals of Blood* (Heinemann, London, 1977).

——— *Writers in Politics* (Heinemann, London, 1981).

White, G. A. and Charles Newman. *Literature and Revolution* (Holt, Rinehart and Winston, New York, 1972).

Williams, R. *Marxism and Literature* (Oxford University Press, London, 1977).

Articles

Abrahams, C. "The Context of Black South African Literature", *World Literature Written in English*, Vol. 18, No. 1 (1979) pp. 8–19.

Abrahams, T. "'Coloured Politics' in South Africa: The Quislings' Trek into the Abyss", *Ufahamu* (1983) pp. 245–55.

Achebe, C. "The Uses of African Literature", *Okike*, No. 15 (1979) pp. 8–17.

Africa Confidential, Vol. 24, No. 14 (1983) pp. 1–4.

Africa Research Bulletin, Vol. 13, No. 6 (June–July 1976) pp. 4060–62.

Alvarez-Pereyre, J. "Black Committed Theatre in South Africa", *Commonwealth*, Vol. 7, No. 1 (1984) pp. 80–93.

Akerman, A. "'Prejudicial to the Safety of The State': Censorship and the Theatre in South Africa", *Theatre Quarterly*, Vol. 7, No. 28 (Winter 1977–78) pp. 46–54.

——— "Why Must These Shows Go On? A Critique of Black Musicals Made For White Audiences", *Theatre Quarterly*, Vol. 7, No. 28 (Winter 1977–78) pp. 67–69.

Asein, O. S. "The Revolutionary Vision in Alex La Guma's Novels", *Phylon*, No. 39 (1978) pp. 74–86.

——— "The Humanism of Ezekiel Mphahlele", *Journal of Commonwealth Literature*, Vol. 15, No. 1 (1980) pp. 38–49.

Babu, A. R. M. "Black American Influence on Africa", *Africa Now*, No. 46 (February 1985) p. 45.

Barnett, U. A. "Africa or the West? Cultural Synthesis in the work of Es'kia Mphahlele", *Africa Insight*, Vol. 14, No. 2 (1984) pp. 59–63.

Birbalsingh, F. M. "Urban Experience in South African Fiction", *Presence Africaine*, No. 129 (1984) pp. 111–21.

Breytenbach, B. "A South African Poet on His Imprisonment" (with Donald Woods), *New York Times Book Review* (1 May 1983) pp. 3–25.

Brink, A. "Commitment I: Writers as Mapmakers", *Index on Censorship*, Vol. 7, No. 6 (1978) pp. 26–30.

Brutus, D. "Dennis Brutus: An Interview" (with William E. Thompson.) *Ufahamu*, Vol. 12, No. 2 (1983) pp. 69–77.

Chennells, A. "Alex La Guma and the South African Political Novel", *Mambo M* (University of Zimbabwe) (1974) pp. 14–16.

Clingman, S. "Multi-racialism or *A World of Strangers*", *Salmagundi*, No. 62 (Winter 1984) pp. 32–61.

Coetzee, J. M. "Alex La Guma and the Responsibilities of the South African Writer", *Journal of the New African Literature and the Arts*, Vol. 9, No. 10 (1971) pp. 5–11.

————— "Man's Fate in the Novels of Alex La Guma", *Studies in Black Literature*, Vol. 5, No. 1 (1974) pp. 16–23.

Cohen, D. "Drama and the Police State: Athol Fugard's South Africa", *Commonwealth Drama*, Vol. 6, No. 1 (Spring 1980) pp. 151–61.

————— Review of *Steve Biko, I Write What I Like*, (ed.) Aelred C. R. Stubbs, *World Literature Written in English*, Vol. 20, No. 1 (1981) pp. 63–66.

Couzens, T. "Sol Plaatje's *Mhudi*", *Journal of Commonwealth Literature*, Vol. 8, No. 1 (1973) pp. 1–19.

Crapanzano, V. "A Reporter at Large (South Africa – Part I)", *New Yorker* (18 March 1985) pp. 50–99.

————— "A Reporter at Large (South Africa – Part II)", *New Yorker* (25 March 1985), pp. 52–97.

Davidson, B. "Brave Forerunner" (review of *Sol Plaatje: South African Nationalist*, by Brian Willan) *West Africa*, No. 3522 (February 1985) pp. 337–77.

De Villiers, A. (ed.) *English in Africa*, Vol. 2, No. 1 (1975) pp. 1–70.

Edebiri, U. "Drama as Popular Culture in Africa", *Ufahamu*, Vol. 12, No. 2 (1983) pp. 139–49.

Editorial Briefings. *Review of African Political Economy*, No. 7 (June 1976) pp. 108–124.

Egudu, N. R. "African Literature and Social Problems", *Canadian Journal of African Studies*, Vol. 9, No. 3 (1975) pp. 421–47.

Elwell, D. "The American Conscience and Apartheid", *West Africa*, No. 45 (January 1985) p. 15.

Fatton, R. Jr. "The African National Congress of South Africa: The Limitations of a Revolutionary Strategy", *Canadian Journal of African Studies*, Vol. 18, No. 3 (1984) pp. 593–608.

First, R. "After Soweto: A Response", *Review of African Political Economy*, No. 11 (July 1979) pp. 93–100.

Fuchs, A. "Towards and Away From Poor Theatre or Athol Fugard's Transgressions", *Commonwealth*, Vol. 7, No. 1 (1984) pp. 71–79.

Fugard, A. "Keeping an Appointment With the Future: The Theatre of Athol Fugard" (with Mary Benson), *Theatre Quarterly*, Vol. 7, No. 28 (Winter 1977–78), pp. 77–83.

Futcha, I. "The Theme of Freedom in Two Early Southern African Novels: *Feso* and *Mhudi*", *Ngam* (Yaounde), No. 384 (1978) pp. 202–29.

Gordimer, N. "A Writer's Freedom", *New Classic*, No. 2 (1975) pp. 11–16.

————— "English Language, Literature and Politics in South Africa", *Journal of*

Southern African Studies, Vol. 2, No. 2 (1976) pp. 131–47.
————— "South Africa's Daughter" (with Anne Collins), *City Woman* (Holiday 1982) pp. 15–30.
Gray, P. "Tales of Privacy and Politics" (review of *Something Out There*, by Nadine Gordimer) *Time*, No. 23 (July 1984) (no pagination given).
Green, J. R. "Alex La Guma's *In the Fog of the Season's End*: The Politics of Subversion", *Umoja*, Vol. 3, No. 2 (1979) pp. 85–93.
Head, B. "Social and Pressures that Shape Literature in Southern Africa", *World Literature Written in English*, Vol. 18, No. 1 (1979) pp. 20–26.
Hope, C. Review of *A Vision of Order*, by Ursula A. Barnett, *Times Literary Supplement* (2 November 1984) p. 1240.
Human, J. J. "A Vision of Order", *Times Literary Supplement* (30 November 1984) p. 1385.
Igbudu, I. "Protest Poetry in South Africa and Mtshali's Refuge under 'The Cryptic Mode'", *Kuku* (1979–80) pp. 35–43.
International Defence and Aid Fund "A New Wave of Cultural Energy: Black Theatre in South Africa", *Theatre Quarterly*, Vol. 7, No. 28 (Winter 1977–78) pp. 57–63.
Johnstone, F. "'Most Painful to our Hearts': South Africa Through the Eyes of the New School", *Canadian Journal of African Studies*, Vol. 16, No. 1 (1982) pp. 5–26.
Kani, J. and Winston Ntshona "Art is Life and Life is Art" (with the African Activist Association and *Ufahamu*) *Ufahamu*, Vol. 6, No. 2 (1976) pp. 5–26.
Karis, T. G. "Revolution in the Making: Black Politics in South Africa", *Foreign Affairs*, Vol. 62, No. 2 (Winter 1983–84) pp. 378–406.
Kavanagh, R. M. "Tradition and Innovation in the Theatre of Workshop '71", *Theatre Quarterly*, Vol. 7, No. 28 (Winter 1977–78) pp. 63–67.
————— "After Soweto: People's Theatre and the Political Struggle in South Africa", *Theatre Quarterly*, Vol. 9, No. 33 (Spring 1979) pp. 31–38.
Kunene, D. P. "Ideas Under Arrest: Censorship in South Africa", *Research in African Literatures*, Vol. 12, No. 4 (Winter 1981) pp. 421–39.
————— "Deculturation: The African Writer's Response", *Africa Today*, Vol. 15, No. 4 (1968) pp. 19–24.
Lindfors, B. "Form and Technique in the Novels of Richard Rive and Alex La Guma", *Journal of the New African Literature and the Arts*, No. 2 (1966) pp. 10–15.
————— "Robin Hood Realism in South African English Fiction", *Africa Today*, Vol. 15, No. 4 (1968) pp. 16–18.
————— "Dennis Brutus's Mousey Tongue", *World Literature Written in English*, Vol. 15, No. 1 (April 1976) pp. 7–16.
————— "Popular Literature in English in Black South Africa", *Journal of Southern African Affairs*, Vol. 11, No. 1 (1977) pp. 121–29.
Mafeje, A. "Soweto and its Aftermath", *Review of African Political Economy*, No. 11 (July 1979) pp. 17–30.
Mbeki, T. "The Fatton Thesis: A Rejoinder", *Canadian Journal of African Studies*, Vol. 18, No. 3 (1984) pp. 609–12.
McGrath, J. "The Theory and Practice of Political Theatre", *Theatre Quarterly*, Vol. 9, No. 33 (Spring 1979) pp. 43–54.
Morris, P. "The Early Black South African Newspaper and the Development of the Novel", *Journal of Commonwealth Literature*, Vol. 15, No. 1 (1980) pp. 15–29.

Mosala, B. "Theatre in Soweto", *Journal of Commonwealth Literature*, Vol. 8, No. 1 (1973) pp. 63–68.

Mphahlele, E. "South Africa: Two Communities and the Struggle For a Birthright", *Journal of African Studies*, Vol. 4, No. 1 (Spring 1977) pp. 21–50.

Mqotsi, L. "After Soweto: Another Response", *Review of African Political Economy*, No. 14 (January–April 1979), pp. 97–106.

Mtshali, O. "Interview With Oswald Joseph Mtshali" (with Ursula A. Barnett), *World Literture Written in English*, Vol. 12, No. 1 (April 1973) pp. 27–35.

Muronda, E. F. "Drama in the Political Struggle in South Africa", *Ufahamu*, Vol. 12, No. 2 (1983) pp. 78–92.

Mzamane, M. "The Study of Literature in Africa", *Marang*, No. 2 (1978) pp. 52–54.

———— "Literature and Politics Among Blacks in Southern Africa", *Pula*, Vol. 1, No. 2 (June 1979) pp. 123–45.

———— "Sharpeville and its Aftermath: The Novels of Richard Rive, Peter Abrahams, Alex La Guma, and Lauretta Ngcobo", *Ariel*, Vol. 16, No. 2 (April 1985) pp. 31–98.

Mzite, D. "Politics in African Poetry", *Marang*, No. 2 (1978) pp. 55–63.

N. M. Review of *Fools and Other Stories*, by Njabulo Ndebele, *West Africa*, No. 45 (January 1985) pp. 55–56.

Obuke, O. J. "The Structure of Commitment: A Study of Alex La Guma", *Ba Shiru*, Vol. 5, No. 1 (1973) pp. 14–20.

Okolo, C. B. "Apartheid As Unfreedom", *Présence Africaine*, No. 129 (1984) pp. 20–37.

Onege, O. F. "The Crisis of Consciousness in Modern African Literature: A Survey", *Canadian Journal of African Studies*, Vol. 8, No. 2 (1974) pp. 385–410.

O'Sheel, P. "Athol Fugard's 'Poor Theatre'", *Journal of Commonwealth Literature*, Vol. 12, No. 3 (1978) pp. 67–77.

Paton, A. "Black Consciousness", *Reality: A Journal of Liberal Opinion*, Vol. 4, No. 1 (March 1972) pp. 9–10.

Povey, J. F. "Three South African Poets: Dennis Brutus, Keorapetse Kgositsile, and Oswald Mbuyiseni Mtshali", *World Literature Written in English*, Vol. 16, No. 2 (November 1977) pp. 263–80.

Rabkin, D. "La Guma and Reality in South Africa", *Okike*, Vol. 8, No. 1 (1973) pp. 54–62.

Rugg, A. "Apartheid Without Tears", *Race Review*, Vol. 14, No. 5 (1983) pp. 180–81.

Schorer, M. "Technique as Discovery", *Hudson Review*, Vol. 1, No. 1 (Spring 1948) pp. 67–87.

Sepamla, S. "The Black Writer in South Africa Today", *New Classic*, No. 3 (1975) pp. 18–26.

Seymour, H. "*Sizwe Bansi Is Dead*: A Study of Artistic Ambivalence", *Race and Class*, No. 21 (Winter 1980) pp. 273–89.

Simonse, S. "African Literature Between Nostalgia and Utopia: African Novels Since 1953 In the Light of Modes-of-Production Approach", *Research in African Literatures*, Vol. 13, No. 4 (Winter 1982) pp. 451–85.

Smith, R. "Allan Quatermain to Rosa Burger: Violence in South African Fiction", *World Literature Written in English*, Vol. 22, No. 2 (Autumn 1983) pp. 171–82.

———— "Autobiography in Black and White: South African Views of the Past", *Commonwealth*, Vol. 7, No. 2 (Spring 1985) pp. 72–82.

———— "Le magazine Drum, voix des Townships noire", *l'Afrique Littéraire*, No.

75 (1985) p. 5061.

Vandenbroucke, R. "South African Blacksploitation", *Yale/Theatre*, Vol. 8, No. 1 (Fall 1976) pp. 68–71.

——— "A Brief Chronology of the Theatre in South Africa", *Theatre Quarterly*, Vol. 7, No. 28 (Winter 1977–78) pp. 44–46.

——— "Chiaroscuro: A Portrait of the South African Theatre", *Theatre Quarterly*, Vol. 7, No. 28 (Winter 1977–78) pp. 46–54.

Vaughan, M. "Literature and Politics: Currents in South African Writing in the Seventies", *Journal of Southern African Studies*, Vol. 9, No. 1 (October 1982) pp. 118–38.

Visser, N. W. "South Africa: The Renaissance that Failed", *Journal of Commonwealth Literature*, Vol. 11, No. 1 (1976) pp. 42–56.

Walshe, A. P. "Black American Thought and African Political Attitudes in South Africa", *Review of Politics*, Vol. 32, No. 1 (January 1970) pp. 51–77.

Unpublished Sources

Adam, H. and Stanley Uys. "Eight New Realities in Southern Africa", South–South Conference, Montreal (14–17 May 1985) pp. 1–8.

Sejanamane, M. "The Crisis of Apartheid: South Africa and Destabilisation in Southern Africa", South–South Conference, Montreal (14–17 May 1985) pp. 1–26.

Smith, R. "Living on the Fringe: The World of Ahmed Essop", 25th Conference of the Association des Anglicistes de l'Enseignement Supérieur, Caen, France (11 May 1985) pp. 1–14.

Index

Kruger, Jimmy, 105
Kumalo, A.N.C., 106
Kunene, Daniel P., 19
Kunene, Mazisi, 117, 147
Kwa Zulu, 126-7

La Guma, Alex, 3, 36-45, 52-68 *passim*, 71, 74, 91, 135, 138, 150, 151
Lacey, Henry C., 100
Land Act (1913), 7, 10-14
Langa, Mandlenkosi, 3, 47, 78-9, 92, 110, 150
Lenin, Vladimir Ilych, 1, 2
Lesson from Aloes, A, 159-61
Letters, 41
Liberal Party, 51, 95
liberal politics, failure of, 95-6
"Liberal Student Crap", 110
liberalism, 8, 9, 24, 33, 56, 95, 109, 110, 112-4
Lifa, 126
literature: "protest", 7; role of, 1, 2
"Little Dudu", 78
"Look Upon the Blackness of My Woman", 99
"Lord, How Long Lord, How Long?", 90, 114
Lovedale Press, 5
Lovedale School, 5
Luthuli, Albert, 58, 159

Makeba, Miriam, 126
Manaka, Matsemela, 157, 159
Mandela, Nelson, 51, 53, 58, 117
Marabi Dance, The, 15-26, 31, 83
Market Theatre, 161
Marx, Karl, 1, 23
Marxism, 6, 19, 21, 65
"Master Harold" and the Boys, 159-61
Matabele, 9-13, 60
Matshikiza, Todd, 45, 125, 126
Mattera, Don, 4, 85, 100-2, 107, 115-18, 137-8, 147, 148, 149
Matthews, James, 3, 4, 73-4, 77, 86-92, 99, 101, 107, 110, 114, 117, 149
Mau Mau, 63, 136
Medupe, 118
"Men in Chains", 81
Mfecane, 5
Mhudi, 3, 6-15, 60, 83, 86, 103
militant politics, 51-2
Mine Boy, 15-26, 34, 59-60, 74
mine workers, 18, 23; black, 24; white, 24
mining, 14
mission education, 5-28
missionaries, 5, 16, 19
Mkele, Nimirod, 80

Modisane, Bloke, 3, 31, 35, 37, 45, 80, 105
Mofolo, Thomas, 7, 16
Motaung, Bonisile Joshua, 150
"Mother's Ode to a Stillborn Child", 78-9
Motsisi, Casey, 74-5, 87
Mozambique, 119
Mphahlele, Ezekiel, 3, 20, 32-3, 34, 45-47, 80
Mtshali, Oswald, 3, 47, 71-3, 76, 78-83, 92, 95, 102, 105-6, 157
multiracialism, 29, 32, 47, 109, 124
Muntu, 7
murder, 15, 20, 21, 37, 62
Mutloatse, Mothobi, 156
Mutwa, Credo, 104-5, 129, 132, 159
Mxenge, Griffith, 159
Mzamane, Mbulelo, 72, 156

Nakasa, Nat, 45
"Namibian Love Song", 118
National Union of South African Students (NUSAS), 95-6
National Youth Organizations, 119
nationalism, 98
Native Life in South Africa, 3, 6-15, 83
Ndebele, Njabulo, 3, 26, 47, 77, 78, 80, 92, 149, 150, 152-4
Nettleton, Clive, 95
Ngoyi, Lilian, 159
Nkosi, Lewis, 29, 40, 75, 125, 151-2
"No children…", 148
"No Time Black Man", 138
Nolutshungu, Sam C., 97
non-violence, 38-45, 51-2, 56, 58
Nortje, Arthur, 45
novels, 66
Ntshona, Winston, 129, 134
Nxumalo, Henry, 37
Nyerere, Julius, 98

O'Sheel, Patrick, 136
"Ofay–Watcher, Throbs–Phase XIII", 84
"Old Man in Church, An", 82

pacifism, 58
Pan African Congress (PAC), 24, 38, 51, 52, 58, 97, 119, 142
"Paper Curtains", 109-10
"Park, The", 86
"Party, The", 86
pass laws, 18, 132, 134
Pass Me the Meatballs, Jones, 92
Patel, Essop, 99
Paton, Alan, 113
People's Experimental Theatre (PET), 136, 142
Petals of Blood, 47, 57-64, 135